FROM HEROINES TO BENEFICIARIES; FROM BENEFICIARIES TO HEROINES?

From Heroines to Beneficiaries; From Beneficiaries to Heroines?

The impact of a small-scale irrigation project on gender in the West Bengal Terai

LOES SCHENK-SANDBERGEN
NIREN CHOUDHURY

IDPAD

MANOHAR
2003

First published 2003

ISBN 81-7304-423-6

Published by
Ajay Kumar Jain for
Manohar Publishers & Distributors
4753/23, Ansari Road, Daryaganj
New Delhi 110 002

Typeset by
Kumud Print Service
Shimla 171 005

Printed at
Print Perfect
Delhi 110 064

This book is dedicated to Mr A.K. Mitra, Senior Technical Officer of the office of the joint-director of Agriculture, Jalpaiguri, West-Bengal, India, who died in 1997. He was an extraordinary man. It is a great loss to miss his professional knowledge and incessant endeavour to implement handpumps to support women in the Terai area.

Plate 1: Farmer ploughing his land.

A Half-acre of Land

I had sold off all my land except for one half-acre.
The landlord said, 'Upen, I'll buy it, you must hand it over.'
I said, 'You're rich, you've endless land, can't you see
That all I've got is a patch on which to die?'
'Old man,' he sneered, 'you know I've made a garden;
If I have your half-acre its length and breadth will be even.
You'll have to sell.' Then I said with my hands on my heart
And tears in my eyes, 'Don't take my only plot!
It's more than gold - for seven generations my family
Has owned it: must I sell my own mother through poverty?'
He was silent for a while as his eyes grew red with fury.
'All right, we'll see,' he said, smiling cruelly.

I bow, I bow to my beautiful motherland Bengal!
To your river-banks, to your winds that cool and console;
Your plains, whose dust the sky bends down to kiss;
Your shrouded villages, that are nests of shade and peace;
Your leafy mango-woods, where the herd-boys play;
Your deep ponds, loving and cool as the midnight sky;
Your sweet-hearted women returning home with water;
I tremble in my soul and weep when I call you Mother.

RABINDRANATH TAGORE, *Selected Poems* (1882-1913)

Contents

Tables

ANNEXURES

Illustrations

MAPS

PLATES

Acknowledgements

The data used in this book were mainly collected during our four years' association (1990-4) with the North Bengal Terai Development Project, Phase II, as sociologists in-charge of the impact research. This project came under operation under the bilateral agreement between the Government of the Netherlands and the Republic of India and was jointly administered by the Department of Agriculture of the Government of West Bengal and the Dutch consultancy firm Euroconsult, representing the Government of the Netherlands. We are very much thankful to the Directorate General of International Development Co-operation of the Netherlands' Ministry of Foreign Affairs for providing us the necessary financial support to carry out the research independently.

We thought it would be useful if a wider audience of scholars could be informed on our findings based on the huge amount of data which were only brought out in internal project reports. The project on which the present publication is based was funded by the Indo-Dutch Programme on Alternatives in Development (IDPAD) in collaboration with the Indian Council of Social Science Research (ICSSR). Therefore, we thank IDPAD for making this publication possible. We are also grateful to Ramesh Jain, director of Manohar, for his substantial contribution to improve the manuscript of this book.

Our special thanks are also due to the various officials down to the block and village levels for their co-operation without which the field-collection of data would have been difficult. In particular we want to mention Dr. Trivedi and Mr. T.K. De, the former Joint Directors of Agriculture of the Government of West Bengal. Their advice, enthusiasm and official support had made our field-study so much easy and pleasant not only for us but also for the entire research team.

The members of the team were: Ranjit Karmakar, Nilotpal Sarma, S.R. Ghosh, Hemanta Roy, Joynal Abedin, S.K. Bhowmik, Pradip Adhikary, Provas Mondal, Md. Enarul Hoque, Amal Dutta, Narayan Ghosh, Biswanath Chakraborty, Mitali Ghosh, Kamal Barman, Murtaza Rahaman and Samsur Alam. They stayed in villages for long periods in difficult circumstances. Moreover, they tabulated the huge amount of data by hand on table long sheets of paper.

Besides, we have been assisted by local village women and girls who worked with us from time to time to assist our regular research staff in interviewing farmwomen. Md. Enarul Hoque in addition, worked as a Research Assistant under the IDPAD programme and helped us in many ways in the collection of additional data and preparation of this book. Namita Choudhury gave valuable suggestions and support and contributed to the computer processing of the data.

Last but not least, we owe our special gratitude to the villagers of the Terai for their cordiality, hospitality and readiness to answer our endless queries. Without their hearty support our field-work would have remained that much dreary and distressing.

The views expressed in this book are entirely ours and do not reflect the policy or views of Euroconsult, the Government of the Netherlands or the Government of West Bengal.

Amsterdam, 10 September 2002

LOES SCHENK-SANDBERGEN
NIREN CHOUDHURY

Abbreviations and Terminology

ADO	Agricultural Development Officer (block level)
Agri-I	Agri-Irrigation Wing of the Ministry of Minor Irrigation
Agri-M	Agri-Mechanical Wing of the Ministry of Minor Irrigation
BC	Beneficiary Committee
BDO	Block Development Officer
CA	Command Area of a scheme
DOA	Department of Agriculture
DTW	Deep Tube Well
HHs	Households
HTW	Hand Tube Well
KPS	Krishi Prayukti Sahayak (Agricultural Extension worker)
NBTDP	North Bengal Terai Development Project/ Small-scale irrigation and soil conservation and soil improvement project, North Bengal Terai.
PDW	Pump Dug Well
RLI	River Lift Irrigation
SC	Scheduled Caste
SS	Sample Survey
ST	Scheduled Tribe
STW	Shallow Tube Well
UR	Unit Rate of Production (per acre production)
Acre	0.4 hectare
Aman (*Amon*)	*kharif* paddy: the most important rice variety which is grown with the monsoon rains

Aus	pre-*kharif* paddy: the rice variety which is grown with the showers that fall in spring
Bargadar	sharecropper
Baris	homesteads
Bidi	local cigarette
Bigha	1/3 of an acre
Boro	High yielding rice variety grown in the dry season
Gua	well
Hat	market
Jotedars	landowner
Katcha channel	earthen channel (unlined)
Kharif	crop grown during period from June-November, rainy season (monsoon)
Lathis	sticks
Mahila Samiti	women's organization
Muri	puffed rice
Pacca channel	lined channel
Panchayat	village council
Pre-*kharif*	March-June, spring/summer crop
Purdah	seclusion of women
Rabi	crops grown in the period from December-March, winter, dry season (irrigation is essential)
Spout	water outlet in a subsurface water transmission system connected to DTW and RLI. Kind of valve.
Tera	bamboo stick to lift water

1. Introduction

> The God of the Engineers is Vishwakarma [male god of the universe]. He has tools in his hands and does the job. He is of mythological value. Every year on 17 September pujas are performed with flowers and incense by all engineers, mechanics and other officials professionally involved in the North Bengal Terai small-scale irrigation project. All over India on the same day Vishwakarma is worshipped.

1.1 BACKGROUND

The project area is located in the plains of the northernmost part of West Bengal state at the foot of the Himalayan mountains, clenched between Nepal, Bhutan, Assam and Bangladesh. If the sky is clear, the snow-covered peaks of mountain tops can be seen from Siliguri, the main city. The Terai area, as this part of West Bengal in India is named, is very beautiful and scenic: small jute stick and bamboo houses lie scattered in patchwork fields of paddy, jute, and vegetables, surrounded by bamboo bushes and palm trees. Poverty is very visible in the type of housing and the lack of material possessions. Households live in homesteads (*baris*) usually with four small shelters (two sleeping rooms, a kitchen and a stable for the cattle) located in a square. The space in the middle of the *bari* square is considered the domain of the women. This spatial set-up hide them behind the outer wall of the hut. It is likely that this typical spatial architecture has been designed in the past as a reflection of *purdah* or patriarchal control. The small shaky houses are made of bamboo and jute stalks with some plastering on the outer walls. The roofs of rice stalks have to be normally renewed every two years if they do not collapse before, damaged by hailstorms or floods. Sometimes, lovely yellow flowers of creepers embellish the roofs of the houses. The only kitchen implements are a *chulha* (oven) made of mud in the floor and a paddy stamper made of stone. Better-off families have a small *pukka* well (*gua*) in the corner of the compound for domestic use and a bamboo stick (*tera*) to lift the water. Ploughs are simple and made of wood. Life is very much adjusted to the bamboo and jute ecology of the area. The marginal and small farmer households try to survive growing rice and vegetables on their small patches of land. Most people have to buy part of their rice (with ration cards), mustard oil, vegetables, salt, pots, pans, and cloth from outside. There are few opportunities to earn a living outside agriculture. It is in this environment that a small-scale irrigation project was implemented.

This book documents the socio-economic impact of the second phase of a small-scale irrigation project, the Indo-Dutch North Bengal Terai Development Project, from a gender perspective. Phase I of the project covered the period 1984-8, Phase II the period from 1988-93, with an extension till December 1994. The project was executed by the Department of Agriculture of West Bengal and financially supported by the International Cooperation Programme of the Government of the Netherlands. It concentrates on the three northern districts of West Bengal: Darjeeling (partly), Jalpaiguri and Cooch Behar (see Map 1).

The main activities of Phase II of the project were the implementation of handpumps, pump dug wells, shallow tube wells, deep tube wells and river lift. In addition a soil conservation programme was undertaken. In comparison with Phase I, new aspects were introduced and financed in Phase II. From 1986 onwards, the development policy of the Netherlands introduced the so-called 'integrated approach', in particular in the fields of water-and-sanitation and land-and-water projects. In the North Bengal Terai Development Project this was in broad outline conceptualized as a focus on human resource development (agricultural extension work, training, demonstration plots) and involvement of women. A small pilot-project was contemplated to try out privatization of a so far government-owned river lift irrigation and deep tube well scheme. One of the assumptions behind the 'integrated

Map 1: Location of project area.

approach' policy at that time was that it would contribute to the success of achieving the social objectives of the project. It was increasingly felt that the technical components, which had dominated technical programmes so far, needed to be complemented with social interventions to enhance what is nowadays called the 'sustainability' of the project.

The aim of the project was to increase especially the production and income of marginal and small farmers, and to generate a better income distribution in the area (Evaluation Mission Phase 1, Vol. 2, 1987). It was also the intention to improve the living condition of women.

It was envisaged by one of the authors who participated in the formulation of Phase II of the project that the implementation of small-scale irrigation schemes might have positive and negative effects on different classes, castes, communities and in particular on gender. During the formulation and conception of the second phase of the Terai project these possible effects were taken into consideration. In view of that, the unique decision was made by a wise man at the India desk of the Development Cooperation office in The Hague, to approve the plan to conduct a socio-economic and gender specific impact study over a period of four years. As far as we know there is no Dutch Development Project in which an impact study of such scope and depth has been carried out.

Is the water harvesting successful with the implemented small-scale irrigation devices? Does the production and income increase of the poor farmer households in the project area? What is the change in the role of women in agriculture, household, and community, when irrigation water is introduced? How do we improve the living conditions of women and in what way we can contribute to empower them? Which negative gender effects would arise, and, if so, what countervailing measures should be taken? These were the questions that came to our mind when we designed the impact study. The findings of the gender part of the impact study form the main content of this book.[1]

The gender impact study is a component of several other gender activities that have been implemented in Phase II of the project and which will be described in Chapter 3 of this study.

Four women students of the Department of Anthropology at the University of Amsterdam studied several gender aspects of the Terai project, and of the area in detail, to collect data for their Master's degree theses (Kranenburg 1994; Loeber 1991; van Westerhoven 1995; Stroes 1997). Their experience and findings are incorporated in the analyses and interpretation.

1.2 MEANING AND RATIONALE

As stated in the outstanding recent study edited by Anil Agarwal and Sunita Narain, *Dying Wisdom*, water has been harvested in India since antiquity (1997, p. 11). Historical and archaeological research show that irrigation systems were constructed and managed by kings, individuals, communities and temples throughout the centuries and even in the third century before Christ. Unfortunately, these systems are long since eroded and in decay for many reasons which are very well analysed in the report. It seems that in West Bengal overflow irrigation in the seventeenth century worked very well until the advent of the British. It not only enriched the soil, but also controlled malaria as the fish in the floodwaters eat away the mosquito larvae. Nowadays the flashfloods in the Terai area are no longer beneficial but devastating as a result of siltation of the river beds at the foothills of the Himalayas, deforestation, and erosion in the catchment areas (Lieten 1995, p. 828). The sad current situation is that after more than fifty years of Independence there is an urgent need to review India's irrigation policy. 'Big is best' was the credo in the early years after Independence and big dams were promoted as 'temples of modern India' (Agarwal 1997, p. 315). Groundwater exploitation has become enormous over the years. Deep tube wells have been installed mainly by rich farmers with the result that water tables fell because of overexploitation with all consequences for drinking water resources. Probably no other group is more affected by the destruction and depletion of traditional water resources than women of poor households (Schenk-Sandbergen 1995).

According to Agarwal the government's record in minor surface irrigation works (defined as projects which a command area of less than 2,000 hectares) has also not been very encouraging (p. 316). The deplorable state of affairs is partly due to the breakdown in the traditional systems of management. Minor irrigation schemes suffer mainly from siltation and neglect. To find solutions for the immense problem Agarwal et al. show that with the effort of Non-Government Voluntary Organizations and local communities, interesting results have been achieved in reviving traditional water harvesting systems.

However, the reality in the Terai area at the start of Phase II in 1989 was that no major local Non-Government Organization existed, to take such an initiative. The Terai project is fully implemented by the Government Departments of Agriculture and Minor Irrigation. As the project is bi-lateral it is a project from 'government-to-government'.

Dutch Development Cooperation is pursuing a Women and Development Policy with clear aims as empowerment and increase of self-reliance for the programmes and projects that are carried out under its supervision.[2] The question may be raised, how to reach the aims of the Dutch Women and Development Policy in the above mentioned context?

This last question is raised in particular in view of the findings in women's studies which can be summarized by the following quotation of Caroline Moser: 'Historically it has been shown that the capacity to confront the nature of gender inequality and women's emancipation can only be fulfilled by the bottom-up struggle of women's organizations' (Moser 1989, p. 11).

According to Moser empowerment of women can only be reached bottom-up by mass women's organizations which have the capacity to mobilize and organize women at the grass-roots. This is a common view in women's studies on the basis of substantial amount of experience and study. We will not challenge this view in general. In fact in the main we adhere to it, but the reality in many areas is that as in the Terai only women's organizations of political parties existed, or elite women's organizations which had a social charity type of character.

The nature of the project can be characterised as a simple, but solid 'old-fashioned' government project. Innovative components of current irrigation management projects, such as the role of NGOs, community participation, training in all its varieties, environmental assessment, indigenous knowledge recording, alternative technologies, credit groups for women, were not included in Phase II of the Terai project. They were not considered in the plan as the potential, capacity, funds, awareness and the perceptions were not available, or ready for it, or sufficient.

It is in view of the above that the meaning of our detailed study on the use, functioning and impact of the 'old-fashioned' government implemented small-scale irrigation in the Terai Development Project has to be seen. Can such a project be successful? Can such a project contribute to the empowerment of women without the support of a powerful and well-rooted women's NGO? In the light of the present assortments and available paraphernalia, which are pre-supposed to be a must in the implementation of water projects, these questions look almost hopeless unrealistic. But, as we will see, the answer will be 'yes': such a project, without tooters and bells can give a substantial contribution to the harvest of water and improvement of the life of the poor and small marginal farmer households, and can strengthen the women of these households to improve their position. In the end it is namely the dedication, commitment, integrity, professional skill and quality of the personality of the people involved in the project that determines its calibre and success. The lessons that can be learned from the Terai case, and the painstaking, indeed often boring, way we carried out our impact study will be hopefully valuable.

1.3 GENDER BLINDNESS

There are only a few empirical impact studies on 'women and irrigation' from the Indian subcontinent (Epstein 1962; Stanbury 1984, 1992; Groverman and Van Walsum 1994). However, there is no lack of general irrigation studies in India, as the selected bibliography of the study of Krishna Bharadwaj on the 'state-of-the-art' of conducted research on irrigation (1990) shows. The same is revealed in a publication of the World Bank Symposium on 'Groundwater Irrigation and the Rural Poor' (Kahnert and

Levine 1993): it contains more than 45 references on irrigation studies in India, and there are many more when we include the Bangladesh and Nepal references. However, it is striking that in both books not one reference can be detected which has in some way to do with 'women and irrigation' in South Asia. It is noted that the only woman scholar who has published a good overview of existing studies on irrigation in India does not point to the missing 'gender and irrigation' research (Bhardwaj 1990).[3]

There is a deeply rooted gender notion among male and female researchers that irrigation is a male domain. The association with the actual construction work of irrigation structures which involves heavy earth moving and dirty clothes has created this image. The male engineering tradition in thinking about irrigation is firmly rooted (Zwarteveen 1993). Therefore, it is certainly not a coincidence that authors of irrigation studies in South Asia are mostly men. The consequence is that conventional irrigation studies are not only male-dominated, but also male-centered, and male-conditioned in content, selection of themes, point of view, interpretation and approach. Fields of male interest are the economic, financial and technical ins-and-outs of irrigation. In particular they focus on economic returns to investment, cost-benefit analyses, technical performance, technology choice, cropping patterns and related agricultural issues. To be fair, indeed, some male authors have gone into the role of irrigation as a mechanism to initiate equity, development and alleviate poverty, but they are a minority (Kanhert 1993). According to Zwarteveen (1993, p. 13) it is no exaggeration that women are a truly forgotten group in irrigation thinking and practice. She states that this gender blindness is partly self-sustaining. Specific women's needs and interests with respect to irrigation have never been accommodated as irrigation, as mentioned in the previous, has come to be defined and conceived as a man's world. Therefore, women's needs and interests are often perceived 'as being of only marginal significance to achieve the "mainstream" objectives'.

For a long time the male focus on irrigation resulted in practice in the unfortunate strict dichotomy of drinking water as a female domain, and irrigation water as the male domain. The compartmentalization of government departments in which drinking water lies mostly under the health department has perpetuated this artificial dichotomy. This splitting up of water sectors had negative effects on success of irrigation projects, as both forms of water usage are in daily life very much related for rural women of poor households and should not be divided, in advance, by gender biased notions and bureaucratic decisions. Therefore, we have explicitly included women, irrigation water and drinking water aspect in our analysis.

Is the lack of 'gender and irrigation' studies specific to South Asia', it is noticeable that in countries where the role of women in agricultural production is visible and recognized, some more studies on 'women, gender and irrigation' have been conducted and published: the African countries (Carney 1988) and countries in South East Asia such as the Philippines (Illo 1988). This shows that the gender blindness for South Asia might relate to the perception of males on economic roles of women. Women are not considered 'water users' as they are not the owners of the land, and their agricultural work is undervalued, or even ignored. Most male scholars possess urban midde-class gender outlooks, mostly based on their own family situation, in which they are the breadwinners, and their wives the mothers and housewives. As we will see in Chapter 3, the prevailing gender ideology that it is lowering to family status if the women work outside, was prevalent among the male planner, decision makers and implementers of the North Bengal Development Project.

More enlightened and less stereotyped male authors tend to reduce women as helpers and supporters of men, or as part-time workers earning some additional money. The 'breadwinner bias' is of course confirmed and reinforced by the overwhelming patriarchal, patrilocal and patrilineal social organization and culture in Indian society. The status-giving seclusion of women, is one of the mechanism that perpetuates male power and male dominance. The *purdah* ideology among the better-off middle classes provokes not only the invisibility and ignorance, but also the low value, of women's productive labour. *Purdah* ideology is also socialized by scholars, which generates the underexposure of the role of women in irrigated agriculture.

On the other hand it is also true that statistics indicate that the formal labour participation rates of women in agriculture in the northern Indian states are very low, and much higher in southern states where *purdah* is less and many women are involved in rice cultivation (Gulati 1975; Sen 1985). Our study still show in detail that the reality of women's labour participation in the Terai area is substantial. However, specifications are necessary, not in the least class-, caste-, or community wise, but also per agricultural crop, season and composition of the family. Moreover, post-harvest operations are often not included in those statistics. These figures give the crops their use-, and cash value and as such these operations are part of agricultural activities. Post-harvest women's work is very well analysed in anthropological women's studies in villages in Bangladesh (White 1992; Chen 1986). Thus there is not only a gap in studies and research on gender aspects in irrigation studies as a result of a double gender blindness, but also a lack of development of successful gender sensitive alternatives to irrigation planning, design and management, as Zwarteveen (1993), has pointed out. In this respect she also blames 'women in development' advocates and NGOs working for, and with women who have criticized irrigation planners for their gender biased approaches (Zwarteveen 1993, p. 14). They give too much emphasis to what is desirable (empowerment of women) and too little to what is possible: and that is often only 'to make sure that the right amount of water is delivered at the right time'. It is obvious that in many government irrigation projects the capacity to change gender inequities is very limited.

Since the past few years the focus in irrigation topics has shifted to privatization of ownership of assets, and community management transfer, in particular of small-scale irrigation devices (Sengupta 1991; Maloney 1994; Kloezen and Samad 1995). This 'new' focus on 'turnover' fits into the global drive for promotion of free-market policies, liberalization, and the pushing of the sustainability concept in development cooperation policies. Rajni Kothari writes in his challenging book *Growing Amnesia* (1993, p. 8), 'perhaps the most serious outcome of the new economic thinking, both globally and nationally, is this undermining of the role of the State'.

Kothari concludes in his spectacular analysis that development is shifting from the state to the market. 'Liberalization' and 'privatization' are the two catchwords that go along with the advocacy of the market (1993, p. 8). His very serious concern is that, among other things, the whole rationale of development as reduction of poverty and promotion of equity dwindles. He warns that it should be realised that the model of liberalization through privatization works against the interests of the poor (1993, p. 74).

As Kothari has noted, developmentalists have created and atmosphere around the concept of 'sustainable development' which gives the socially concerned a sense that their cause has prevailed, while (according to him) this is impossible without a fundamental change in the ethics and values of development (1993, p. 104). We share his concern, given the prevailing poverty and agrarian production relations and conditions in India. Regarding privatization and its effect on women, we are very worried that in particular the poorest women of marginal farmer households and the landless women will be adversely affected.

In 'management oriented' studies no attention (Uphoff 1991), or less that half a page, is spent on women (Maloney, p. 299), stating that their involvement in the management of the scheme will be crucial for its success. 'Why', 'how', and 'when' is not elaborated, nor explained.

With the intrusion of the 'community participation' and 'community managed and government supported' approach in the world of development cooperation there is some response from women scholars and activists. There is a growing pile of richly illustrated journals, workshop reports, embassy brochures and scattered case-studies on 'women and water' and 'women and water management'. However, most of these studies relate to water supply management in drinking water and sanitation projects.

1.4 NEW INTERESTS: WOMEN (GENDER), LAND AND WATER RIGHTS

The discourse on gender analysis in development planning has contributed to an increasing interest in women and water management issues. Central to this analysis are questions as, who uses, who has access, and who controls resources and who benefits from the resources and who is disadvantaged. More participation of women in decision making and management of any kind of activity which is male-dominated is encouraged and promoted, to acquire more access and control over resources by women, which is hoped to result in more 'empowerment' for women.

Recently, the interest in the subject 'women and water' is expanding in international women's platforms and donors. The paradigm of gender concern has shifted to themes as 'women and management of natural resources' and 'land and water rights' for women. A need is expressed in action plans and policies to secure women's rights to land, water and other natural resources (Fourth World Conference on Women, Beijing 1995). The main reason for the current donor concern of women's rights to land and water is the awareness that the environmental crises have a severe impact on livelihood systems of in particular women of poor households whose survival resources and their rights to these resources, are quickly eroding (Rights of Women 1997, p. 1).

It is said that the worldwide articulated concern for the degradation of the environment has to open the eyes of the international development world to draw attention to the theme of rights of women on land and water. That is surprising as it is known from anthropological studies that, for example, in South Asia women have according to state laws and succession acts all rights to inherit land, but hardly any married women owns land (Sharma 1980; Rahman and Van Schendel 1997). A study conducted by one of the authors of this book on land rights in Laos shows that the right of the majority of women to land is secured by the matrilineal society in which three social aspects are decisive: kinship and descent, post-marriage residence, and customary inheritance rights (Schenk-Sandbergen 1998).

Moreover, many eminent peasant, tribal and women's struggles, uprisings and movements have fought for fair rights on land, water and forests (Kelkar 1992; Agarwal 1994). Till now, the role of women in peasant struggles and uprisings and ecological movements (Chipco) was and is very impressive. It is in this historical context that in the next chapter on the historical role of women in the important peasant movements of the Terai area will be sketched. Before women became 'handpump beneficiaries' in the North Bengal Terai Development Project they probably were peasant heroines fighting for their rights of land and water. The main line of thinking in the book and the red thread is, if and in what way gender supportive project interventions can empower or strengthen women from 'above', to emancipate them so that they can struggle from 'below' to become again heroines in the future. Therefore the title of the book is: From Heroines to Beneficiaries; From Beneficiaries to Heroines? The questionmark reveals that we are cautious, as we realize that it is too ambitious to think that this process can emerge over a short time span with such limited activities that were possible in the project.

In view of the above it is amazing that the impact of irrigation on women is such a step-child in empirical studies and that gender aspects related to irrigation are so underexposed and invisible. Is irrigation not directly related to food, to production of rice, wheat, vegetables? Would this not have the interest of women of poor households in India, where millions of children and adults are suffering from undernourishment? And, is it not reiterated in women's studies that women feel very responsible for the daily food production as a consequence of the division of labour between the sexes?

The subject is even becoming more relevant as political parties in India increasingly in the 1990s seem to realize that food is an important issue for the majority of the Indian electorate. They hurry in drawing up 'food manifestos' to promise a variety of cheap food schemes for the poor. Instruction is even given by the New Delhi authorities to the Planning Commission to undertake a major exercise in providing food security.[4] And, it is easy to see why. General economic policies of liberalization and privatization, and the rise of prices of essential commodities have worsened the poor's purchasing power to buy food; the more as in many places in India daily wages—in particular those paid to women—remain far below the official minimum. Rural women of poor households are hit the most as they have to purchase food for the family.

Irrigation water is an important means to increase food production and it is our experience that the rural women of poor and landless households are very aware of that. In the Tungabhadra Canal Irrigation Project in which one of us worked, the women say, 'We know the problems of water better than men. We have to transplant rice, to irrigate vegetables, to provide drinking water to our children and cattle. Let us manage the water (Schenk-Sandbergen 1998, p. 1).'

1.5 WOMEN AND IRRIGATION STUDIES

The few academic studies on the impact of irrigation on women show that irrigation schemes can have a wide ranging effect on women's life and labour. Let us first look at the negative findings. It is argued that an increase in household income (which irrigation provides) may draw women out of the paid agricultural labour force (Sharma 1980). It is indicated that in particular in traditional *purdah* observing societies irrigation can lead to the withdrawal of girls and women from the agricultural labour force to the more highly valued practice of female seclusion (Stanbury 1992). In women's studies this process is called the domestication of women. An increase in family income can improve the total well-being of the family, but at the cost of greater female dependency on male earners. Stanbury differentiates this picture by indicating that the impact of irrigation is of course different for women of different castes and classes: irrigation benefits do not reach all women equally. She states that irrigation has increased the gap between the opportunities available to landless and landed women. She shows that in her village in north India the participation of landowning women has increased but she predicts that it is likely that the landless Harijan women will lose their primary source of cash income, wage work in agriculture, as irrigation has accelerated rural mechanization. She also reveals that for the lowest classes of women labour saving devices purchased by their employers in the field of water, fuel and fodder procurement, have reduced wage labour opportunities. Stanbury concludes that despite the increase in cash and greater contact with urban centres, village women remain relatively isolated from economic activities and decision making. As reason she mentions the custom of *purdah* and the cultural features surrounding it.

However, Scarlett Epstein (1962) who has studied the impact of irrigation in two villages—one with, and one without irrigation—in Karnataka indicates positive effects on women of irrigation. She found that village women achieved greater independence with irrigation through increased income from livestock raising. In her unirrigated control village women had to depend on their husbands who obtained a new source of income from wage labour in the nearby town.

Groverman and Van Walsum (1994) describes the impact of bore well- and surface water lift irrigation on women in Andhra Pradesh. They found a shift in the gender division of labour due to the change from a traditional mixed cropping pattern to a pattern emphasizing the monocropping of cash crops. They noticed that women remain in charge of 'traditional' food crops and men take responsibility for 'modern' cash crops. Moreover, they indicate a shift in control over production to men, due to a shift from a subsistence oriented economy towards integration in the market economy. As we will see later in our study in which the same will be revealed, men go for bank loans, buy seeds, and purchase pesticides and fertilizers. Agriculture is being taken away from women as they are almost cut off from the new methods of cultivation. The modernization of agriculture and the decrease of the value of women's work because it is linked to sustenance, and non profits, have been described in an impressive way by Vandana Shiva (1988). Groverman and Van Walsum also report that irrigation has provided more work for women labourers in agriculture but the shift from payment of wages in kind to payment in cash has affected the food security of the households of agricultural labourers. They also point to the increased use of pesticides, 'which may affect the health of women more than men' (1994, p. 89). Their pilot study shows that the gender impact of irrigation interventions depends largely on contextual variables and such variables should be taken into account when designing and implementing a specific irrigation intervention.

Summarizing the above a positive impact might be that women also benefit from more production and consequently more income for their families. Negative consequences might be the withdrawal of women from productive labour, re-enforcement of a *purdah* (seclusion) ideology, deterioration in the status of women, more inequality in gender relations, loss of agricultural skills, more work load, less decision-making power, more indebtedness and more pressure for women of poor households to do agricultural wage labour (Agarwal 1981, 1986; Shiva 1989; Menon 1995; Sen 1982; Kelkar 1981; Groverman and Van Walsum 1994; Zwarteveen 1997).

1.6 THE NEED FOR 'ENGENDERING' IRRIGATION STUDIES

Why is there a need to 'engender' irrigation studies? The most obvious reason is of course to study the possible positive and negative effects of an irrigation scheme on women. The knowledge of the negative effects will hopefully contribute to a better gender aware planning and management which might reduce the chances of negative effect. However, also the positive effects should be strengthened in order to support the improvement of living conditions and process of empowerment and emancipation of women.

The question, 'why there is a need to engender irrigation studies' can be replied from various angles.

First there is the reality that rural women of various castes, classes and communities participate to a high degree in food production, and agricultural cultivation and that change in production of crops by means of irrigation will have an impact on them in their farm work, domestic labour, motherhood role, and development. Labour force participation is very much determined by women's responsibility for child care and other domestic work.

Second, decisions over and cost for irrigation schemes and paying of water fees will directly influence the daily expenses and life of women that their children's future development opportunities in the long run. That in itself should urge scholars to take up gender and irrigation studies without delay.

Third, the need for the engendering of irrigation studies has a very crucial social purpose in terms of contribution to Women in Development Cooperation policies. Gender experts are sent to all places in the world in order to strengthen women in irrigation development, but they desperately lack basic information and detailed studies on the impact of irrigation in various ecological, socio-economic and political contexts to formulate alternatives in making irrigation planning and management more gender sensitive. Moreover, in development projects time and money is often not allotted to conduct a serious gender study as a basis for drawing up recommendations for action and intervention in inception and formulation reports. Often this compels Women in Development experts to propose the general conventional wisdom to start a gender awareness training course for the male staff of the project.

It is our conviction that relevant gender aware irrigation activities, in particular for poor farm women, can only be proposed when they are based on serious specific in-depth gender studies in which eventually mixed methods of anthropology and (sustained) participatory appraisals can be applied.

At the practical, operational level, the 'engendering' of irrigation studies has an important 'learning-by-doing' component in itself. From the beginning of our research we consulted, discussed and communicated with policy makers, managers, implementors, and the farm women of poor households at different levels on the content and meaning of the research. As views and perspectives have been shared and exchanged with the responsible government officials from the Indian and Dutch side, a surplus-value was already generated in the process while conducting the studies: the wider raising of gender awareness. Asking attention for the women and irrigation component of the research is in itself a tool to generate awareness on gender components. This opened doors to operational clarity regarding the advisable project support for women's involvement in various activities of the project. Nowadays, manuals and check lists for gender planning in irrigation projects are drawn up to involve women in all phases of a project (SAWA 1993). But, in fact this is often done without a context, without the basic knowledge and insight of the ideological and socio-economic impact irrigation has on the women of marginal and small farming homes in various historical, ecological, socio-economic and political conditions. One should be cautious not to fall into the trap to assume that irrigation is by its nature always good for women, or to be on the safe side that it will not worsen their situation. These assumptions have to be studied first in context and on the basis of these findings the gender planning recommendations and instructions can be drawn.

More specifically, this volume may contribute to the ongoing theoretical debate in women's studies and feminist anthropology on how to achieve an optimal 'gender planning' with the aim to strengthen and/or to empower women in development interventions. Related to this, we hope that this study will reveal in what way 'empowerment' can be operationalized in a specific irrigation intervention context. An earlier article on the gender aspects in the Terai project (Schenk-Sandbergen 1991) in which the question 'what is the scope for empowerment in a bilateral government project' was raised, was used in the reader of the gender awareness course for staff of the Development Co-operation Department of the Ministry of Foreign Affairs. There, it was presented as an example of what today will be labelled as 'best practice'. Let us see if this qualification can still be given some years later when the impact of the project has some time to crystallize.

One thing is clear. There is a definite need to conduct empirical studies that analyse the content and relevance of gender concepts in a given local setting. The findings might help to develop successful alternatives in irrigation development, in which the women's view is articulated. We consider it a challenge to show how in the framework of the North Bengal Terai Project a sound gender impact study has been conducted, and how its findings, besides contributing to gender theories and policies, might be translated in social relevant recommendations for a 'gender specific strategy' not only for the present phase in the Terai but for a wider range of irrigation interventions. We are adherers of the credo that research should contribute to, and reflect on, practical development policies and foremost concrete implementation (Hommes 1970). With this approach we hope to bridge the gap that often exists between scholars, policy makers and consultants.

Finally there is a need for the engendering of the so far male-colonized irrigation subject from the angle of the relevance of scientific development. A deconstruction of the existing viricentric bias in 'irrigation' studies and a blend between the male and female perspective on the subject will be an enrichment. In other fields of social science the 'engendering' of conventional male-dominated subjects has brought forward tacit dimensions and innovative concepts (Schenk-Sandbergen 1995). It is hoped that our study will yield similar results as concepts as 'empowerment', changing gender division of labour, gender sustainability, gender relations and unequal power relations between men and women will be its key ingredients: concepts that represent and reflect the women's perspective on irrigation.

The importance of our study should also be seen in view of the global economic transformation process of 'liberalization' and 'privatization' policies which are widely promoted and implemented by the Indian government. Also in the Terai project after eight years of experience with implementing small-scale irrigation technology which has had remarkable success in reaching the target groups (landless, marginal and small farmers, and women), 'privatization' of the larger irrigation devices—the deep tube wells (DTW) and the river lift irrigation (RLI)—is pursued by the donor in the current third phase. 'Privatization' is assumed to be the best development strategy for 'sustainable development' and perceived as a necessity, in spite of the fact that the capital costs in the Terai project are financed from the state budget of West Bengal (mainly through the additional Dutch donor contribution) whereas the recurrent costs such as maintenance, repair and fuel subsidy are borne fully by the West Bengal state government. The latter is also responsible for organizing operations and maintenance. However, due to an enormous increase in irrigation works (Dutch Project, World Bank Project and regular state implementation), scarcity of funds is mounting, and although this is of course a question of policy priorities, the West Bengal government does not seem to be capable of financing its operation and maintenance obligation.

It is assumed that cost recovery from farmers can only be achieved by privately-owned, but commonly managed, irrigation systems (Schenk-Sandbergen 1994).

If this transformation will expand, it will no doubt have a structural effect in the near future on farm- and landless women in the project area. It seems realistic to expect that we can be pessimistic on the nature of the effect, unless other profound changes which respond to class and gender interests and rights will be initiated.

1.7 METHODOLOGY OF THE GENDER IMPACT STUDY

Let us now briefly describe the nature of the socio-economic impact study on which the gender material in this volume is mainly based. The impact-study consisted of two components:

A longitudinal in-depth study at eight locations, where in a total of 273 households were visited repeatedly between 1989 and 1993;

A one time sample survey, which covered 1,524 households (see Map 2 for the research locations).

The in-depth study documented in detail changes over a period of four years in the living conditions of selected farm households visited after each agricultural season. The in-depth study concentrated on the changes in cultivation and farm income, as a result of the availability of irrigation water and the extent to which the target groups of marginal/small farmers and scheduled castes/tribes were reached. Community and class are the analytical categories in the general study. The classification of communities is based on the existing caste and community composition. For the classification of class we had to follow the classification of farmers as used by the Department of Agriculture in West Bengal and consequently in the North Bengal Terai Development Project (see Table 1.1). The classification is based on hectares but in practice acres and *bigha's* were more useful to differentiate the farmers' classes. Therefore, acres and *bigha's*

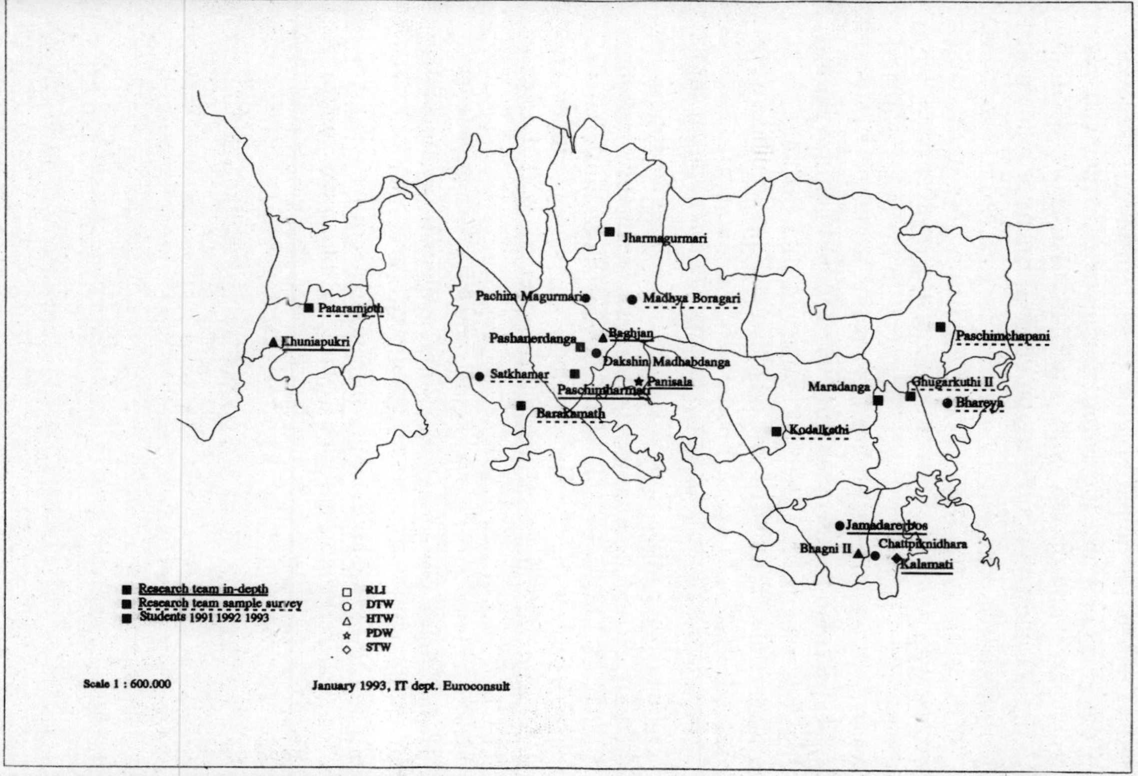

Map 2: Location of research and surveys.

are also mentioned in Table 1.1. The classification problem will be discussed in Chapter 5.

In addition, the in-depth study tried to identify the conditions for success and failure of the different irrigation facilities. It also tried to assess the impact of the newly-introduced irrigation on the workload and the living conditions of women in the 'beneficiary'[5] households, and especially to explore whether the project had contributed to the empowerment of women in the project area.

In irrigation projects the target groups are mostly the land owners, with a prioritization of marginal and small farmers. The landless are assumed to gain indirectly from the anticipated increase in agricultural production. In our study we focussed explicitly on landless women (and men) to find out how far the project has benefitted them. Changes in their livelihood, in particular the availability of paid employment opportunities, were assessed.

The sample survey was undertaken to put the in-depth study in wider perspective and thus covered the same fields. In addition, it tried to identify the various constraints—administrative, technical, social—which might have hindered the optimum use of the various schemes. The sample survey encompassed the entire project area and concerned the three agricultural seasons of 1992-3.

The methodology of the in-depth study is the so-called 'before-and-after' methodology which has the qualitative advantage that the conditions of selected households can be compared before and after the installation of the irrigation facilities.

In order to be able to compare the sample survey with the

TABLE 1.1: CLASSIFICATION OF FARMERS BY SIZE OF HOLDING

Class	Hectares	Acres	*Bighas*
Marginal	0-1	0-2.5	0.1-7
Small	1-2	2,5-5	7-15
Middle	2-4	5-10	15-30
Large	>4	>10	>30

in-depth study with respect to the size of the sample in comparison with the total number of irrigation schemes installed under Phase II of the project, Table 1.2 is presented.

The table shows that the size of the handpump sample in the in-depth study (0.3 per cent) is much smaller than that of the other components. This has been rectified in the sample survey (see for criteria of selection of sites, Annexure 1).

Ten research assistants and associates, of which the majority are born and raised in the Terai as sons of farmers, have stayed during long time spells in the villages working under difficult conditions: they resided in deserted pump houses without electricity and furniture, and in a Christian orphanage which was converted into the Cooch Behar field research office. The research assistants have visited each of the 273 households at least 10 times: first they have documented the base-line situation (1989-90) and subsequently visited the same households at least once in every agricultural season (pre-*kharif*, *kharif*, and *rabi*) over three years (till 1992-3). Many of them have become 'adopted sons' of the respondents, but sometimes they were kept 'hostage' by the farmers to put pressure on the officials of the Department of Agriculture for example to get installations repaired.

TABLE 1.2: SAMPLE SIZES IN-DEPTH STUDY AND SAMPLE SURVEY AND TOTAL NUMBER OF IRRIGATIONAL FACILITIES (PHASE II)

Irrig. Schemes	Sanctioned number (Phase II)	In-depth study			Sample survey		
		Size of sample		No. of HH	Size of sample		No. of HH
		No.	%		No.	%	
Hand Tube Well	24.030	85	0.3	85	825	3.4	825
Pump Dug Well	300	3	1.0	8	15	5.0	49
Shallow Tube Well	150	3	2.0	15	15	10.0	74
Deep Tube Well	16	1	6.0	75	3	18.7	176
River Lift Irrigation	30	1	3.3	60	5	16.7	354
Landless				30			46
Total				273			1,524

We, the authors of this book and supervisors of the research, have regularly paid visits to the fieldwork locations, in connection with the fieldwork of the assistants, and have spoken to about 25 per cent of the households. Our visits served the purpose of getting personally acquainted with the living conditions and the ways in which the project had an impact on these conditions, of as many women and men as possible. This has resulted, e.g. in a sizable body of qualitative data, some of which we present in this study.

In order to ensure that reliable data on women would be collected in the research, separate detailed questionnaires were drawn up only for women in the base-line study. The questionnaire used for the follow-up study contained a special section on women and a special questionnaire for landless households.

The drawing up of a special questionnaire for women, however, does not at all guarantee that the 'women's perspective' will be reflected in the research. This is mainly due to the double male dominance in interview situation in which women are asked questions by a male interviewer, and answered by male persons around in the village. It happened that women often started to give the replies and then in the middle of a sentence they stopped talking when a male relative or a neighbour turned up. The team developed several ways to avoid this kind of male dominance by asking to see the kitchen in the house or to take chance to interview women whose husband, male neighbours, of relatives were not around. To avoid tension from the male interviewer side, local village women and girls were recruited to interview women respondents. The approach at the village/scheme level was based on the common knowledge in women's cross-cultural studies that date collecting on women requires a specific methodology. One of the pre-conditions of this methodology is that women investigators should gather data from women, as they have more access and a better communication with other women. Women respondents feel more free and unconstrained to talk on their gender-specific problems in the presence of other women (Golde 1970; Whitehead 1986; Warren 1988; Schenk-Sandbergen 1992).

In the beginning of the in-depth study a few women anthropologist were recruited and joined the team, but they left soon as

Plate 2: Local trained village women of the research unit.

their parents did not like them to stay overnight in the field. Therefore a solution was found involving local village girls and women to conduct interviews with women. The selection of local women was not a process of our free choice. The head of the village council, or panchayat leader had to be approached, and he would strongly recommend a daughter, wife or female relative for the work. It seemed impossible to ignore his wishes and approach poor educated girls and women directly. However, in one village we were lucky to include a fearless woman in the team representing the spirit and mentality of her courageous sisters who fought in the Tebhaga and Naxalite peasant revolts in this area.

The local women got an on the spot training to conduct the interviews by the 'learning-by-doing' method in the beginning under the guidance of the experienced male field workers. In a short time the local girls and women were able to do the interviewing on their own (see Plate 2).

As no computer was available at the start of the in-depth study, the collected data were processed manually. A technological

TABLE 1.3. LOCATION AND NUMBER OF HOUSEHOLDS COVERED BY THE IN-DEPTH STUDY

Location	Type of Irrigationfacility	No. of households interviewed
Jamardabos, Dinhata I	Deep tube well (DTW)	75
Paschim Harmati, Mainagura	River lift system (RLI)	60
Bhangni II, Dinhata	Hand tube wells (HTW)	
Bagjan, Maynaguri	Hand tube wells	85
Velkujot, Kharibari Phansidewa	Hand tube wells	
Kalamati, Dinhata II	Shallow tube well (STW)	15
Panisala, Makliganj	Pump dug well (PDW)	8
Landless Labourers		30
Total		273

revolution, and a big leap forward in human resource development, took place in the research office with the purchase of a computer at the end of 1991. Unfortunately, this innovation was too late to relieve the research staff of this tedious, labourious work of the in-depth study. The sample survey heralded a new era of D-base processed data, Lotus graphs, and figures.

During the base-line survey in 1989-90 special emphasis was given to data on the women of 243 beneficiary households under various irrigation schemes. In addition, women of 30 landless labourer households were also studied Table 1.3 shows that in total 273 women were selected for the in-depth study. This number decreased to 261 households at the end of the survey, as a number of families had outmigrated.

In the sample survey one respondent from each household, usually the head of the household, acted as the key informant. Table 1.4 describes the age and gender characteristics of these informants.

The sample survey gives a good insight in what happens as 14 male and one female interviewer go in the field with notions to interview the head of the household. The result is that 1,412 men and 66 women are interviewed as the main respondents. Only 4.5 per cent of women (most of them younger than the male informants) were approached (came forward) to act as key

TABLE 1.4: AGE AND SEX OF THE KEY INFORMANTS

Scheme	Hhs.	Sex of Informants				Age range (years)	
		Male		Female		Male	Female
		No.	%	No.	%		
RLI	354	346	98	8	2	16-80	21-60
DTW	176	174	99	2	1	16-78	35-40
HTW	825	770	93	55	7	16-80	22-65
STW	74	73	99	1	1	17-70	36
PWD	49	49	100	0	0	16-70	–
Total	1,478	1,412	95.5	66	4.5	–	–

informants; out of 66 female informants 55 belonged to handpump beneficiary households. However, to correct this gender bias we collected gender-specific data in the sample survey from the interviewed males by including specific questions for the women of the house.

The total population of 1,478 households in the Sample Survey belonging to different irrigation schemes is 8,466 which means an average household size of 5.7 persons. The class distribution per irrigation device of the 1,478 household is given in Table 1.5.

The class wise distribution in the sample survey reveals that the hand tube well (HTW) sample has more than 80 per cent marginal farmer households; it is followed by deep tube well (DTW) and river lift irrigation (RLI). Also, more than half the pump dug well (PDW) sample has marginal farmer households.

TABLE 1.5: CLASS-WISE DISTRIBUTION OF FARM HOUSEHOLDS IN THE SAMPLE SURVEY

Scheme	Total HHs	Marginal		Small		Middle		Large	
		No.	%	No.	%	No.	%	No.	%
RLI	354	222	62.7	90	25.4	34	9.6	8	2.3
DTW	176	124	70.4	38	21.6	10	5.7	4	2.3
HTW	825	666	80.7	130	15.8	27	3.3	2	0.2
STW	74	15	20.2	37	50	15	20.2	7	9.6
PDW	49	26	53	16	32.7	7	14.3	–	–
Total	1,478	1,053	71.2	311	21	93	6.3	21	1.5

Taking all schemes together the marginal and small farmers constitute the major part of the sample (92 per cent). The middle and large farmers make up the remaining 8 per cent.

The implication of the nature of the sample survey is that our analysis has a strong focus on women of poor households and that the impact of irrigation on different classes of women can only be traced for a small group of women from middle- and large farmers households. These figures show that the North Bengal Terai Development Project has reached the target group, the poorer farm households belonging to Scheduled Castes and Scheduled Tribes, for whom this project has been primarily sanctioned.

The material of the book is not only based on the findings of the statistical data of the questionnaires of the in-depth study and the sample survey, but—as mentioned earlier—even more on the qualitative data collected during field visits over the years and talks with women in the area at the veranda of houses, sitting near the handpumps and observing their use. On our way to pumphouses we had talks with village leaders, members of water user committees and small groups of women. Discussions with all involved staff from the agricultural extension worker level to the Director of Agriculture were intensive and frequent. Also the reactions in the workshops we organized to inform the grass root workers on the findings of the research has greatly contributed to our insight and understanding of the social relations and change process in the Terai. In this way much qualitative data has been collected which we hope can flavour our presentation of tables with a vivid and colourful touch.

1.8. CONTENT AND AIMS OF THE GENDER IMPACT STUDIES

The scope of the in-depth study and the sample survey was wide since it had to deal with women from diverse communities and various types of irrigation technology: handpumps, deep tube wells, river lift irrigation, pump dug wells and shallow tube wells. As anthropologists we have not limited our focus strictly to agriculture and irrigation but have developed a rather flexible set of questions covering 'women, irrigated agriculture and development' in a broad sense.

To obtain a clearer understanding of the key variables influencing gender roles and relationships in irrigated agricultural systems we have addressed the following themes in our questionnaires, talks and interviews:

- The context of the location; community, class, landownership, land size, cropping pattern, productivity, income and changes in it, access to and control over irrigation water, use and performance of the schemes.
- Position of women in the family; family size and composition, ages, age of marriage, dowries, fertility pattern, education, main occupations in the household.
- Women's domestic and economic roles; household labour to indicate the workload and time spending with special attention for the impact of handpumps, division of labour in order to make women's role in agrarian production visible, changes in work-load and wage labour, changing perceptions on wage labour.
- Women, patriarchy and empowerment; the decision making role of women in agricultural and family matters, financial autonomy of women earning wages, freedom of movement, gender composition of water user groups.
- Constraints and gender perception of problems, interests, solutions and ambitions of the interviewed women for future development.

Briefly summarizing, this book aims:

- To describe the eminent history, difficult life, hard work, few joys and many problems of mainly women of marginal and small farmers' households living in three districts and in the project area of the Indo-Dutch North Bengal Terai Development Project.
- To analyse which changes have occurred in women's household- and agricultural work, gender relations and gender

ideology due to the implementation of a predominantly irrigation-oriented project.

- To show whether irrigation development can be a mechanism to improve the living conditions of women and girls and reduce male dominance and subordination of women.
- To indicate how farm women (and men) of poor households can be strengthened (empowered) in general, and specifically within the realm of irrigation development anticipating the future drive for privatization and withdrawal of the state.

1.9. ORGANIZATION OF THIS VOLUME

In the next chapter we will sketch in brief the historical and socio-political context by highlighting the illustrious role tribal and peasant women played in the revolutionary peasant movements and uprisings of the study area. The variety in background of the main communities, as Rajbansis, Namasudras, and tribal women will be indicated, but has to remain sketchy because of lack of data. The gender history, gender activities and the gender capacity in the implementing government organizations of the North Bengal Development Project are described and analysed in Chapter 3. In Chapter 4 the basic gender data of the project area will be central, presenting the findings of the impact research on socio-demographic aspects, kinship, residence patterns, inheritance, marriage, motherhood, and problems as dowries and illiteracy of poor farm women. Chapter 5 concentrates on the changes that were evoked by the use of irrigation water on the labour participation in household and agriculture labour. Moreover, we analyse if traces of domestication could be found. The perception of the women on their changing roles as housewives and farm workers will be revealed. Chapter 6 analyses the impact of irrigation on the workload of women, the changing gender division of agriculture- and domestic-labour, and wage labour pattern over a time period of four years. In Chapter 7 special attention is given to the impact of the Terai small-scale irrigation scheme on women of landless households. Did they get more employment, more labour days and a better income position? Very important is the question if and how far the Terai project could act as a mechanism to reduce patriarchal power by reducing male dominance in decision making in agriculture and the family. Are women strengthened to get more access and control over the resources like land and water? Some answers are given in Chapter 8. The achievements and constraints of other gender project activities as for example farm women training, the appointment of women extension workers, and the role of women in water users' committees is recorded in Chapter 9. In Chapter 10 the main gender findings are summarized at the theoretical and operational level. A reflection on gender-specific strategies and interventions in small scale irrigation projects is given that may be useful for future projects.

NOTES

1. The findings of the general socio-economic impact study have been documented in project reports and documents of the Research & Evaluation Unit of the NBTDP: Report No. 13, Summary In-depth Study (1989-90 to 1992-3); Report No. 14, Report of the Sample Survey (1992-3); Report No. 15, Overview main Findings Socio-Economic Impact Study, Arnhem, The Netherlands, Euroconsult. See also, Niren Choudhury, and Loes Schenk-Sandbergen (1994), 'Irrigation and Rural Development: the Impact of Small-scale Irrigation in the North Bengal Terai Region' (manuscript).
2. See Action Programme Women and Development, Ministry of Foreign Affairs, Directorate-General for International Cooperation, The Hague 1986-7, and Sector Papers, Women and Development, Policy on an operational footing: main points and checklist, Directorate General for International Cooperation/Ministry of Foreign Affairs, the Netherlands, March 1989
   No. 1, Women and Agriculture
   No. 2, Women and Water & Sanitation
   No. 3, Women and Health
   No. 4, Women and Energy, Forestry & Environment.
3. It shows the conditioning of female scholars in the male approach and content of science which is a widely discussed topic in women's studies, but cannot be elaborated here (Harding 1983; Mies 1983).
4. Tilak D. Gupta states in his revealing article that obviously a factor for the rethinking on the 'myth' of food self sufficiently in India is that Food Corporation of India's storehouses were, and are, bursting out of their hinges with a record amount of food surplus. However, the surplus

is mounting up as the poor have no purchasing power to buy food grains and other food commodities (p. 9, *The Telegraph*, 8 February 1995).

5. In this context we use the word 'beneficiary' as this is the usual terminology in project documents and in the daily practice of the government line department. We feel reluctant to use the word as it has strong connotations of welfare and of bestowing favours on a passive people.

2. From Heroines to Women Beneficiaries: Historical Context

2.1 HISTORY, GENDER AND DEVELOPMENT

Arriving in the Terai, one disembarks at the cities Bagdogra or Siliguri. A quick look at the streets and market places shows that this is a male dominated society. In the markets only a handful of obviously poor women sell vegetables and forest products; in the streets 80 per cent are men, the others poor servant women, school girls, ragpicker girls and younger women accompanied by their husbands. The processions behind the bier of a deceased person which marches dispersed in between the awful crowded traffic at Hillcart road are only male, because 'Women are soft, and cry, therefore they stay at home'. Waiters in hotel are males, only a few women are room maids. The act of changing traveller's cheques at the State Bank of India in Siliguri shows that out of the 200 male employees there are 12 women, of whom the two I spoke with were older widows. This rather gender polarized visible world is a reality, but it does not say much on power in class and caste terms. Out of the 80 per cent males in the streets perhaps 70 per cent are poor rickshaw pullers, petty traders, shop servants, sweepers, etc. The powerful hide in white ambassadors and maruti jeeps and are relatively invisible.

The scene does not change much in less urbanized smaller towns as Jalpaiguri, Cooch Behar, Alipurduhar or even smaller rural places: not even Naxalbari. Now Naxalbari is a small neglected place where the small railway station looks deserted and in decay, but in the past this tiny village was the cradle of historical events and became a landmark in the protest movements of the poor peasants and peasant women of India.

Thanks to a male historian who has recorded and documented the heroic role of women in this peasant movement, we have some knowledge about the strong, powerful and autonomous position of peasant women at that time (Sen 1985). It awakens us to the fact that the gender position of (rural) women has detoriated in the Terai region over time. It urges us to search for the historical dynamics that transformed the heroines of the past into 'handpump women-beneficiaries' in a Indo-Dutch small-scale irrigation project.

As will be revealed below, the gender history of the Terai area illustrates very well that the view commonly held that women have traditionally been oppressed in Third World societies, and that 'development' and 'modernization' are the keys to strengthen and to empower them is for the majority of women a misconception. The opposing view will be presented here, asserting that women's status in the Terai was relatively high in the past, but has deteriorated due to introduction of the structure and ideology of male dominance, as corollaries of the integration of mainstream upper-caste Hindu gender ideology with capitalist transformation processes. This finding is not a new perspective. In particular the anthropologist Eleanor Leacock has collected substantial cross-cultural evidence to demask the myth of male-dominance in traditional Third World societies (Etienne and Leacock 1980; Leacock 1981). In this context we can also refer to studies which have documented the destruction and undermining of matrilineal and matrilocal societies in India and Laos (Agarwal 1994; Schenk-Sandbergen 1995a).

In a development project as the Terai small-scale irrigation project, aiming to 'empower', and pursue 'autonomy' for, women according to Dutch development policy, it seems relevant to be aware of the historical dimensions and dynamics of these concepts and to understand the local context. We shall, therefore, highlight the heroic role poor peasant women and their tribal sisters played in revolutionary movements in the Terai. We will also analyse what they gained or lost by it. When we look in the mirror of the past, we become more cautious about introducing approaches in the small-scale Terai project, such as organization, mobilization, participation and accommodating women's needs and interests.

Similar concepts were of course the vital forces behind the immense struggle of the women (and men) in the revolutionary movements of respectively forty and twenty years ago to improve their downtrodden conditions. The crucial difference, however, is that at that time these thoughts and ideas came from below, from the people themselves, whereas at present they are introduced from above by the project with the expectation that they will be taken up by the people themselves.

The women in the Terai have gone through a revolution in which they have heavily suffered and sacrificed much to fulfil what is at present in Moser terminology identified as 'their practical needs' such as a fair share in the rice harvest, and access to, and control over, land, and 'strategic interests' as stopping wife beating and sexual harassment by landlords. From their historical experience they know perhaps better the meaning of what is now called 'practical' and 'strategic' gender needs and interests than gender experts working with the Moser framework (1989).[1] The recalling of fragments of history will show that peasants in the Terai might have not too positive associations with concepts like community participation, organization, now packed in 'sustainability' and community participation, and community management terminology. It might not be a surprise when these associations evoke very painful experiences in which the peasants finally were the losers. Their convictions, beliefs and culture are shaped by these past events.

Therefore, a valid question in development projects that should be asked before any project will start is, 'how do the so-called "new" and "innovative" concepts fit in the historical and socio-cultural context of the specific location?' This implies that the process of repression and destruction of existing values and attitudes, on which collective efforts for survival and improvements in the past were based, should be known and understood. That is a solid ground to present and implement project objectives adjusted to the historical, cultural heritage. In this respect parallels can be drawn with other fields of development. It is for example self-evident that applied technology as a respected concept is based on studies of indigenous technology and knowledge, while historical, sociological and anthropological aspects are often ignored in projects aiming to organize and mobilize people for development. We do not propagate the historical and sociological approach as an instrumental functional approach, with a reductionist aim to increase the success of a project. It is more intended to create respect, sensitivity and modesty in the project atmosphere and accordingly an implementation. It is a misconception to assume that history is for the historian and anthropologist, and development for the consultant. The two should always go together, and that should be reflected in the available intellectual capacity of the expertize in a project. Eric Wolf (1979) demonstrated that most historical notions of Western people are totally ethnocentric. They are not aware of the rich and formidable history of the Asian, African and Latin American continent.[2] On a much smaller scale we see the same when foreign funded projects are conceptualized. It is as if the 'target' people have no history (see Plate 3).

Thus, not many foreign and Indian consultants from other states visiting the project field of the North Bengal Development Project will be aware that the Rajbansi 'beneficiary woman' they talk with during their field visits, might be the daughter of a woman who was jailed, molested or shot in the Tebhaga or Naxalbari uprisings. The reason might have been that her mother fought for her right to get a fair share of the rice yield as *bargadar* (sharecropper) of the *jotedars* (landowner), or to get land to which she was entitled under the Land Reform Acts of the state.

A comprehensive history of the people in the three districts (Darjeeling, Jalpaiguri, Cooch Behar) of the Terai area has still to be written. Fortuitously, there are several important studies in which the rich peasant and tea estate workers' protest movements of the area have been documented (Dasgupta 1975; Ram 1971; Sen 1985; Singh 1995). All these studies have a strong focus on the main features of Bengal's agrarian system in the colonial period and provide considerable insight why capitalist relations in agriculture remained weakly developed in West Bengal, uptil now (Sen 1985). These historical backgrounds are of course relevant as background knowledge for a well-considered assessment of the scope and limits of the Terai Development Project, aiming to generate agricultural develop-

Plate 3: A handpump 'beneficiary' or a heroine?

ment with the implementation of irrigation as the main mechanism.

Before coming to the gender aspects of the peasant movements some basic facts are necessary. In Jalpaiguri district the Tebhaga peasant revolt flamed up in 1946-7. And Phansidewa, Naxalbari and Kharibari were the cradle areas of the vigorous Naxalite struggle of 1967, now project areas where handpumps are implemented for marginal households. It is noteworthy to remember that the office of our research and monitoring study unit is at a stone's throw of the campus of the North Bengal Terai University where radical students became important cadres of the Naxalbari peasant movement (Sen 1985, p. 60).[3]

The Tebhaga movement demanded reduction in the share of the landlords from one-half of the crop to one-third. The peasant struggles in 1967, 1969, 1970, were, broadly speaking, 'tenants' struggles for the occupation of *benami* land (or land transferred by landowners to fictious persons in order to evade the ceiling law).

The fearless and dynamic role of peasant and tribal women in the protest movements is documented by Sunil Sen (1985). In his preface he ingenuously confesses that it is his objective to tell the story of the working women in Bengal who have remained invisible in history because the professional historians have generally ignored or underestimated the role played by labouring women in the popular movements. He has really written a book out of his heart, making a fist for the women's movement and women's development in Bengal.

From the historical role of women in the Terai peasant protest movements we learn much about the autonomy of women, gender relations and gender ideology of the years since independence. This can help us to understand the changes in the role and position of women in irrigated agriculture over the years, and now. Sunil Sen writes on their situation during the Tebhaga movement in 1946 (p. 41),

> The agrarian struggle made a deep impact on the peasant women, notably Rajbansi and tribal women. Partly this can be explained by the fact that they enjoyed greater freedom than Hindu and Muslim women. The Rajbansi women moved freely in the *hats* [markets] selling

vegetables and rice: widow-remarriage was allowed; the man marrying a Rajbansi girl had to pay bride price.

Also Charu Chandra Sanyal reveals in his charming ethnographic study of the Rajbansis, their division of labour and the important role of women in agricultural production and the household and local economy (1965, p. 32),

> The women never till the land with the plough. But they help the men to weed the jute, paddy or tobacco land, to prepare and sow paddy seeds for the nursery of winter paddy [*aman dhan*], to transplant *aman* seedlings in the fields and help cutting the paddy plants when the paddy is ripe. The women also look after the kitchen garden, the cattle byre and remove the refuse to the dung heap. They go to the weekly market to sell the produce and to make purchases. They also go to nearby jungle to collect dry logs, make cow-dung cakes and expose them to the sun to dry and collect clean jute stems from the jute washing field to store them as fuel. In fact a Rajbansi women is the main worker and a great asset to the family.

Although, in 1965 Sanyal states about well-to-do class women,

> The woman of this class does not usually go to the weekly market [*hat*] although she does not observe *purdah*. She is free to move about but rarely speaks to an unknown visitor nor approaches him. But she does all household work herself. Cooks are not engaged to prepare food. It is the duty of the woman to cook and serve the food.

These quotations indicate that a 'Sanskritization' process in which the behaviour, values and attitudes of the Hindu upper-castes were adopted by more well-to-do Rajbansi women was on its way. Nowadays, this pattern has stretched out to women of poor classes and a few Rajbansi women in the age-groups between 15 and 40 who can be seen selling and buying in the market. Moreover, the bride price has been replaced by dowry which is a general indication for the decrease in status of women as we will explain in Chapter 4. Is this the outcome of the integration and intruding of the original peasant/tribal gender relation with the dominant Hindu gender ideology transferred through formal education and modernization (mass media, radio, TV, movies)? The relevant point is that gender relations in tribal communities are usually assumed to be more equal and more symmetrical than in Hindu culture (Fernandes and Menon 1987; Kelkar and Nathan 1991), due to the important productive role tribal women fulfil. And, it should be noted, although we will discuss this below, that it is likely that Rajbansis have a tribal origin (Sanyal 1965).

The autonomous, independent position of peasant and tribal women is illustrated by a description in the study of Sen. He mentions that tens of thousands of peasant women in hundreds of villages in Bengal were at the core of the Tebhaga peasant struggle. Armed with *lathis* (sticks), bow and arrows, shouting slogans, peasant and tribal women marched in processions, joined in carrying the rice crop from the sheds of the landowners and gave shelter to underground activists. They acted independently, and took decisions to surround the police forces and to organize warning systems (Sen 1985, p. 40). Besides the class struggle aspects, they fought a fierce gender struggle. Mahila samitis (women's organizations) were organized and local women leaders emerged. They made a stand against wife beating and demanded better treatment by their husbands who looked down on them. The latter is in contradiction with the earlier claimed more equal status between men and women of the peasants and tribes. However, this should be seen in a relative perspective as Kelkar and Nathan (1991) state in their study on tribal women in Jharkhand:

> With regard to women, Jharkhandis, including women themselves point out that women in tribal society do not have as low a status as women in plains Hindu society. Both in the family and in society adivasi women certainly have a more prominent position than do women in developed class society in the plains. But this relatively superior position should not blind one either to its rapid erosion, or the 'traditional' inequalities. (p. 22)

Also Sunil Sen points to the class aspect of subordination of women, which tells much on the class character of gender relations around 1946, but which still matters in the area. He notes that although rich peasants participated in the Tebhaga movement, their wives, sisters and daughters were seldom seen in meetings and demonstrations. He concludes that women in affluent peasant families are more suppressed by gender ideology than women of the poor agricultural classes. Relations between men and women in a poor peasant family are more equal owing to their common hardship and poverty.

He also notes that in particular in the North Bengal districts the women activists mainly came from the Rajbansi community, often played the leading role and among them widows, who had nothing to lose, came forward as leaders. 'In Debiganj in Jalpaiguri district Punneswari Debba, a Rajbansi widow took out a procession of women as the men, arching the situation, had not dared to start the movement' (p. 40).

The final gains for women in the Tebhaga struggle were almost nothing, but Sen states that thousands of peasant women were awakened to political life. According to him there was a growth of political consciousness that became evident as time passed. The women's movement of the Communist Party, the Mahila Atmaraksha Samiti (MARS) formed in 1943, played through the years, shifting through different political orientations, an important role mobilizing peasant and working class women for the democratic movement.

Women were even more militant and fearless in the Naxalite revolutionary movement in 1967. This movement started with a minor incident in the small village Naxalbari, but the incident became a turning point in the history of the left movement in India.[4] Mao-Tse-tung had prognosed that 'the spark will start a prairie fire' and that happened: till now the flames are not extinct in other parts of India. Whatever the historical interpretation of this often named 'spring thunder' struggle—it lasted only fifty-two days—which unfortunately turned soon into a terrorist annihilation of landlords, it arose out of protest against the worst forms of feudal exploitation, inequality and indignity despite two decades of independence at that time.[5] Many women attending Naxalite meetings were killed in sudden attacks by police firing. Sunil Sen records the short stories about female activists in the movement and their remarkable courage in the face of fierce oppression.

Besides the earlier mentioned rise in political awareness, what other achievements can be mentioned which impacted the position or status of women? Land reforms were carried out under the pressure of the revolt movements but laid the basis of the small peasant agriculture in West Bengal. And, Sunil Sen raises again a crucial gender point when he states, 'Few writers have cared to examine the impact of small peasant agriculture on the social consciousness of peasant women.'

Lenin did, and his opinion was that a small peasant economy cannot raise the social status of women. This insight was shared by the West Bengal Congress Agrarian Reform Committee and they pleaded in the beginning of the 1970s for a cooperative organization as a pre-condition to reclaim wastelands and to allot it to the agricultural labourers (Sen, p. 83). When we look around in the outskirts of Siliguri and Bagdogra twenty-five years later, where devastating poverty of the people is rampant, and long patches of dry waste land are laying idle along roads and railway tracks, we may ask why this recommendation has not been followed all these years. Why have people, and in particular the women, not organized, or not been organized by government or NGOs, to start planting fuelwood, fruit trees and vegetables on this government land?[6] This will be very supportive for the numbers of non-workers among female agricultural labourers which are steadily increasing. A small study on women's participation on Forest Protection Committees in North Bengal very near Siliguri (Sarugarh) shows that women can be organized to plant, and to maintain tree-growing as most of them are members of the committees and a few are even members in the executive committees and do the work very well, despite male chauvinism and harassment by male bureaucrats (Mukherjee n.d.).

Since the struggle for land reached its climax in 1969, and waned after the formation of the Left Front Government in 1977, the women's organizations turned to the panchayats which were invariably male-dominated (Sen 1985, p. 83). According to Sen it would be illusory to think that women can have exactly the same place as men in the three tier panchayats in hierarchial society. The danger is that the panchayats develop as male-bastions and rural women will be left out of development programmes. Our encounters with women-panchayat members do not justify such a pessimistic view as they were very able to raise their voice, as will be described in Chapter 8.

2.2 GENDER VARIETIES, COMMUNITIES AND CLASS

After these small historical reminiscences in which the context of women in the project area is sketched, let us now look in more detail into the composition, variety and differences between groups of women in the Terai area.

The distribution of households by community shows that almost 68 per cent belong to the category of Scheduled Castes (SC) and Scheduled Tribes (ST).[7] In the Terai the SC mainly consist of Rajbansis and Namasudras: the first one are now considered a Hindu caste belonging to the local indigenous population of the area and form proportionately the largest group of households. The Namasudras are Hindu refugees and migrants from Bangladesh. The in-depth follow-up study shows that 30 per cent belong to general Hindu castes, and only 2 per cent are Muslims. There are in the in-depth study proportionally many Muslims taking part in the river lift irrigation scheme, and many tribals among the households using the deep tube well scheme, but the sample survey shows that this is an incidental representation.

The representation of the communities in our in-depth study and sample survey reflects more or less the percentage of SC and ST together, respectively 57, 48 and 34 per cent of the total populations of Jalpaiguri, Cooch Behar and Darjeeling districts.

Table 2.1 shows the caste/community origin per scheme as compiled from the sample survey. The total sample contains 1,000 households belonging to SC and ST communities. This is almost 68 per cent of the 1,478 surveyed households taking part in any of the irrigation schemes, and similar to the proportion revealed by the in-depth study. However, the representation of the Muslims—265 households—is 18 per cent, and much higher than in the in-depth study. Other Hindus—213 households—form a smaller share in the sample survey: 14 per cent. The figures are presented per irrigation device.

The table reveals that the social stratification and social hierarchy, and the related socio-political climate of the Terai area is unusual for Indian conditions by the notorious absence of Brahmin and Kshatriya and other twice-born castes. In the Terai area social inequality is based less on religious and cultural

TABLE 2.1: DISTRIBUTION OF CASTE/COMMUNITY OF THE INFORMANTS ACCORDING TO IRRIGATION SCHEME IN THE SAMPLE SURVEY

Caste/Community	River Lift Irrigation		Deep Tube Wells		Hand Tube Wells		Shallow Tube Well		Pump Dug Well	
	HHs	%	HHs	%	HHs	%	HHs	%	HHs	%
Rajbansi SC	176	50	34	19	293	35	17	23	19	39
Non-Rajbansi SC*	77	22	52	30	235	29	4	5	3	6
Muslim	22	6	61	35	115	14	43	58	24	49
ST	8	2	26	14	51	6	5	7	-	-
Others**	71	20	3	2	131	16	5	7	3	6
Total	354	100	176	100	825	100	74	100	49	100

Notes: * Non Rajbansi Scheduled Castes are for the majority the so-called Namasudras, an SC group originating in Bangladesh.
** Others means general Hindu castes.

grounds, than on disparities in land ownership. Caste hierarchy and the related oppression are diffuse and scattered. Caste based feudal patron-client relations are not marked: class relations cut through caste divisions as the community composition of the 30 landless households shows. There is no dominant landless caste or community, but the landless are dispersed: Muslims 14, Rajbansi 10, Scheduled Tribes 3, and general Hindu 3 households. The community-wise distribution in the sample survey for the interviewed 46 landless households shows a similar pattern: Muslims 21, Rajbansi (SC) 20 and general Hindu 5 households.

In particular since Partition in 1947, the three districts of our study have become a melting pot of various refugees and migrant communities and groups such as the Namasudras and a large number of Nepalis, and groups from Bhutan. In particular the groups of Bangladeshis who lost everything in the past, and had to work hard for their survival, have developed tough livelihood strategies. They have become dominant in villages in the Terai region.

The continuous shift in the village population after 1947 and thereafter at interval—especially after the Indo-Pakistan wars in 1965 and 1971—can be briefly illustrated with data we collected in one of our survey villages, namely Paschim Harmati. As Table 2.2 shows, the migrant communities who have settled down in this village belong to all communities. We do not have community-wise immigration figures but a general pattern of migration and settlement in the village can be given.

It can be said that migrants (after 1947 and in particular 1971 with the independence of Bangladesh) far outnumber the original

TABLE 2.2: MIGRATION TO PASCHIM HARMATI VILLAGE

Year of migration to the village	Number of HH	Percentage
Before 1947	77	21.5
1947-65	72	20.1
1966-70	72	20.1
1971 and after*	137	38.3
Total	358	100.0

Note: *Till the time of the Base-line Survey in May 1990.

inhabitants in the village. The village has grown 'unnaturally' into five times its original size during the last four decades. This phenomenon of sudden increase in the size of population has caused an acute demand on cultivable land leading to a gradual reduction in size of holdings.

2.3 BACKGROUND AND PORTRAITS OF FARM WOMEN

The Rajbansi and the Namasudra women are numerically the largest groups in our study. As mentioned earlier the Rajbansis and Namasudras are officially classified as Scheduled Castes (Harijans) which raises associations with untouchability, and severe suffering from poverty and religious degradation, and, in particular for women, of a double exploitation by caste and gender. The plight of Harijan women in India is widely documented (Trivedi 1976; Bhave 1988). However, the exploitation and degradation that SC women elsewhere in India face, is certainly not the case in north West Bengal. Sekhar Bandyopadhyay writes in this connection something very interesting in his article on the history of the Namasudras (1994). He emphasises that untouchability in its strict sense was never a problem in Bengal. So-called untouchables suffered less in Bengal compared with Harijans in other regions of India. He does not explain why this is the case; but it might be an effect of the more secular political ideology in the area which could also emerge as the twice-born castes form only a small minority.

Due to lack of information we can only sketch some scattered background information on women of these two communities. In addition we rely on our impressions, observations and talks during field visits.

2.3.1 Rajbansi women

Swaraj Basu has written a fascinating account of the creation of the Rajbansi identity in Bengal (1994).[8] Indeed, their origin puzzled us for a long time as they are officially known as Scheduled Castes, but in their style of life and in particular in their gender relations characterized by relatively equal relations between men and women. We, as experienced anthropologists, recognized obvious signs of tribal culture. Rajbansis themselves have claimed for a long time Kshatriya identity and this can be interpreted as a kind of emancipatory movement to show self-esteem. It fits in the general Indian pattern in which people of lower castes claim Kshatriya descent (Mukhopadhyay 1990).

The following notes of a field visit may reveal something of the living conditions of Rajbansi women and households at the time of implementation of the second phase of the Terai project. In the fieldnotes attention is given to the handpump programme and irrigation practices at the household level:

Field visit 11 May 1989, district Darjeeling, block Kharibari-Phansidewa, villages Dubanuchi and Guabari.

45 Rajbansi families live in the village. The mud houses are well maintained and plastered. Nice decorations with figures of flowers, peacocks and geometric designs are drawn on the walls by the women. The villages are absolutely clean. No rubbish or waste piles can be observed.

There is a handpump installed by the Public Health Engineering Department for drinking water purposes. There are 11 handpumps implemented under the Terai Indo-Dutch Project, 15 more have been sanctioned already.

The family of Singh has got a handpump under the programme. They have six children and live here together with the brothers of Mr Singh. They have 1 *bigha* of land near the handpump but not near the homestead. It is just 20 metres from the road. They were sharecroppers and cultivated 3 *bighas* of land. The harvest was shared with the landowner on a 50-50 basis. Because of 'operation *barga*' [land reform] they got the *patta* [land use title] right. This means that the owner cannot sell the land to somebody else. So tenure of land has been assured on a permanent basis for them. The landowner decided to divide the land in two equal parts: 1.5 *bighas* for them, and 1.5 *bighas* for himself. They cannot survive with 2.5 *bighas* of land; therefore Mr Singh is doing wage-labour at the tea-estates. He is not picking leaves as that is women's work, but he plants young tea saplings. He earns Rs 9 a day [at the date of interview the minimum wage in West Bengal was Rs 18 per day]. This work is available 90 days per year. A side-benefit of labour in the tea garden is that one can collect firewood for cooking purposes from the estate.

They took a loan under the Dairy Scheme to buy a cow. Now they have four cows and one ox. They sell a little milk a day [1 litre, Rs 4].

Plate 4: Rajbansi family.

Mrs Singh fetches water from their own handpump. In that case she makes 5 to 6 trips a day. The land of the vegetable garden near the handpump is now completely fallow and looks very sandy. They plan to grow chillies, cucumber, beans, etc. They buy the seed under the Comprehensive Area Development Scheme. They hope a seed dealer will be posted nearer to the house. They know how to grow vegetables because they had already a 'rain-fed' vegetable garden. With irrigation they hope to increase their income from Rs 2,000 to Rs 3,000. Their investment also increases, they don't know exactly by how much [Rs 600 ?]. Mrs Singh states that she does the same work as her husband, i.e. the pumping, weeding and plucking in the vegetable garden. She also works on their former sharecrop land. All the agricultural work is done by both of them: 'we work together'. However, the marketing is done by Mr Singh. He will go to a nearby *hat* [market] and sell their vegetables there, or they will sell it to a merchant who comes to buy the vegetables (see Plate 4).

There is only one detailed ethnographic study of the Rajbansis of North Bengal, by the anthropologist Charu Chandra Sanyal (1965). He has covered almost all the subjects of a classic ethnographic study. Material culture, birth- , marriage-, death customs-, social relations, religious beliefs and supernatural agencies, proverbs, songs, quarrels between villagers, dialect and vocabulary are painstakingly recorded.

2.3.2 Namasudra women

The second group we found in our sample in this area were the Namasudras. The common knowledge of many people is that they are refugees and immigrants from Bangladesh, hard working, and skilled farmers. They bought land from Rajbansis to settle as small landholders. Almost nothing is known of their history after Partition when the majority fled from Bangladesh. Numerically, the Namasudras were the largest Hindu caste in Eastern Bengal. Sekhar Bandyopadhyay, in his study on the Namasudra movement in Bengal, 1872-1947 states that the Namasudras had a very low social status among the Hindus of Bengal: they were perceived as untouchables. There was a considerable social distance between them and the high caste Hindu landowner reflected by the specific class situation in

Bangladesh. In 1911, about 78 per cent of the Namasudras lived on agriculture as 'farm servants, cultivators or field labourers' (p. 95). On women he only mentions that the Namasudra movement went through a form of cultural adaptation in which they sought symbols that would indicate a higher ritual status (p. 98). In that line they forbade their women from visiting market places.

The following notes from field visits give an impression of the life and work of Namasudra women and households in the time the second phase of the Terai project was implemented.

Field visit 11 May 1989, district Darjeeling, block Kharibari-Phansidewa, villages Dubanuchi and Guabari.

On our way we see a row of women working in the paddy fields [transplanting]. In the village are 11 pumps scattered in clusters of three to four houses, and implemented in different years. The agricultural department had to follow this scattered selection in the beginning because of the political pressure of the block panchayat. In 1989 they could convince the panchayat that it is more efficient to install at one time 20 handpumps and the next year the same cluster in another village.

In the village are three pumps for drinking water of the Public Health Department: two are out of order. Fifty families, originally from Bangladesh are living in this ward of the village.

The house we visit of a Namasudra family has a beautiful vegetable garden full of beans. The size of the beanplot is 0.6 *bigha* and they will get Rs 1,500 if they sell all the beans. This is possible because of the handpump they got two years ago. They have in total 1.5 *bighas* near the homestead. The paddy nursery is also located in the vegetable garden and irrigated by the pump. The mother of the house tells us that she is waiting for the rains to transplant the rice. She does all the work in the vegetable garden with her husband and a labourer. The labourers are women from the landless Poddar [merchant] community. She is not working in their other fields. The trees and bushes in the garden are sufficient to meet their need for cooking fuel. She sells 1.5 litre milk a day [Rs. 6]. The money is spent on household needs.

The neighbours got a handpump 20 days ago. The platform has yet not been constructed. The wife of the house uses the water for all purposes. Before the community handpump was installed they had a *katcha* well. They have closed that after the handpump came, as the water in the *katcha* well was not potable or safe. They were suffering from diarrhoea. Now it is much better. There is a primary health centre at a distance of 2 kilometres. They think that the quality of the water under the Indo-Dutch Project is better. It has no bad smell. The wife of the house has also more privacy when bathing because their handpump is more out of sight from the road. In this village there is no culture of making bath rooms with bamboo mats. Women are not shy in this village, only on questions like: 'how much land do you have?' she keeps quiet and smiles. The men emphasise that their women are not allowed to do any wage labour. People have a large variety of fruit trees [mangos, papayas, palm trees with coconuts, etc.].

Tuesday 12 December 1991, visit to two villages Kodalipara and Danagach in Kharibari block.

The handpump of the family we visit in the village Kodalipara has been installed one year ago: it looks already very rusty. The owners themselves do not paint the pump. Probably a provision in the budget has to be made for that. The household consists of four people [father, mother, son and daughter]. They came from Bangladesh: the father of the owner fled in the 1971 India-Pakistan war to another district nearby. Four years ago the family settled in this village together with relatives. They had some land in Bangladesh which they sold and with that money they could buy 2.5 *bighas* paddy land and 2 *bighas* vegetable land [price of 1 *bigha* is Rs 2,000].

There was some tension [but no physical violence] in the allotment of the handpump in the village because the locals [Rajbansis] wanted to have handpumps too [when we pass the Rajbansi locality by jeep it gives a very poor impression and besides the land is absolutely barren, brown and dry]. The soil of this locality is very sandy but the farmers succeeded in making nice vegetable gardens. White radish is growing very well: besides we see nice rows of Chinese cabbage, brinjal and some kind of green cabbage. Husband and wife irrigate the crop by fetching water from the handpump in buckets and digging *katcha* irrigation channels to the fields. They have invested Rs 175 in a half-*bigha* radishpatch on fertilizer, seeds and pesticides. Now they sell the radish for Rs 1 a kg. It is estimated that this household will get Rs 500 out of it. The name of the mother of the house is Jamuna Bosu. She works with her husband in the vegetable garden. She is busy washing the crop to make it look more attractive in the market. Her husband will go by bicycle and sell all the radish and bundles of green cabbage in the afternoon. She never goes to the market. They have a plough, a bullock and a cow. She makes fuel from the dung of her animals. Sometimes she collects other dung cakes. Nevertheless I see some firewood in the kitchen. They have two rooms [houses] which need to be repaired. There are two girls around 13/14 years: one studied up till the seventh standard, the other did not. The girl had to stop her studies because for secondary education she has to go to a town nearby and transport is not available. It is not considered decent for a girl to walk such distance at her age.

We visit Mrs Mazumdar in the village Bandar Ganj in Gram Panchayat Bidhan Nagar. Some women have got the handpump in this village in their name under the special allocation programme for female headed households.

The location is near the banks of the river where they were washed away a year and half ago due to a flood. They are from Bangladesh and had settled on the river bank. There are two small houses in which 13 people live surrounded by a very neat vegetable garden; bordered by a pineapple field at one side. Long beans, potato and wheat are cultivated. The owner and his wife also earn their income as agricultural labourers. They have two sons and two daughters. His brother has seven members in the family and does not own any land.

The Mazumdars have irrigated 2 *bighas* of land by using a rubber tube which can reach very far in the field. They both work very hard in the vegetable garden [I see their small son also helping] but they also use wage labour [his brother] at a wage of Rs 15 daily.

The farmer on the other side of the road has a very small house with beautiful big orange marigolds in front of it. He shows his bamboo tube which functions as a *pukka* channel. He bought a cartload of manure for Rs 65 and additional oil cakes as fertilizer. He likes to buy a sprayer. Now he is too poor to buy pesticides but shows that he sprinkles his crop with a bucket of water.

2.3.3 Tribal women

The third important group in the area are the tribal women. The Scheduled Tribes form numerically a minority in the project area and consist of dispersed small sub-tribal groups as the Santhals, Rabas, Garos, Oraons and Mundas. Many of them are migrants from other states (Orissa and Bihar); in order to survive they had seasonally migrated to West Bengal to work in the tea gardens. Later they settled in the north of West Bengal. Their living conditions are very poor as the field notes show:

In the next village we visit the house of Mrs Dhamniamee. She has

Plate 5: Tribal grandmother with grandson.

four daughters and a son. She looks undernourished and is pregnant with the sixth baby. It is noticed that her children suffer from scabies. The small girl in her arms is scratching all the time on the wounds on her arms. All the other children suffer also from scabies and look dirty. The household has a handpump but it is not regularly used for bathing the children as the mother feels to weak to do that. They are from a tribal community [ten families in this locality]. They came here in 1957 to work in the tea gardens and managed to buy some land and start farming. Now nobody of their group is working any longer in the tea gardens. They have 5 *bighas* paddy land and 5 *bighas* vegetable land. The vegetable garden looks well and it is irrigated by bamboo tube. Dhamniamee is looking after it. She grows also potatoes. She herself goes to the market. She takes the vegetables in a basket on her head. She went today and will go on Saturday again. Her bullock was stolen some time ago. Now they have to save every *paisa* to buy a new bullock, therefore they are not eating much from their own vegetable garden. She wishes to have a brick house (see Plate 5)

2.3.4 Muslim women

Class differentiations between Muslim women are notable but in general Muslim women belong to the very poor sections of the village communities. In contradiction to the situation in Bangladesh, Muslim landless women in the Terai area are allowed to do agricultural wage-labour in the field. Their labour market is not totally restricted to post-harvest operations in the *bari* (house-compound) of a woman employer. The following fieldnotes give an impression of some aspects of their lives.

Visit 6 February to Paschim Harmati, Mainaguri block to a Muslim ward where 42 Muslim families live.

A woman with a green *sari*, and a dark face has no children and only a husband. They have only half *bigha* of land. She grows wheat, paddy, potato, bitter gourd. She went for wage labour in the past but not now as she is not feeling well and very weak. Her husband also does not feel well. She has a cow as survival. She gets 2 to 3 litre milk a day. She can sell 1 litre a day for Rs 6. She and her husband take the cow for grazing. They cut grass growing between the wheat on other farmers' land and give that to the cow. This is allowed and nobody will object. Two months ago she sold four chickens for Rs 18 each to buy medicines. She has no money to buy new ones.

Plate 6: Marginal farm women from Muslim community.

We visit the house of the Muslim panchayat woman representative, Nunihar. The big compound contains four houses: they are of bricks and wood and have iron sheet roofs. The friendly patriarch of the house with his white Hadji cap explains that Nunihar is his daughter-in-law but that she is not there at the moment. The family are big landowners. He has 25 *bighas* of land [the whole family 100 *bighas*]. It is remarkable that the poor women just accompany us to the courtyard and sit down and look and listen to our talk, nobody tells them to go.

We interview two women with children (see Plate 6): Motinakatun, is a marginal farm woman, the family has 2 *bighas* of land. She has one son, and three daughters. She came to this village 17 years ago to marry here, from a village at 12 km distance. The other woman is landless and an agricultural wage labourer Asiakatun: she has three daughters, and three sons. In the season she has 20 days a month work and off-season [now] only six days. Nevertheless, she states that she has more work because of the river lift irrigation, to grow cauliflower, cabbage and bitter gourd. They voted for Nunihar. Asia's main problem is food and she has a daughter of 16 who has to be married. It will cost Rs 2,000 to 3,000 and they cannot afford that. She has two *saris* [the one she is wearing full with holes] and one blouse. The blouse her husband got as wage from the landowner. For marriages she borrows a *sari* from a richer neighbour. For fuel she collects leaves and twigs. She and her children collect when she comes home from work. She also fetches water as her husband gets cramps in his stomach when fetching water. No men will collect fuel and water for it will lower their status. Muslim fathers have no role in deliveries. May be they will take care of the younger children at that time.

One year ago a new Anganwadi opened; it is a bench of bamboo in the open air under a tree. The mothers show us the registration cards. Registration of vaccinations and supply of Vitamin A, DPT, Polio, and some post natal care is mentioned on the cards. The Anganwadi has a food programme consisting of maize, molasses and mustard. The women have attended an Oral Dehydration demonstration organized by the Anganwadi.

NOTES

1. This is an ironic remark pointing to the fact that the concepts 'practical and strategic gender needs' developed by Moser became a kind of Holy Bible in Women and Development studies and training courses on gender planning.

2. After three million years of waiting we have luckily also a women's history of the world dealing with all the continents. Marilyn French has written a 1,311 page volume under the title, *From Eve to Dawn: A Woman's History of the World* (1995).
3. They were suspended by the Vice-Chancellor of the University and arrested by the police.
4. According to Singh (1995) the Naxalite movement started with three share-croppers, supported by 150 CPI(M) followers, armed with *lathis*, bows and arrows and carrying party flags, who lifted the entire stock of 300 maunds of paddy from the *jotedar's* (landowners) granary without leaving him a share (p. 3).
5. See the study of Prakash Singh (1995) for detailed figures on share-cropper/landowner percentages in Naxalbari and Kharibari-Phansidewa (pp. 5 and 6).
6. In a somewhat different context of forest areas the study of Menon and Viegas reports that there are very successful so-called 'Forest Protection Committees' in the south of West Bengal (Purulia, Midnapore and Bankura districts) in which the government works together with the population and in particular with the tribal women in villages who have organized themselves in FPCs (Viegas 1993). In tangible benefits the FPCs have full usufructuary rights in the protected forest areas as well as a 25 per cent share in the net sale of timber at the time of felling.
7. Communities of former Untouchables and people from other communities originally living in the forests are registered in a special government schedule by which they are entitled to certain measures of positive discrimination with regard to schooling, employment and other social facilities.
8. This is not the place to comment on his analyses but it shows that the colonial literature on caste and the identity it gave to people was an outcome of a close interaction between colonial ethnographers and the indigenous, usually high caste, informants which were highly biased by all sorts of prejudices based on their notions of purity-pollution scaling of various groups in the caste social hierarchy scale (Basu 1994, p. 55).

3. The Project: Gender History

3.1 THE PROJECT AREA

As stated in Chapter 1, the project area is located in the plains of the northernmost part of West Bengal state at the foot of the Himalayan mountains, between Nepal, Bhutan, Assam and Bangladesh.

The North Bengal Terai Development Project covers the districts of Jalpaiguri and Cooch Behar as well as the two southern blocks of Darjeeling district. For a long time it was a restricted area; foreigners mainly came to visit Darjeeling,[1] could only enter with a special permit till 1992. The political instability in the past caused by the Naxalite movement, the Bangladesh refugees and lately the actions of the Gurkha Liberation Front are the background of the long restricted area status of the area.

Four and half million people live in the project area, most of them (85 per cent) in rural settlements. The rural population density is high: 435 per square km and the landholdings are generally very small. Of the farmers 60 per cent possess an average landholding of less than an acre; another 25 per cent of the farmers owns between 1 and 3 acres. Moreover, 30 per cent of the population is landless and depends on share cropping, agricultural wages and employment in the informal sector. The farm system is predominantly based on subsistence cultivation, rice being the major crop. Yields are generally low and plough tilage is mainly dependent on manual labour.

The cultivable area is 1.25 million acres and represents half of the total geographical area. Most of this is developed. The cultivated area has remained stagnant for a long time with little scope for expansion as the tea-gardens and the forests in the northern part of the districts form a clear demarcation line. Rainfall is abundant in the Terai—3,354 mm per year—but it is irregular. Evaporation moreover is high and the soil is coarse. Irrigation is therefore essential during *rabi* and pre-*kharif* season. Irrigation is also used to make up for deficiencies in rainfall during the *kharif* season.

In the past the traditional way of fetching water for domestic use and irrigation for the vegetable garden was to make a *pukka* well and to lift the water with a bucket on a bamboosweep. For irrigation purposes *katcha* wells were dug if the groundwater table allowed, or water was fetched with vessels from ponds, water tanks and rivers. The vessel which was used for drawing water from rivers had a half boat like shape. Big bamboo sticks were used to lift the half-boat from the river.

The cropping pattern varies for different parts of the Terai. The traditional rice varieties are *aus* (broadcast in pre-*kharif*) and the rainfed *amon* (*kharif*). High-yielding *boro* paddy is a recent introduction and is cultivated in the dry season and is dependent on irrigation as well as other agricultural inputs as chemical fertilizers and pesticides which require much financial investment.

As mentioned earlier, more than half the population in the Terai is classified as Scheduled Caste (the Rajbansis and the Namasudras being the most important group) or Scheduled Tribe (presented by groups such as the Santhals, Rabas, Garos, Oraons and Mundas).[2] In addition there are many refugees and migrants from Nepal, Bhutan and Bangladesh (Pal 1985).

As mentioned earlier, the social hierarchy and socio-political climate of the Terai area is unusual because of the absence of Brahmin and Kshatriya dominance. Caste hierarchy and related oppression are diffuse and scattered, the majority of the population being landless or marginal and small farmers (Dasgupta 2000). Sustainable livelihood-systems are deeply rooted in survival strategies of the marginal and poor members of farm households. Tactics of risk avoidance and coping with a stratified agrarian structure are well developed. Terai has a long historical record of peasant movements, revolts and land reforms (Ghose 1983; Kohli 1987; Lieten 1993; *EPW* 1981; Dasgupta 1986). *Zamindari* relations have also been wiped out by the natural fragmentation of land due to inheritance, immigration, in-flow of many refugees from Bangladesh, and of course land reforms. Therefore caste based patron-client relations are not marked (known in Bengal as the Jhodhari system): class relations cut through caste divisions. In particular groups of Bangladeshis who lost everything in the past, and had to work hard for their survival, have developed tough strategies. They have become dominant in villages in the Terai region.

The Government of West Bengal has been constructing minor irrigation works in the Terai for a long time (Choudhury and Mukhopadhyay 1988). In terms of people, water and soil fertility the potential of the area is substantial, but marketing and transport infrastructures remain important bottlenecks. By now it is considered almost self-evident among the population that the government has to provide productive assets: to a certain extent it is perceived not as a favour, but as a right. The political ideology of the ruling Communist Party (CPI, Marxist), which has strong support in the locally elected panchayat councils at village, block and district level, has endorsed this and is reflected in a serious commitment to improvement of the living conditions of the poorest and women in Bengali society (Lieten 1992; 1994). According to the Dutch sociologist Lieten it is even possible that in West Bengal a process of *re-peasantization* has been in operation. According to him West Bengal is the only state where the percentage of (male) agricultural labourers has declined between 1981 and 1991 and where the ratio of agricultural labourers to peasants has come down (1994, p. 529).

3.2 THE NORTH BENGAL TERAI DEVELOPMENT PROJECT

It is difficult to say how far the Terai small-scale irrigation project is representative of large bilateral projects in India. It is undeniable that the Marxist-Communist political climate in West Bengal is different from that of other states (except may be Kerala). It is my experience that that has an impact on perspectives and attitudes of the involved government officials; many of them have a high level of social awareness and concernedness for the weakest sections (Westergaard 1987). The evaluation mission of 1987 was very positive about the results of Phase I: with dedication, social awareness and craftsmanship the project have been implemented by the Bengal authorities and officials.

However, in the field of gender the usual stereotype values and perceptions of the prevalent gender ideology are dominant.[4] Many other ecological, socio-economic and cultural differences can be indicated in comparison with other rural development projects in India supported by Dutch Development Cooperation. Nevertheless, I think that wider generalizations can be made on the basis of my findings in the Terai project, as there are also many similarities and universal aspects related to the agrarian social structure, social hierarchies, gender ideologies and relations.

The objective of the North Bengal Terai Development Project is to improve the standard of living of small and marginal farmers in the project area by increasing agricultural production, as well as to contribute to a more egalitarian income distribution. Towards this end small-scale irrigation facilities were provided under the second phase of the project (1988-94), in particular river lift irrigation schemes that had a planned command area of 200 acres, deep tube wells to serve 100 acres, shallow tube wells (STW) serving 10 acres of land, pump dug wells (PDW) with a capability of 7.5 acres and at the end of the scale hand pumps expected to irrigate 0.35 acre. During the second phase of the project 24,025 handpumps;[5] 300 pump dug wells; 150 shallow tube wells; 12 deep tube wells and 27 river lift irrigation installations were installed. Moreover, 436 lined channel units (the so-called 10-acre units) were constructed to convey the irrigation water. Demonstration plots for extension work also form part of the project activities. It is estimated that the project served approximately 2,75,000 persons, and that the total of area newly irrigated was in the vicinity of 19.320 acres.

Handpumps are privately owned and managed. Marginal farmer household are selected with 1 *bigha* of land near the homestead were selected. The pumps are usually installed in villages in clusters of 25. Female headed households get priority in getting a handpump, and a number of them have been given in the name of the woman of the household (in 1994 almost 10 per cent). Unlike the smaller facilities, the river lifts and deep tube wells remain the property of the state. They are managed and maintained by government staff, in cooperation with the users, who are formally organized in Beneficiary Committees (BC). The selection criteria for the river lift and deep tube wells spells out that at least 65 per cent of the land in the command area should be owned by either marginal or small farmers. For the shallow-, and dug wells a contribution of 25 per cent of the investment costs is required from the beneficiaries. They are owned and managed by clusters of about five households.

Important additional and supportive activities of Phase II were training, research (in 1992-3, 474 men and 73 women were trained by the Department of Agriculture) and some marketing support.

The institutional aspects of the project are as follows. The Terai project is executed by the Joint Director of Agriculture posted in Jalpaiguri, representing the Department of Agriculture. He is assisted by the Department of Minor Irrigation. The Joint Director is responsible for all activities of the department in the three districts. Under him Principal Agricultural Officers are posted in the three district headquarters, and under them are seven Subdivisional Agricultural Officers heading the offices, including several Subject Matter Specialists. All together the Joint Director Agriculture, has a professional staff of 170 men plus about 500 extension workers. The Department of Agriculture also looks after soil conservation, demonstration plots and training of farmers and farm women. In the beginning of Phase II the training was given by an NGO but problems arose and the local branch of the Communist Party occupied the building and demanded their departure. The Department of Minor Irrigation has two wings: the agri-mechanical wing responsible for the implementation of handpumps, pump dug wells and shallow tube wells, and the agri-irrigation wing responsible for the river lift irrigation, deep tube wells, and the so-called 4-hectare units (masonry distribution canals to avoid seepage of water from the river lift and deep tube well systems). The Superintending Engineer has two Executive Engineers under him who supervise the Assistant Engineers heading the Subdivisional Offices. The Steering Committee in Calcutta is the leading policy and decision making organization. Its 'full' members are six Ministers of various departments and 'invited' members are the Secretaries of the various involved departments and, Chief Superintending and Executive Engineers, all men. At the project level the Advisory Committee handles project planning, implementation and in theory also monitoring. The distribution of the facilities over the districts is decided by the Steering Committee. The distribution of facilities at the district level is decided by the Zilla Parishads at the block and village level the respective layers of panchayats are involved.

A Netherlands Project Coordinator, a consultant from Euroconsult, visited the area four times a year to monitor the progress of the project. He reported his findings in Calcutta to the office of the Secretary of Agriculture and to the Dutch Embassy in New Delhi. Other short-term missions by Dutch consultants in training, marketing, computer programming and research supported the project.

All materials and irrigation equipment are manufactured and assembled in India. Construction is tendered to local contractors who should give priority to local landless women in recruiting unskilled labour.

3.3 GENDER HISTORY OF THE PROJECT

During the time of formulation of Phase II (March 1987) the South-Asia desk of the Dutch International Cooperation Department welcomed the request from the Indian Ministry of Agriculture for the funding of the North Bengal Terai Development Project. At that time it offered a potential shift in the nature of Indo-Dutch Development Cooperation policy, to reduce import- and budget support and to increase project support,[6] reflecting the major Netherlands development policy objectives: macro-economic self-reliance and direct poverty alleviation (IOV Evaluation Report 1994).[7]

As indicated in Chapter 1, in Phase II of the Terai project the usual technological, economic and financial components were funded, but in comparison with Phase I, new aspects were financed as the Dutch Development Cooperation had started since 1986, the so-called 'integrated approach'.

It was the conviction of the mission members that the best

chances for success of social interventions in the Terai project could be expected by relying on the existing institutional set-up of the regular government departments, and the favourable socio-political climate in the project area. An effort from the Dutch side during the formulation mission of Phase II, to post a Dutch team-leader in the field was resisted by the Bengal authorities with self-confidence. The project was conceived in the spirit of self-reliance and autonomy in March 1987 (NBTD Report Evaluation 1987).

As the better-off class always has a better chance to grasp power by dominating irrigation facilities which will benefit them, it was certainly felt by the mission members who formulated the second phase that clear social, economic and gender selection criteria and procedures should be formulated, to ensure that the earmarked target groups (marginal- and small farmers, land-less and women) should be the beneficiaries. In out line it was comprehended that the components of the Dutch driven integrated approach, were no alien concepts for the Indian counterparts, but roughly in accordance with their state policies and the 'social justice' atmosphere in the departments.

In the framework of the already mentioned 'integrated development' policies the Dutch government had appointed a 'Women and Development' sector specialist at the embassy in Delhi in 1986. She found in 1987 that in all reports and studies that have been produced on the Terai project at that time, women were mentioned in two sentences, of which the main message was: 'women do not participate in agriculture'. Being familiar with the Indian situation she doubted the validity of this statement, and insisted that in the work plan for Phase II gender activities should be included. One Indian and the Dutch author of this book were assigned to formulate recommendations to improve the living conditions of women in poor households in the area. The Women in Development terminology of 'empowerment' and 'autonomy' was not yet used at that time, but the intention and way of working consisted of an approach and methodology which became popular some years later.

In 1987, we found at first view that the project was pretty gender-blind; not a single women was involved in its planning, implementation or management. In the first round of discussions the male staff expressed their replies on our questions of, 'how to involve women in the project' in the conventional male perception, 'that women have nothing to do with the project as they are not participating in agriculture and therefore not in irrigation'. Obviously the patriarchal Hindu upper-caste gender ideology (that it lowers the social esteem of the family when its women work outside) conditioned their replies. We can call this the '*purdah* reflex' of males and the conformation to social expectations related to their class status and the perceived status of the person asking questions. It will do here to note, that it cannot be denied that *purdah* functions in the Terai as a set of values at different levels, and that the context in which it will be observed differs according to class, religion, education, family and age. *Purdah* can in brief be defined as the main mechanism in a patriarchal society for men to have access and control over natural and social resources. Its main effect is to restrict opportunities for women to develop and that it limits their access to and control over their products of labour and resources. Yet the '*purdah* reflex' seems often to be a light veneer, and in casual talk it often took little effort to get the admittance of all types of male government staff that women are very important, and do most of the farm work in India, and that their husbands are lazy and waste money smoking and drinking. and that women cannot be left out.

During the formulation mission to draw up recommendations for women's activities, we went to the villages and spoke with 19 women whose households had received a handpump or pump dug well or whose land was located in the command area of the deep tube wells in the first phase of the project. We made case-studies and found that many women have internalized the upper caste ideology that it is not dignified to participate in the cultivation of the fields.[8] The positive moral and social value given to women not doing outdoor agricultural work was a realistic constraint in getting information on the real participation of women in agriculture and irrigation in interview conditions, where, because of time pressure only one-time talks could be arranged. This experience boosted us the more with the thought that a gender in-depth study was an absolute must to chip away and find out more. On the other hand, there were groups of landless women who immediately frankly admitted that poverty compels them to earn wages: even a mother and two daughters of a Muslim sharecropper household told us during field visits in 1987 that they are willing to do any work in the fields when called, but the owners of the land (men) do not call them because of traditional notions.[9]

From the short scouting visits it became clear from our observations that the role of women in agricultural production was substantial. To show the involvement and the contribution made by women in shaping the economic status of the family, we presented two case-stories in the evaluation report (NBTD Report of the Evaluation 1987, Annexure 3). We learned that in better-off land-owning families the income generating activities from agriculture of the men are supplemented by those bari-based directly productive activities of women such as as rice processing.[10] The variations in the participation rates in work one's own crop-field or in paid village labour or wage labour outside the village seemed to be mainly dependent on the economic condition of the household and much less related to community or religion. To have a better assessment of the gender activities that could be proposed to improve the concrete material conditions of women, and to pursue a better power resource basis three broad classes of rural households were roughly categorized in terms of labour and income:

1. *Women of landless households*: households which cannot subsist without female and children's paid village labour.[11] The women and children are indirectly involved in the project because the work in the command areas of the river lift irrigation, deep tube well and handpump beneficiary households irrigation facilities is partly done by them. They are for the majority women of scheduled caste and tribal origin and very poor Muslim women.

2. *Marginal and small farm women*: The households can subsist because of the female unpaid family labour and paid village labour during certain seasons. These women work outside the

house in the vegetable garden and many of them work also in their own rice and jute fields. They belong to the Rajbansi and Namasudra communities. Muslim marginal farm women are usually not allowed to work in the paddy fields or vegetable garden.

3. *Middle and large farm women*: Households which for social esteem reasons withdraw their women from paid village labour or work in their own crop lands, and in some cases partly from unpaid family labour. The women are mainly involved in *bari* post-harvest processing and therefore directly effected by the river lift irrigation and deep tube well irrigation if their land is in the command area. Sometimes hey supervise female labourers or do some work with the help of labourers in the vegetable garden. The majority are of Rajbansi or Bangladeshi origin.

3.4 GENDER ACTIVITIES IN THE PROJECT

Besides the attempt to get a better insight into the life and work of women in the Terai, and the study on the impact of the implementation of small-scale irrigation on it, the following concrete material and 'empowerment' recommendations for gender activities were made[12] and included in the planning of the project.

The recommendations were also based on theoretical considerations. Caroline Moser (1989) has developed the concepts of gender needs/interests, strategic gender needs/interests and practical gender needs/interests. She explains that there is an important distinction between *women's interests,* and *gender interests*.

> The concept of 'women's interests' assumes compatibility of interest based on biological similarities. In fact the position of women in society depends on a variety of different criteria, such as class and ethnicity as well as gender, and consequently the interests they may have in common may be determined as much by their class position or their ethnic identity as by their biological similarity as women.

Moser states clearly that women may have general interests in common which should be called *gender interest,* to differentiate them from the false homogeneity imposed by the notion of 'women's interests'. Gender interests can be divided in strategic and practical ones. Strategic gender needs are needs which are formulated from the '*analysis of women's subordination to men*' (Moser 1989, p. 10). They pursue a more equal organization of society, in terms of both the structure and nature of relationships between men and women. Strategic gender needs may includes abolition of the sexual division of labour; removal of discrimination such as rights to own land or property, or access to credit; the decrease of the burden of domestic labour and childcare and political equality. Strategic gender needs are 'feminist' by its nature, and so is the level of consciousness required to struggle for them.

Practical gender needs are those which are formulated from the concrete conditions that women experience, in their *engendered* position within the sexual division of labour, and deriving out of this their practical gender interests for human survival (Moser 1989, p. 11). Practical gender needs do not challenge the prevailing forms of subordination of women, even though they directly arise out of them (Molyneux 1985, p. 233). In light of this we may conclude that empowerment of women can only be realized through strategic gender needs and interests.

When we apply these concepts to the Terai irrigation project we first have to identify the practical gender needs for different categories of women in the project area. To answer this question detailed and specific feminist anthropological research and insight is required. The implementation of irrigation facilities is in fact a practical gender-neutral interest for both men and women. It is in the interest of both to have more water to increase agricultural production. However, only by studying carefully the division of labour by sex and the nature of women's productive and reproductive labour can the need be assessed for specific practical gender-interests.

The next and more complicated question is: what are the strategic gender needs and interests of different categories of women in the project area? A thorough knowledge of gender relations, gender ideology and *purdah* context will be an absolute necessity for an insight into the ways and means by which strategic gender needs can be supported and the empowerment of women encouraged. *Purdah* is part of the gender ideology, a pattern of prescribed behaviour for a woman, including veiling her face and body, restricting her movements outside the home, and above all, maintaining a respectful and deferential demeanour within the home (Sharma 1980; Mandelbaum 1988; Liddle and Joshi 1986;[13] Chen 1985). *Purdah* embodies in extreme form the principles of hierarchical division and social segregation of women and men, principles which have strong religious legitimation and sanction. Liddle and Joshi reveal that *purdah* can be seen as an instrument of patriarchal control and the control of property and income.[14] Marty Chen (1985) writes: 'Whereas *purdah* is useful in describing the status of women, patriarchy is more useful in analysing how and why men control and dominate women.'

Ways and means have to be invented that will reduce the whole patriarchal set-up which subordinates women, especially in poor households to realise strategic gender needs. Often the gender relations in poor households are more equal than in better-off households: *purdah* is a luxury that very poor castes and classes cannot afford. But poor women face the restrictions of access to labour markets by *purdah* imposed on them by the patriarchs of the richer landholding families in the village.

It will be revealed below that an incorporation of practical gender interests (for women) may awaken and stimulate an awareness of strategic gender needs. I agree with the view of Lilian van Wesemael that both types of interests can support each other in a dialectical way and that they should not be seen as a contradictory set of concepts (Wesemael 1988) in which practical gender needs have a much lower status in feminist eyes than strategic ones. They will be briefly described and the assumptions of their effects in material and ideological terms will be indicated. If and how these recommendations were implemented over a span of five years will be discussed in Chapter 9.

The following gender activities were planned in the formulation of Phase II:

(a) to install 20,000 handpumps (planned 13,500 in the preparatory documents)

(b) female headed households which belong to marginal farmers (operational landholding less than 1 hectare, and 1 *bigha* consolidated land for vegetable growing near the homestead) will be given preference to get a handpump
(c) the site of the handpump should be selected in consultation with the women of the house
(d) construction work of the project (pumphouses, 4 hectare units, etc.) should provide wage labour to local landless women (and men)
(e) to appoint women extension workers (two per block) in the 27 blocks of the project area
(f) to train female agricultural labourers and farm women of marginal and small landholders to improve agricultural management and operations
(g) to appoint a woman in the advisory committee of the project
(h) to appoint women in the water-users committees that should be formed in the command areas of river lift irrigation and deep tube wells
(i) to construct a women's corner in a central marketplace with water and sanitary facilities.

3.4.1 Installation of handpumps

The proposal to install 20,000 instead of 13,500 handpumps was based on the findings of our small investigation during the formulation mission. The proposed increase in number of handpumps was accepted without any problem by the male staff members. The justification for the increase of the number of handpumps was that besides the objective of providing irrigation water they can contribute to the saving of time and energy of women's domestic labour by providing drinking water which makes time free for women to do productive labour; to the improvement of the nutritional status of the children as more vegetables can be grown; and to a better health condition of children and adults as the drinking water is more safe than the water in traditional open dug wells, to make the environment greener and more beautiful (see Plate 7).

The traditional way of lifting water with a bamboo stick (*tera*)

Plate 7: Drilling a bore-hole for a handpump.

from a small dug well (*kuwa*) costs a lot of time, physical energy and strain, in particular for women and children. In some villages the health department has installed public handpumps and dug wells for drinking water to be used by a cluster of households. A change in water source use was noted with the instalment of individual handpumps under the first phase. Drinking and cooking water was fetched from the pump as it is easier, quicker and costs less physical strain. Also the drinking water for the cattle (30 litre a day for a cow or bullock) is fetched in the majority of the cases by handpump. Water for bathing and washing clothes is in many cases still taken from the dug well, if available. The disadvantage of this change in water use may be that because of less regular use of well water, the well gets silted and the water becomes unsuitable for drinking. In Cooch Behar district many households have no small dug well in their compound but fetch it from a community well. For them the handpump is an even further improvement of the daily water supply needed.

Regarding the nutritional status in the area we collected information from a female paediatric specialist, then employed in the government hospital in Cooch Behar. She said that according to the season 40 to 80 children are admitted daily to the hospital because of malnutrition and water-born diseases.[15] Children also suffer from a shortage of protein and calories. The vegetable growing can help to improve these conditions. During field visits we saw that mothers plucked green cabbage for their own dinner from their vegetable garden which they irrigated with the project handpump. This shows that not all the vegetables are sold for cash and that a portion is used for home consumption. Water-borne diseases come mainly from open water resources like traditional wells.

Regarding the 'empowerment potential' of the implementation of handpumps we had some indications that they can initiate somewhat more freedom of movement. New crops and vegetables can be grown and that enlarges the traditional gender 'division-of-labour' crop horizon a little bit. New crops are not yet associated with the male or female domain of the division of labour. We spoke with women who were never allowed to take part in rice and tobacco cultivation, but now with the pump there was no objection as the crops were not yet gender specific in its symbolism of male and female crops.

Another thought in view of 'empowerment' regarding hand-pumps was that time is saved and can be used to earn cash. That in itself bears a potential for a less vulnerable position in which poor farm women are not only dependent on cash earnings of agricultural labour. This will certainly reduce the power of the upper-caste patriarchs who have control over access to paid village and wage labour.

At a later stage we introduced the notion that handpumps should be registered in the name of the woman of the house, and a quotum be achieved in a certain time (10 per cent). The strong notion at the level of the administration is that only the formal owner of the land can be the owner of the handpump, and have water rights and so only men can become owners of handpumps and a few women and widows who have inherited some land. The proposal to make women the owners of handpumps as they use them most, a thought similar as 'land to the tiller' which is a very accepted thought in the Terai, did not appeal in the beginning to the male staff of the project, but was over time accepted, and had an unexpected favourable effect which will be discussed in Chapter 9.

The following field notes describe a visit to two female handpump owners,

Field visit Thursday, 15 March 1990: visit to the village Bagjan, Mainaguri block.

A cluster of 25 handpumps is installed. The houses of two women beneficiaries [Savitri and Bharati] were revisited. They got the handpump in their name as the land [1 acre and 0.6 acre] is also registered in their name. The sisters inherited the land of their father as there were no sons in the family. Savitri is growing chillies with the water of the handpump. She has bought the seeds in the market. She is using the water also for bathing and washing, but they are not drinking the water because it has a bad smell. The main change so far for her is that she could reduce the number of trips to the water source from 12 to 3. The time saved is spent on irrigation. The advantage is of course that she expects to get a better income. Her biggest problem is that they have no plough or bullocks of their own. She is asking to do something about it. Her sister shows me her collapsed roof: she has no money for repairs.

These field notes show when a small intervention can generate a whole chain of supporting needs which however are not incorporated in the project. It shows the limitations of the 'integrated' approach as conceptualized in the policy of the project.

The handpump programme has been implemented since 1987 with speed. In the beginning of 1995 the number has already increased to 28,025. The impact study has to show in what way in the long run the handpumps have supported women.

3.4.2 Female headed households

Female headed households which belong to the marginal farmers will be given preference for grant of a handpump. A woman head of a household during field visits expressed her gladness with the handpump and a special recommendation has been made for this small group of women.

Friday, 16 March 1990: visit to the village Tambari, Phansidewa, district Darjeeling.

In the village 30 handpumps have been installed. We visited some households which got the handpumps one year ago. Wonderful fields with vegetables could be seen everywhere. We visited a female headed household. Three pumps out of 30 are given to female headed households in this village because the land is registered in their name. The family migrated long ago from Bangladesh. Her husband died about 10 years ago. She got the pump one year ago and since then her income increased because she could grow much more vegetables. We see neatly planted pumpkins, chillies, tomatoes etc. She has three sons all attending school, and three daughters. Twice a week she goes to the local market and sells a small quantity of vegetables [later we met her at the market and she had sold a small quantity of coriander leaves]. She has a nice plot with stringbeans which she irrigates with the help of her daughters.

In women's studies the subject of 'female headed' households is a central one. In a study on this category of women in India, Kumari (1989, p. 3) writes that they are 'essentially deprived and underprivileged and form the last of the chains in the process of feminisation of poverty'. In her study in villages near Varanasi women become heads of families due to the outmigration of the husband, or widowhood or desertion; divorce was non-existent (Kumari 1989, p. 95). According to the estimations of Visaria and Visaria (1985, p. 54) the incidence of this in India is comparatively low: about 10 per cent national average. Preference to households headed by women as handpump beneficiaries was accepted with some discussion in which the argument was used, 'there are hardly women of this category in the area'.

An important reason for the willingness to give preference to female headed households in the patriarchal context is that the land is in the name of the female head of the household. A woman without a husband becomes a kind of 'honourable male'. There is a decisive and crucial pre-condition for the Bengal agricultural officers to carry out this recommendation and that is that only the registered person who is the owner of land is considered as a beneficiary: in 90 per cent of the cases males. Female household heads are perceived as legal landowners and therefore entitled to water rights through the ownership of hand tube wells. From a theoretical point of view the handpumps fulfil a practical gender need for female headed households. As regards strategic gender needs, the handpump water is an essential asset to increase home consumption and vegetable production. In this way this small category of women might become more self-reliant in the subsistence and cash economy. They quite even sell their produce themselves on the market, which is exeptional. In this small way a change has occured in the deeply anchored gender relations, to the advantage of this specific group of women. We see that women are capable of growing their own agricultural products and they intrude in one of the main strongholds of patriarchal dominance: the market. The appropriation of strategic public physical spaces by men is an outcome of the whole set-up to subordinate women and therefore every woman entering the male-dominated public space is an agent of change. In this context we proposed special facilities for women in market places. It is likely that in the long run the economic conditions of the few female headed households in the project area will be strengthened. In short we may hope that in the long run this recommendation contributes to the empowerment of woman-headed households.

3.4.3 Site selection of handpumps by women

The stipulation that the site of the handpump should be selected in consultation with the women of the house was stated in the basis document and was accepted by officials. Although this recommendation appears matter of fact, for Indian conditions it means some decision making by the women on an economic asset, to which in turn is somewhat challenging the decision making power of the official beneficiary, the landowning male of the household.

If we analyse this point at the level of our theoretical framework we can state that the consultation in site selection may be called at first view a practical gender need. Women are the ones who use the pump most frequently because of the division of labour, and it is therefore convenient if the pump is installed at a place according to thier choice (and technical criteria). A closer look may reveal that this probably practical need perceived activity can be a first step to a more strategic gender need, e.g. to have a say in other decisions related to productive and reproductive labour.

3.4.4 Project construction work and female landless labourers

The project generated some employment in the construction of the pumphouses for the deep tube wells and the river lift irrigation. The 4 hectare units require of at least 150 meter brick and plastering work (see Plate 8). The stipulation was accepted that contractors should recruit unskilled labourers from the local population. In this way construction work should provide wage labour to local landless persons. However, unequal wages for women is shown from the previous field report.

Field visit 21-9-1989: Mainaguri, village Paschim Harmati.

The river lift irrigation-pumphouse has been constructed and the underground tubes and pipes are connected recently, but the three engines have to be installed. During construction local people were employed to do the unskilled labour. The ten women employed as construction labourers earned Rs 16 a day: the men Rs 20 a day.

Irrespective of the construction work that will create some

Plate 8: Four-hectares unit irrigation channels.

employment for men and women of landless households, we may expect that the irrigation facilities generate more agricultural work. This is of utmost importance for the landless households and in particular for women. To survive they have to contribute to the family income but the rigid division of labour has resulted in a highly segregated labour market which offers much fewer labour opportunities for them. They may not face much patriarchal control over their labour by their own husbands but the men from rich households control the paid labour opportunities in the village and dictate the norms of *purdah* and status that often discourage women from seeking wage employment outside the village (Chen 1985, p. 25; Westergaard 1981, p. 14). Therefore any traditional agricultural employment generated by the irrigation facilities can be an important contribution to get more labour but it can also give more resources to landholding patriarchs to have more power in imposing control on the labour of landless women.

The practical gender need and interests of this category of women are perceived and acknowledged by the officials and translated into the concrete demand to contractors to recruit local landless women in construction works. This in itself is again a small contribution to create work opportunities out of the scope of traditional channels, and shows the social and political sensitive climate of Bengal to be concerned with the weakest sections.

3.4.5 *Appointment of women extension workers*

It was strongly recommended on the basis of several obvious arguments that women extension workers (two per block) be appointed in the 27 blocks of the districts, as the total extension work is carried out in the Terai area (and in the whole of Bengal) by about 500 male village extension workers, Krishi Prayukti Sahayak (KPS). The appointment of women extension workers can be presented as a practical need and interest of marginal and small farm women. In fact no objection was made against this suggestion in 1987 and we had good hopes that after some time a start would be made with the training of women in this work. To create labour opportunities for women in a male dominated field of employment might mean more chances for empowerment of women who will be appointed as extension workers but also for the women who will be trained and informed by them. However, practical arguments were used to explain the difficulties that are involved. The following discussion (see Coordination Report, April 1989) is an illustration:

> One KPS organized a special extension day for women in his village. He noticed that the women felt the need to know more on agricultural methods and kitchen gardening. 15 women attended the meeting. The KPS were very much in favour of appointing women KPS to inform the women on nutrition and kitchen gardening but they raised the problem of transport. They cycle from one village to the other but for women that is not possible. They admit that it is not a question of physical constraint but of cultural values. Cycling by girls is done in Siliguri, but not in rural areas.

There is a deep internalization of *purdah* notions in the imagination of the implementing officials in which KPS can only be males. Gender ideological stereotyping enforced even the assumption that in the 'Government Notification of Recruitment Rules for KPS', it is specified that *only men* were eligible to apply for the post of KPS. But the State Recruitment Rules signed by the Governor in July 1985, state that the qualifications required for recruitment to the post of KPS should be persons having passed school final examination, or preference should be given to candidates with higher secondary examination in agriculture; and a knowledge of Bengali/Nepali (in case of hill areas of Darjeeling district), spoken and written. After studying the content of the notification the officials immediately admitted that women are persons and that there were no formal constraints any longer on the recruitment of women. How the realization and procedures discussed with the Minister of Agriculture in Calcutta worked out over time will be shown in Chapter 8.

3.4.6 Training of female agricultural labourers and farm women of marginal and small landholders

The training of farm women was from the beginning accepted as a useful activity, but the number of courses in comparison with those allotted to men was only 10 per cent. Efforts to increase the number of training courses for women revealed the well-known constraint that women as non- landowners are not perceived as beneficiaries 'More courses for women mean less courses for men, and as the land is in the name of the men, they are the eligible beneficiaries. As only "beneficiaries" are entitled for training it will be difficult to include women in such quantities in the training programme.' Finally, it was agreed to include courses for vegetable growing farm women with a duration of five days. The course content was adjusted accordingly.

It will take time to organize courses for landless women labourers as they are not usually conceptualised as beneficiaries, although they are very much involved in the project as they have to do the work in the command areas of the irrigation facilities.

The need for the training of women can be illustrated by the following event. During a visit to the training centre (KVK) we asked one of the farmers there to whom he would communicate the things he would earn during training when he returned home. He replied with a big smile, 'I will communicate everything during the day to my brothers and father and male neighbours; and . . . at night I will communicate some of the information to my wife.'

3.4.7 Appointment of a woman in the advisory committee of the project

In order to incorporate the women's point of view in the management and decision making of the project we suggested the appointment of a well-known rural women's leader or other capable woman in the Advisory Committee. As mentioned earlier the members and invited members of the committee are ministers and secretaries of departments and the main engineers in the project. Although the Minister of Scheduled Castes and Tribes Welfare is a member, the Department of Social Welfare and Women's Affairs is not represented. The Committee is a powerful organization and decides on the allotment and distribution of facilities in the districts. The point was raised many times during visits with the Joint Director of Agriculture but he always stated that it was very difficult to find a suitable woman within government circles involved in the project, as it should not just be a token appointment.

3.4.8 Appointment of women in water-users committees

Water users' committees should be formed in the command areas of river lift irrigation and deep tube wells. Much can be said about the formation of water-users committees and the rôle they have to fulfil. There is an official memo from the Government of West Bengal from 1979 (an amendment of 1992) in which it is stated that local committees for distribution of irrigation water should be reconstituted with the following members: the local MLA, Panchayat Samiti, Gram Panchayat, AEO of the Block and the Sub-assistant Engineer of the Block or the operator of the installation. In addition the members as mentioned will in their first meeting of the committee select and co-opt five representatives of the cultivators in the command area (not more than one representative from one spout): two representatives will come from the category of small and marginal farmers. This official regulation does not at all reflect the community participation perception that was envisaged in the Dutch integrated approach, let alone that it would deal with the participation of women in the water-users committees. It will take a long time of awareness raising and understanding to constitute participatory water-users committees. It will take no doubt a much longer time to appoint women representatives of marginal and small farmers' households to advocate their rights and interests regarding irrigation. This point will be the more urgent in view of the envisaged 'privatization' of now state-owned but already community managed irrigation devices. Women will be highly involved in the financing of operations and maintenance of irrigation devices, and, not the least, in payment of the high water fees which will be required when the subsidy which is furnished now will be withdrawn. The fact that most women are not landowning, and therefore not perceived as beneficiaries, will contribute to ignore them in the management and decision making process of the irrigation schemes.

3.4.9 Construction of a women's corner in a central marketplace with water and sanitary facilities

Supportive to the project is a proposal to improve market infrastructures. A proposal for the improvement of a special market has been developed. Additionally, it is suggested that one corner of the market will be reserved for women sellers in the market, and this corner should have its own water and latrine facilities. As said before, markets are the spatial domain of men and *purdah* assures that women have little access to these places. It is mostly tribal women and heads of families who are seen at local markets. In may be assumed that a reserved women's corner can give some protection to women and that facilities for drinking water and sanitation may increase the duration of their stay. Usual poor men and women have to sell immediately and are hardly able to take their time in bargaining because of lack of facilities as shelter in the rainy season or drinking water, and for women lack of toilet facilities.[16]

A planned corner in the market may increase the bargaining power of women although it is not meant to mean that women would be restricted to that part of the market. However, in practice in view of the functional and spatial segregation of the sexes it is not likely that women will mix with men.

NOTES

1. Darjeeling was a famous former hill station. In the hot summer time British officials sent their wives and children to Darjeeling to have some fresh air. I found the hill station in spring 1987 and 1989 in a dilapidated condition: the 'alternate-day-strikes' which were part of the Gurkha protest movement had throttled almost all economic activity and tourism.
2. There are 59 Scheduled Castes and 38 Scheduled Tribes in West Bengal (Census 1981, SC and ST, Amendment Act, 1976).
3. In view of that the Land Reforms in West Bengal (A.K. Ghose 1983; Atul Kohli 1987) and in particular Operation Barga (Leeuw & Pluyms: Review of Agricuflture, *EPW*, 16, 1981) and the Comprehensive Rural Development (CADC) Programmes (Dasgupta 1986) have to be mentioned.
4. See for an explanation of the concepts gender and gender ideology Henrietta L. Moore, 1988.
5. An additional lot of 4,000 HTWs was approved in August 1994, raising the number of HTWs to 28,025.
6. Until the mid-1980s about two-thirds of total Netherlands aid was provided as macro-economic support, made up of import support in particular (DFI 1,405 million over the period since 1980), mostly fertilizer support, and of project assistance in the field of water transport (DFI 382 million). Almost all this support met with the Government of India's declared demand. About one-third of total Netherlands aid was directed towards poverty alleviation programmes. Apart from project aid in the Rural Water Supply Sector (DFI 334 million) and in the Land and Water Sector (DFI 107 million), budget support of DFI 484 million was provided to improve the position of the poor.
7. Between 1980 and 1992 India received DFI 3,500 million development assistance from the Netherlands and was by far the largest recipient of Netherlands aid. For India the Netherlands was the fifth bialteral donor (10.5 per cent of all bilateral aid or 5.2 per cent of total aid) IOV rapport. While the total development assistance increased by more than 53 per cent during this period (from DFI 3,360 million to DFI 5,160 million per year) India's share decreased from 9 per cent in 1980 to a mere 5 per cent in 1992. Since 1980, the share of non-project aid in the development programme with India has gradually decreased, from 98 per cent in 1980 to 75 per cent in 1981-6 and to about 50 per cent in the period 1987-92.
8. Kirsten Westergaard (1981, p. 14) writes on her research in villages in Bangladesh that are near the Terai area: 'In the villages studies it was thus found that the ideological superstructure reinforces the subordination of women to the extent that their inferiority is believed by the women themselves.'

9. At a theoretical level (see Marty Chen 1985) this case is very interesting because if manifests exactly patriarchal control over poor women's labour by the village men of rich households. They control the paid labour opportunities within the village and dictate the norms of *purdah* and status that discourage women to find wage-labour outside the village.
10. Post-harvest activities are crucial once the paddy has been brought to the homestead: this means drying, threshing, winnowing, cleaning and the time-consuming work of parboiling. Everywhere women spend hours every day to use a foot-operated hammer-like implement for the dehusking. They are also responsible for the storage of the domestic and cash stocks of rice.
11. Marty Chen makes the significant distinction between paid village labour and wage labour. She points to the fact that in Bangladesh wage-labour includes agricultural and non-agricultural labour for cash or kind outside the village but including the fields of the village, and, therefore, traditionally male. Traditionally women are restricted to agricultural and non-agricufltural labour for cash or kind inside the village. In the Terai the same distinction is significant (1985, p. 17).
12. This terminology overlaps the concepts of Caroline Moser of practical and stratetic genger needs and interests which were used in an earlier article (Schenk-Sandbergen 1992). We feel it a bit overdone to focus on Mosers 'theoretical framework' although it certainly helps sharpen our analytical understanding of the proposed recommendations.
13. Mandelbaum, 1988 is primarily concerned with describing and trying to account for the observance of *purdah* among Hindu and Muslim in the '*purdah* belt' of northern India, Pakistan and Bangladesh. He adopts a noncritical, cultural relativist perspective and his functionalist explanations are largely tautological. An outstanding theoretical analysis of '*purdah*' is given in the book of Liddle and Joshi, 1986.
14. Marty Chen quotes in her interesting paper the following definition of patriarchy from Cain et al. 1979, p. 2: 'patriarchy is a set of social relations with a material base which enables men to dominate women'.
15. See for an interesting article on malnutrition of rural children and the sex bias in an other part of West Bengal (Sen and Sengupta 1985).
16. Men can urinate and defaecate at any place in the streets or open field, but women can only relieve themselves before sunrise and after sunset.

4. Basic Gender Data and Status of Women in the Family and Community

> The Sun will start rising in the West if the malefolk start washing clothes, cleaning utensils and the house, collecting firewood and fetching drinking water regularly. These are meant for us. But, why should we do all these things ? Even if we starve we are not allowed to work as Khetmajdur [casual agricultural labourers]. What work we are to do and how to do it are decided by the Samaj [society] and my Vater [husband]
>
> PARBATI, 38 years, Scheduled Caste, in Roy 1992, p. 130

4.1 GENDER, CLASS AND COMMUNITY

In this chapter we will sketch the general condition of women in comparison with men in the Terai. Therefore, we will present facts and figures to indicate gender gaps and to present gender indicators reflecting the disadvantaged and detoriating position of women. We are concerned about the conditions and position of women in the Terai project and attempt to strengthen them as far as activities within the realm of the small-scale irrigation project allow.

For the in-depth study seven locations were selected where new irrigation facilities were introduced under the North Bengal Terai Development Project. In addition to households with access to land and hence the new irrigation facilities, a number of landless labourers were interviewed as well in these seven locations (see Table 4.1). In total 273 households were selected initially. This number decreased to 261 households at the end of the survey, as a number of families outmigrated. Two women of marginal farmers households have joined a non-beneficiary household because their husbands died. Obviously they were not able to continue their own small farms on their own in the project area.

The women's base-line study was based on interviews with women in the five types of irrigation schemes implemented, and women and girls of 30 landless labourer families. As mentioned in Chapter 2, our findings show that there is a dominance of SC Rajbansis in the composition of the deep- and shallow tube well (DTW and STW) and handpump beneficiary households (HTW). The character of the deep tube well population in Jamadarerbos is flavoured by the substantial tribal community having land in the command area. The Muslim community is predominant in the population of Paschim Harmati where river lift irrigation (RLI) and pump dug well (PDW) schemes were implemented. The women of landless labourers households are mainly Muslims or belong to the Rajbansi community.

Table 4.1 reveals the representation of number of households classwise at the time of the base-line and end of the indepth study.

As of each household a woman was interviewed, Table 4.1 shows the representation of women respondents over the four class categories. In the river lift, deep tube well, and shallow tube well schemes 50 per cent of the women can be classified as farm women of marginal households. In the handpump clusters we selected about 75 per cent women members of marginal households. The proportion of women of small and middle households is much smaller compared to the percentage of women in the marginal category. Women of the richer households (middle and big farmers) are represented most in the pump dug well schemes.

The findings of the in depth study show that there was no correlation between community and class, neither in 1989-90, nor in 1992-3. A Rajbansi woman can be a member of a marginal, small, middle, or big farmers' household, and she can be landless. For all communities it can be stated that the majority of women interviewed are from marginal farms. It is remarkable that out of the 26 interviewed landless women, 12 are Muslim. Poverty obviously compels them to break the ideological constraints of their community.

TABLE 4.1: DISTRIBUTION OF HOUSEHOLDS BY AGRARIAN CLASSES IN THE BASE-LINE AND FINAL YEAR OF THE IN-DEPTH STUDY AND IRRIGATION FACILITIES

Scheme	Total HHs		Marginal		Small		Middle		Big	
	1989-90	1992-3	1989-90	1992-3	1989-90	1992-3	1989-90	1992-3	1989-90	1992-3
RLI	60	61	32	30	12	15	12	13	4	3
DTW	75	72	41	35	17	21	13	12	4	4
HTW	85	81	69	61	12	17	4	3	0	0
STW	15	14	7	6	4	4	3	3	1	1
PDW	8	7	2	0	2	2	1	2	3	3
Landless	30	26	0	0	0	0	0	0	0	0
Total	273	261	151 (62%)	132 (56%)	47 (19%)	59 (25%)	33 (14%)	33 (14%)	12 (5%)	11 (5%)

The distribution of the households by community shows that the Rajbansis constitute a little less than half of the sample followed by Muslims, general Hindus, other Scheduled Castes, mainly Namasudras, and the Scheduled Tribes in order of their numerical strength.

4.2 SEX-RATIO, AGE, MORTALITY AND MOTHERHOOD

Sex-ratios (the number of women per 1,000 males) are important indicators to assess the overall position of women in society. Low sex-ratio figures point to higher mortality to whom women and girls are exposed. The sex ratio was in the 1981 Census for the total population of West Bengal 911, showing a disadvantaged position of women. The average of 911 is an aggregate of rural and urban sex-ratio, the figures being 875 for the urban and 947 for the rural population. In 1991 the Census data show a slight improvement in the sex-ratio as the average has come to 917. In our small sample of the follow-up study the members of males and females are basically too small to estimate a reliable sex-ratio. However, to indicate a trend derived from the research, the data show that there is reason for concern about the women's well-being in the Terai region. The sample survey in particular indicates an alarmingly low sex ratio, 876, far below the West Bengal rural average of 947 (Census 1981).[1] The in-depth study sex-ratio is 944: about the state's rural average.

Table 4.2 shows the number of households and respondents on which the sex-ratio figures of the in-depth study and sample survey are based.

The sex-ratios presented in Table 4.3 show that for each irrigation device of the project, the in-depth sub-populations consist of less women than men, except in the shallow tube well scheme.

TABLE 4.2: POPULATION, HOUSEHOLDS AND MALE/FEMALE DISTRIBUTION, SEX-RATIOS

Study	Population	No. of HHs	Sex		Sex ratio
			Male	Female	
In-depth	1,624	261	836	788	944
Sample survey	8,665	1,524	4,617	4,048	876

TABLE 4.3: POPULATION AND SEX-RATIO IN THE IN-DEPTH STUDY

Scheme	Male		Female		Sex-ratio	
	1989-90	1992-3	1989-90	1992-3	1989-90	1992-3
RLI	196	204	182	191	929	936
DTW	249	245	231	234	928	955
HTW	259	255	243	238	938	937
STW	40	38	49	46	1225	1,211
PDW	30	36	24	28	800	778
Landless	63	58	62	52	984	897
Total	837	836	791	789	945	944

The remarkable point of our sex-ratio findings is that the low rate in the Terai area is not caused by the factors that are repeatedly reported for other states, such as neglect, malnutrition and poor health care of the girl child below 15 years (Miller 1981). The distribution of population by age and sex points to an interesting pattern which is revealed in the base-line study.

Table 4.4 shows that in 1992-3 the number of girls under five years outreaches the number of boys by 20. This means that the usual pattern in India of high mortality rates of girl-babies as a result of sex-discrimination and neglect of girls is not valid for the Terai area. In the age category 5 to 15 years the proportion of girls is slightly less than equal with boys in the same age-group. An obvious decline in the number of women compared to men is clearly seen in the age group 15+. Obviously, possible causes of high female mortality have to be traced in this 15+ age group.

As will be shown below our data reveal that 95 per cent of the girls are married at the age of 15 years. It is our impression that in particular too early motherhood in combination with a often dramatically weak physical condition of the mothers and lack of ante- and post-natal care, and a high mortality risk during childbirth might be the major causes for the low sex ratios in the category of women above 15 years (Gopalan 1985; Chowdhury 1985).

Malnutrition and undernutrition of children and adults of landless and poor families is very visible. Daily a paediatrician

TABLE 4.4 DISTRIBUTION OF POPULATION BY AGE GROUPS AND SEX IN THE SAMPLE SURVEY

Scheme	Male						Female						Total					
	–5		5–15		15+		–5		5–15		15+		–5		5–15		15+	
	(a)	(b)	(a)	(b)	(a)	(b)	(a)	(b)	(a)	(b)	(a)	(b)	(a)	(b)	(a)	(b)	(a)	(b)
RLI	32	23	45	60	119	121	35	25	43	51	104	115	67	48	88	111	223	236
DTW	33	21	70	66	146	158	46	34	65	63	120	137	79	55	135	129	266	295
HTW	33	34	70	62	156	159	38	43	69	64	136	131	71	77	139	126	292	290
STW	5	7	5	7	30	24	10	7	11	12	28	27	15	14	16	19	58	51
PDW	4	6	8	10	18	20	3	2	8	7	13	19	7	8	16	17	31	39
Landless	12	7	17	19	34	32	12	7	17	16	33	29	24	14	34	35	67	61
Total	119	98	215	224	503	514	144	118	213	213	434	458	263	216	428	437	937	972

Note: (a) = 1989-90; (b) = 1992-3

in the medical college of Siliguri has to admit malnourished children. Her data show that babies of low-income groups of one year have already a weight 30 per cent below the usual standards. They suffer in particular a shortage of minerals and vitamins. She has no data according to sex but it is in this social context that in particular the vegetable growing with the support of the handpump irrigation water gets an additional value. It is observed that mothers prepare the home-grown vegetables also for their own consumption. The retardation of girls and boys builds up during childhood, and this means for women that they have few reserves at the lifestage of pregnancy, deliveriy and lactation. A study by the paediatrician shows incredibly underweight mothers. Many poor women said they were not able to work because of total weakness. A study among a very poor group of stone-cutter women in the outskirts of Siliguri shows that women have a strong feeling that they are not even able any longer to breastfeed their babies (van Westerhoven 1995). This phenomenon has also been reported in studies in slums of Calcutta (Sen and Sengupta 1985). The study of Westerhoven shows although we cannot speak of discrimination of female babies in a broad sense, a small sex bias in breast-feeding matters. Boys are longer and better breastfed than daughters and this may cause sizeable differences for the future physical development of boys and girls.

In addition, the high incidence of diarrhoea among children and adults in the districts of the North Bengal Terai Development Project is another prevailing cause for the undermining of health and a constant drain of energy. Testing of water samples from wells, which are the usual public and private drinking water sources in the Terai, indicated that many are highly polluted. Chlorination with bleaching powder is not done by the people, or the public health authorities. Although the water quality of the handpumps implemented by the project has so far not been scientifically tested, the observations of the paediatrician, field-investigators and the agricultural grass-roots workers is that handpumps provide safe and good quality drinking water. Talks with beneficiaries of handpumps during field visits also indicate that they emphasize that their children's health condition has considerably improved since use of handpump water for drinking began.

It will be unrealistic to expect that in this study improvements in the sex-ratios as a result of better agricultural production and income can be demonstrated: the time span is too short. Besides, studies show that better living standards may even result in a wider gap in the nutritional status between boys and girls, as the parents are then able to give even more preference to boys in food and education (Sen and Sengupta 1985, p. 22). Only a follow-up study over a very long period can reveal whether a small-scale irrigation project can contribute to an increase in production and income that will contribute to better nutrition for girls and women.

The low sex ratios in the age category 15+ reflect the universal trend of higher mortality rates for women of poor households due to child-birth under riskful conditions. We have identified three factors to illustrate this trend: limitations of medical facilities in the village, impure status of deliveries, and early resumption of heavy agricultural work.

The following field notes show the circumstances of the very limited medical facilities among Muslim women in a river lift scheme:

> In the river lift irrigation scheme we visited a Muslim woman named Muzamad. Her children are all born on the floor of the house: no traditional *dai* [midwife] was even helping her. The first baby died because the cord was cut with a sharp piece of bamboo. Her mother-in-law cut the cord of the other babies twice with a blade. Till now the Muslim women deliver babies in the same way and are cut off from professional help and information.

In the in-depth study we have asked how babies are born: with the help of a trained midwife, a traditional midwife or in a hospital. In the *rabi* season of 1993, 44 babies were born in the river lift irrigation, handpump and deep tube well population, 6 of them in the hospital (from the more well-to-do classes) but 31 at home. From the 31 midwives who were present at the deliveries, 30 were untrained traditional *dais*, and only once a trained midwife was called. Traditional *dais* are mostly elder community women with much practical experience (Jeffery 1987).

It is the task of the midwife to sever the umbilical cord with a cutting instrument. Field visits show that the use of the fine green bamboo split about one foot long with sharp edges is still used. The green skin is stripped off a standing bamboo tree and washed with cold water immediately before use and it is thrown away after the cutting of the cord. The midwife does not change her usual clothes, nor wash her hands, nor boil the string of the bamboo strip nor even washes them with plain hot water.

In seven other cases the babies were born with the help of female relatives. In each village we could identify on average three *dais*. The expenses for a delivery in the hospital are at least Rs 200 and could be as much as Rs 500. A delivery in the house comes to Rs 50 to 100. The renumeration of the *dai* varies, it can be unboiled rice, Rs 10 to 20, some *pan-gua* (betel leaf and areca nuts), sometimes a cheap *sari* or some mustard oil. It depends on the pecuniary strength of the family.

Moreover, deliveries are from a religious point of view impure events which contribute to circumstances in which poor rural women give birth which enhance maternal deaths. One of the most dramatic consequences is that sources of support from other women are scant and local perceptions of female physiology involve the creation of very negative self-images (Jeffery 1989). In the Terai project area the information collected showed that notions of the impurity of deliveries are still existing. Two Namasudra households of somewhat better-off farmers could afford the luxury of building a temporary shelter from bamboo and paddy straw for the delivery. This is the so-called 'lying-in-room' in which the door either faces east or south. The mothers delivered the babies on a bed of straw with the help of a *dai*. After the third day of the delivery the males destroyed the lying-in-room by making a fire of the materials. This symbolizes the impure status of childbirth. No male members were allowed to enter this room during the whole period of confinement. They withdrew to the outer yard of the *bari*. In these two cases a factor in the arrangement seemed to be that the old mothers of the house insisted on this traditional birth custom. This custom is not practised by the Rajbansis, which shows that they observe less the Hindu dogma on purity and impurity.

The eminent study of Charu Chandra Sanyal (1965) teaches

us a lot on birth customs, pregnancy, delivery, and care for mother and child 30 years ago. Both the expecting mother and the father had to observe certain customs related to uncleanliness.[3] Sanyal writes:

> When a woman becomes pregnant [Gao-Bhari] she is not considered unclean and is allowed to go about her régular works and do all cooking and household duties without restriction. She may eat whatever she likes. But she is not allowed to go about alone at night nor attend any funeral, nor go to eat in a house where a post-funeral ceremony is being performed lest evil spirits get possession of her. She should not go out on Tuesday and Saturday and should not cross any river. It is believed, this may do some harm to the child in the womb and may even cause its death. (1965, p. 61)

However, it is interesting that also for the husband of the pregnant woman certain taboos exist,

> It is forbidden to carry a funeral bier or to go to attend cremation. He is not allowed to sacrifice any animal with his own hands nor to go about fishing. He should not kill any animal. He should not also take his meals in the house where a post-funeral ceremony is being performed.

This shows again the relatively equal gender relations in the Rajbansi community during the 1960s. However, after the seventh and ninth day when the stump of the cord attached to the child falls off, both the mother and father are considered unclean. Neither is allowed to touch the well or enter the kitchen. In former days the father also did not do field work for the first seven days. After seven days the ceremonial bath of the mother either in a nearby pond or near the house well takes place. In the latter case some other woman draws the water for her as she is still untouchable. She changes her clothes. Water in which a *tulsi* (*ocymum sanctum*) leaf is dipped is sprinkled on her, on the child and on all articles of the lying-in-room. The uncleanliness is then over. Even then she is not allowed to touch the well, but allowed to enter the cow-shed and to do other household duties except cooking, and she can take her usual meals. In poor houses where there are no other female members, she is also allowed to cook. Usually a temporary well is dug for her use. In the same evening a ceremony is performed at the *thakur bari*: the corner of the inner yard of the house where the *tulsi* plant is growing.

After seven days the father gets his hair shaved, his nails are pared and his clothes are washed. He is considered clean after the evening *puja* at *thakur bari* is done. He then resumes work in the field (Sanyal, p. 65). However, one month after childbirth the untouchability is completely removed with a short ceremony in which the hair of the child and the father is shaved and the nails of the mother are pared (Sanyal, p. 67). The husband is then admitted to sleep again with his wife.

Another negative factor influencing the health of mothers, according to our field notes, is that in particular landless women often resume wage work soon—say one week—after delivery.

4.3 KINSHIP, RESIDENCE, INHERITANCE, MARRIAGE, DOWRIES

4.3.1 Kinship, post-marriage residence, inheritance

Patriarchy in the Terai is reflected in residence-, kinship-, and inheritance patterns. Patrilocal residence patterns are almost an iron law. All young brides migrate after marriage to the village of the bridegroom and parents-in-law. This makes the position of young women very vulnerable as they have to adjust to a new family, and are dependent on their acceptance and tolerance. Patrilocal residence is perceived as natural, almost as God-given. But, there are societies in the world where post-marriage patterns are the reverse which greatly contributes to a relatively high status of women.

A study of matrilocal Lao Lum groups in Laos by one of the authors of this book shows that the main argument for matrilocality is that women feel more secure, loved, protected and at ease when their own mother and sisters are around, in particular in situations of risk and emotional events as child birth. Nobody can look after the daughter so well as the own mother. The perception in Laos is that the matrilocal social organization is based on the maximum care daughter and mother can give to each other (Schenk-Sandbergen and Choulamany-Khamphoui 1995a).

It is likely that matrilocal systems also existed in the Terai-area especially among the Rajbansis who might have a tribal background (Mukhopadhyay 1990). We found only one case of matrilocality of an older more-well-to-do Rajbansi woman in the project area who said that thirty years ago her husband came to live in her house. This may be evidence for the theory that Rajbansis originally came from Assam as it is known that matrilocal and matrilineal relations are existing. Kinship patterns, reflected in family names, are transmitted along the male line from father to son(s). Inheritance patterns of land and house and other resources are almost 100 per cent patrilineal. We could also not trace any customary inheritance right for women. We came only across two cases where women had inherited small plots of land from their father as there were no sons in the family. Perhaps it is superfluous to state that women have in India since 1967 the legal right to inherit land, but very few will insist on it for reasons described in many studies (Sharma 1980; Agarwal 1994). This social set-up, in combination with devasting poverty, generates a low status for women as they do not own assets as land, house, and income. As we will see these basic social aspects, and kinship, post-marriage residence and inheritance patterns are the main causes that women are not considered water users or beneficiaries. Moreover, *purdah* notions and restrictions make it difficult to get access and control even over their fruits of labour. The men go to the markets and sell the products the women, or both, have grown.

4.3.2 Marriage and community

Marriage is universal among rural women. The outcome of the follow-up study shows that of the women of the age group 15+ of all the schemes almost 90 per cent of the women are married or widowed.

The Table 4.5 points to the fact that the age of marriage for girls in the project area is still very low: around 15, though the percentage of unmarried girls over 15 years has increased by 3 per cent in the past three years. Only among the Scheduled Tribes is the percentage of unmarried women above 15 years, 25 per cent which may indicate that their age of marriage is higher than in the other communities. The impact of the Christian con-

TABLE 4.5: MARITAL STATUS OF WOMEN BY COMMUNITY

(*in %*)

Community	Unmarried Adults (15+)		Married (15+)		Widowed (15+)	
	1989-90	1992-3	1989-90	1992-3	1989-90	1992-3
Rajbansi SC	11	10	79	73	10	17
Other SC	8	10	70	72	22	18
Muslims	4	14	79	76	17	10
General Hindus	12	15	64	63	24	22
Schedule Tribe	23	25	72	70	5	5
Total	10	13	75	71	15	16

version in the deep tube well area we selected in Cooch Behar district, may be the reason for a different attitude towards the age of marriage.

Most marriages are arranged, and the wife and husband see each other for the first time at the marriage ceremony.

4.3.3 Dowry

Field visits have revealed that during the past years households of marginal and small farmers are increasingly confronted with the very serious problem of dowry when a daughter has to be married. Dowries are on the increase in the whole of India, and also in the project area (Krishnamurthy 1981; Paul 1955; Schenk-Sandbergen 1986). It seemed that only ten years ago the Rajbansis had a system of bride price in which the parents of the bridegroom had to give presents to the parents of the bride as a compensation for their loss of a daughter and her labour. This bride price system reflected esteem for the girl. Now it has turned the other way round and we found that Rajbansis, Namasudras, Muslims and even tribal groups gave dowries. It is a well-known fact that the overall trend in increase of dowries has a detrimental effect on the existing, already vulnerable position of women. The question how far the observed increase in dowries in the Terai area might have an impact on the worsening of the food priority and health care of girls cannot be answered. What we can indicate, however, is that dowries compel parents of daughters to sell or to lease-out the small plot of land they possess. With that they loose water rights and therefore a basic survival resource.

Dowry is quickly spreading in the area and marriage becomes for all communities also in the Terai a problematic event with many detrimental consequences in terms of status of women and increasing impoverishment. The dominant dowry pattern of the upper-caste Hindus is seeping into the conduct of the poor farmers households. In particular in the marriage season the common people are daily confronted with immense marriage and dowry expenses which are shamelessly displayed by upper-caste affluent families in Siliguri. We watched such a marriage feast in the best hotel in town.

> The father of the bride rented 54 rooms, VIP hall, garden, swimming pool in the hotel and relatives from all parts of the world and India were flown in. Cooks, barbers, shoe shiners, laundry and decoration workers, waiters were hired. Thousands of guests, women decked in silk and gold, attended the dinner. Two orchestras were playing on two flower decorated podia. It was said that in addition the father of the bride paid Rs 3,00,000 cash for the dowry. This fanfare is watched by the personnel of the hotel who earn a maximum Rs 1,000 per month, and all the labourers who worked for days with respectful craftmenship [80,000 small lights were installed for flashing light decorations] but who earn even less than Rs 1,000 per month. Most of them were angry about this waste of money, but on the other hand it is difficult for them to ignore the power of the event when it comes to marrying off their own daughter.

To be more precise we asked in the in-depth study, 'if there is a grown-up daughter in the household, and if yes, how much expense is or will be incurred?' Fifty-one households had a grown up daughter and we have collected the expenses for the dowry itself, the wedding feast and other related expenses.

The minimum for the feast and other expenses as a *sari*, blouse and *dhoti* for the in-laws are Rs 500. However, the data show that in the majority of cases this expenses will mount up from Rs 1,000 to 7,000. A dowry in a marginal farmer's household will cost at least Rs 2,000 and includes the minimum presentation of a wrist-watch and a bicycle to the bridegroom. The dowries of Rs 10,000 to 15,000 involve in most cases the cash to start a small shop or to purchase a rickshaw. They are given by middle and rich farm households in the riverlift and deep tube well schemes. The marginal farm households in the handpump schemes are not able to spend such high amounts as even small amounts have already detrimental consequences for their financial position.

We came across sad cases where because of poverty no dowry could be paid. The girl of the house was just taken away to marry somewhere else and nobody knew where they had gone.

We talk with Mrs Sajoni Roy, also an old widow. She lives with her only—slightly mentally handicapped—son in the hut. She has removed the upper part of the pump and keeps it in her house to avoid stealing. The pump has to be repaired but she has no money. She has 1.5 *bighas* of land. She sold 0.5 *bigha* for the marriage of her daughter of 15 years. There was no money for a feast or for buying a wedding *sari*, furniture, etc. The in-laws came and took her daughter. She does not know where she is at the moment. She uses the water of the pump in *rabi* season to grow *kumrai*, *jhinga*, *karala*, pumpkins and chillies. The seedlings of the *amon* paddy are almost on the verge of transplantion. The paddy will provide four months food. She cannot buy fertilizers but collects cowdung from the roadside to make manure in her compost pit.

Dowry may be perceived as an ideological gender issue, but in the sea of poverty in which it is adopted it is almost the only way for all those poor and unemployed boys to get any modern asset as a wrist-watch, bicycle, cassette radio. The tendency to look at dowries as a commodity without social and emotional connotations is also coming up in the Terai area and has lead to suicide of young brides. The following case shows that the harassment of the in-laws to provide more dowry became too much for a family as the following field notes reveal,

Field visit Gram Panchayat Biniwada, Velkujote, 9 February 1995.

The pradhan of the panchayat is said the following on the important role of the women's organization nowadays. There is a Mahila Samiti from CPI[M], the dominant political party in the village. Activities? On 1 February a young mother with a small infant committed suicide by taking poison. She was constantly tortured by her mother- and sister-in-law, beaten up, denied food, etc. She had not brought enough dowry. The Mahila Samiti [and men] marched with 250 people to the police station and reported the case and got the mother-, sister-in-law and husband arrested. This happened in Debaganj, a village under the Gram Panchayat.

It is sad that the women who fought almost 20 years ago so militantly for their share in the land reforms but also for their gender emancipation, have to march now to a police station to unveil the terrible atrocities of dowries.

The burden of dowries is an increasing reason for loss of land, or mortgaging of land, cows and other assets. How did the 51 households with grown-up daughters meet the expenses for the marriage? 19 farm households were able to contribute to the dowry with their own saved money, 6 households took a loan from kin and friends. In 3 cases kin and friends contributed money as a gift. Twenty-three households are compelled to sell land: 2 had to sell 0.5 *bigha*, 12 farmers had to sell 1 *bigha*, 3 households 2 *bighas* and 6 households 3 *bighas* of land to provide the money for the dowry of their daughters. Six farm households had to mortgage their land to fulfil the dowry demand of the in-laws.

The following field notes illustrate the consequences for the status of the land owner when he has to mortgage his land:

In one case a marginal farmer owned 5 *bighas* of land. He mortgaged 2.5 *bighas* for the marriage of his first daughter, and the other 2.5 *bighas* for the dowry of his second daughter. He is working now as a sharecropper on his own mortgaged land. Besides the 50 per cent share of the harvest which he has to give to the farmer to whom he mortgaged his land, he also has to pay back an additional amount to him in order to repay his debt and to get back his land in the long run.

Hopefully the use of irrigation water in the project area may generate higher yields, which will enable the farmer to pay back the mortgage debt earlier.

4.4 HOUSEHOLD SIZE AND COMPOSITION, FEMALE HEADED HOUSEHOLDS

4.4.1 Size of the household

The average household size in the project area is 6.2 persons in the in-depth study, and 5.7 in the sample survey. The in-depth study reveals a correlation between family size and economic status: the poorer the household, the smaller the family. The general trend is that of small nuclear families among landless (4.2 members) and marginal and small farmers (5.1), and larger joint and extended families in medium (9.7) and large farmers households (6.5).[4] The data show that there are not many differences in the general pattern per community, while during the time span of the in-depth study not many differences could be traced either.

Regarding changes in household size, the data show that there is a slight increase in the average size of the household for all communities over the three years from 6.18 to 6.44 members per household (excluding the landless households). Class-wise, households of landless, marginal, small and big farmers have somewhat increased, while the average size of the household of middle farmers came somewhat down.

TABLE 4.6: SIZE OF HOUSEHOLDS ACCORDING TO CLASS AND SCHEME

Scheme	Class	HHs	Total pop.	Size of HHs
RLI	Marginal	222	1,127	5
	Small	90	580	6
	Middle	34	231	7
	Large	8	83	10
	Total	354	2,021	6
DTW	Marginal	124	649	5
	Small	38	258	7
	Middle	10	70	7
	Large	4	43	11
	Total	176	1,020	6
HTW	Marginal	666	3,579	5
	Small	130	920	7
	Middle	27	224	8
	Large	2	16	8
	Total	825	4,739	6
STW	Marginal	15	73	5
	Small	37	223	6
	Middle	15	98	7
	Large	7	44	6
	Total	74	438	6
PDW	Marginal	26	126	5
	Small	16	79	5
	Middle	7	43	6
	Total	49	248	5

Source: Sample survey.

Table 4.6 shows that the size of marginal farmers' household in all the schemes is uniformly five. The size of small farmers household is five in pump dug well schemes, six for river lift irrigation, and seven in deep tube well and handpump beneficiary households. The middle farmers household size varies from six to eight to six for pump dug well, seven for river lift irrigation, deep tube well, shallow tube well and eight for handpump beneficiary households The large farmers usually have a bigger household with eight to eleven members, except that among shallow tube well beneficiaries the large farmers have relatively small households. This is rather unusual for a big household. But as our sample is small (seven households) we cannot say whether this is the regular feature of shallow tube well owning big households or not. The results of the sample survey confirm that the higher the agrarian status of a farmer the bigger is his household, irrespective its community.

An interpretation of household size figures leads to the conclusion that the majority of the families are small and consist of father, mother and three children. The poorer the family the smaller the family. The majority of landless families have only two children. From talks with women it was revealed that the fertility of women is high, but child mortality frequent.

It was too far out of the scope of our study to collect precise data on child mortality but we asked some questions on family planning.

4.4.2 Family planning

We asked in 214 households of the in-depth study (handpump beneficiary households, river lift irrigation and deep tube well) whether in the household any woman observed family planning, and to make the subject clear we asked separately if any man in the household observed family planning.

In 46 households of the total 168 it was stated that the women went for sterilization operation (27 per cent). Women of all communities, also the Muslim women, are motivated and took the decision to reduce their number of children. The fieldnotes in Paschim Harmati of January 1995 show that poor Muslim women have undergone the family planning operation on their own initiative,

A small woman with a purple *sari* has three children [one girl, two boys]. After the third child she herself took the initiative to go to Mainaguri hospital to have a 'family planning' operation. She felt: 'we are so poor I cannot feed and clothe all these children. We have no land, even a rented hut, so more children we cannot afford.' Her husband left the decision to her. The types of labour she does for wage labour are: stripping jute, weeding jute and wheat, husking. Now she is called today for making *muri*.[5] In the afternoon I see her making *muri* in the compound of a richer woman.

On the other hand talks in the villages also revealed that son-preference is an important factor in the decision to use family planning methods. The following field notes illustrate this point.

Field visit Velkujote, 9 February 1995.

We arrive in the village. At the entrance is the UNICEF handpump. We embark on a small beautifully decorated house where an old woman is making small mats for parties. We go to Laksmi's house. We have an interview with Bedhu Singh, a young woman who seems to be the daughter-in-law of Laksmi. Bedhu married nine years ago and had three children: one boy and two daughters. The boy died as he was born premature. The daughter on her hip is 1.5 years and breastfed. She does not think of family planning as long there is no baby boy. She married at 15 and it was an arranged marriage.

And what about the men? The figures show that around four times more women than men went for an operation: only 11 men of 168 households (6 per cent). In practically all cases the respondents told us that sterilization was the only way of family planning known to them.

4.4.3 Composition of the family

The composition of the family has also its impact on the division of labour in the domestic domain and in irrigated agriculture. Women in joint families can divide motherhood roles, domestic and agricultural work between them. Women in nuclear families have a much heavier workload.

Nuclear families constitute 64 per cent of the sample survey

TABLE 4.7: TYPE AND SIZE OF HOUSEHOLD

Scheme	Total HHs	Nuclear				Joint				Extended			
		No.	%	Pop.	Size	No.	%	Pop.	Size	No.	%	Pop.	Size
RLI	354	233	65.8	1,127	4.8	74	20.9	571	7.7	47	13.3	323	6.9
DTW	176	108	61.4	529	4.9	48	27.3	343	7.1	20	11.4	148	7.4
HTW	825	531	64.4	2,671	5.0	223	27,0	1,608	7.2	71	8.6	460	6.5
STW	74	41	55.5	193	4.7	29	39.0	217	7.5	4	5.5	28	7.0
PDW	49	35	71.4	163	4.7	6	12.2	33	5.5	8	16.4	52	6.5
Total	1,478	948	64.1	4,683	4.9	380	25.7	2,772	7.3	150	10.2	1,011	6.7

Source: Sample survey.

Note: Joint household means here family of father and sons or of brothers living in a common household. In an extended household any relative, usually affinal or relatives of mother, lives in the household.

(average size 4.9), joint families 26 per cent (average size 7.3) and extended family 10 per cent (average size 6.7). However, reality is not so clear-cut as the formal classification suggests. In the selected villages it was often found that family units live together in one compound and can statistically be classified as nuclear. However, actually and functionally these families were in many respects joint: they pool the means of production and labour (Mukherjee 1977). In order to be entitled to government benefits, farmers know that they should be classified as marginal and small farmers. Therefore, they divide the land owned by the father of the family on paper, and register this transaction in the Land Register at the Gram Panchayat. Women in such types of semi-joint households, however, continue to work together in agricultural and domestic labour. In particular the processing of rice (food) is a commonly undertaking. Even when there are separate kitchens in a 'compound' family the general conditions are mostly much better than in 'pure' nuclear families.

In some cases family size is also influenced by cases of polygamy. In one Rajbansi village we came across two cases of polygamy. One case consists of two sisters: the first one initially did not give birth to a son and hence the husband married the second sister. Subsequently the first wife had a son but not the second. They live in the same house, there is no jealousy. To give birth to a son is a must.

Table 4.7 shows that the proportion of nuclear household is quite high in all the schemes, though it is slightly smaller in shallow tube well households, among whom joint household constitute about 39 per cent. Similarly, the proportion of extended households is slightly higher (16.4 per cent) among pump dug well beneficiaries than among others. The average size of nuclear households is 4.9, that of the joint household is 7.3 and of extended it is 6.7. Irrespective of schemes, the size of a type of household is more or less uniform.

4.4.4 Female headed households

Out of 261 households, only 10 are female headed in the in-depth study: nine women are widows and one is married. All women who are household heads, except one, earn their own

Plate 9: Rajbansi widow

living as agricultural labourer, cultivator or maid servant. The percentage of female headed households in the sample survey is even less: only 4.5. Findings of the follow-up study show that female headed households can only be found in households of the landless and marginal farmers of the handpump scheme. As an illustration of the living conditions of these women the following notes may be illustrative:

We talk with Mrs Kadam, she is an old, very thin, widow and a little bit deaf. She has three sons but since two years they all live in Siliguri. They do not give her any money. They have mortgaged the land next to the handpump [1 *bigha*] and took the money themselves. It is a secret how she survives. Other women standing around while taking the interview confirm that they do not help her or give her food because they are too poor themselves. We visit Mrs Kadam's small house and compound with her place of worship. Her kitchen has been destroyed by the tornado and she keeps the leftover bamboo sticks of her former kitchen in her hut. If she can get, she does agricultural wage labour. With the handpump water she cultivates vegetables and could sell

TABLE 4.8: CHARACTERISTICS OF FEMALE HEADED HOUSEHOLDS

Community	Class		No. of HHs		Marital status		Main occupation	
	89-90	92-3	89-90	92-3	89-90	92-3	89-90	92-3
Rajbansi SC	M-1	M-3 L-1	2 L-3	6	Widow-2	Widow-6	Agl	Agl-1 HW-1 Nagl-1 Cult-1
Other SC	M-1	–	1	–	Married-1	–	Agl cult	–
Muslims	M-3	M-3	3	3	Widow-2 Married-1	Widow-2 Married1	HW-2 Ser-vant-1	Ser-vant-1 Cult-2
General	M-2	L-1 L-1	3	1	Widow-3	Widow-1	Agl cult	Agl

M = marginal; L = landless; Agl = agricultural labour; HW = housewife; Nagl = non-agricultural labour; Cult = cultivation.
Note: There is no female-headed household in STW/PDW.

some pumpkins. Now the handpump does not function and she has no money for repair.

The above findings on female headed households show that the category is very small and should not be exaggerated in gender policies in the Terai project. However, this small category should certainly get priority in the selection for handpump beneficiary households. Table 4.8 shows the details of the female headed households per community, class, marital status, and main occupation.

As could be expected of the 10 female headed households, 9 are widows. Most of them survive with wage work as agricultural labour (see Plate 9).

4.5 EDUCATION

As training was one of the components of the project it seemed relevant to investigate literacy rates in our studies in a gender specific way according to class and community.

Table 4.9 shows that the literacy rate of females in West Bengal is 20 per cent less than that of males according to the 1991 Census.

TABLE 4.9: LITERACY RATES *(in %)*

	Male	Female
West Bengal Census, 1991	67	47
In-depth Study	76	54
Sample Survey	66	36

The same gender pattern was found in the in-depth study, although it is noteworthy that the literacy rates for the age-group above 5+ are higher than the state average for both men and women. On the other hand, in the sample survey the average for men is equal with the state average, while the female literacy rate is 11 per cent lower. However, this means that the comparison of literacy rates between males and females in the sample survey indicates a substantial difference of 30 per cent less for females.

The literacy rates for the landless are significantly lower: for men 56 per cent, and women only 22 per cent.

Higher literacy rates and better school attendance often relate to an improvement of socio-economic conditions of households. Higher production and a better income in the project would—in the long run—hopefully contribute to a higher educational level, in particular for girls. However, the in-depth study shows that in comparison with the base-line data of 1989-90, in 1992-3 more boys than girls were sent to primary school. This difference in school attendance is difficult to explain, and may be due to cultural and demographic circumstances. Sex discrimination is not as bad as in other states of India, but still these figures indicate the priority in educating sons over daughters. The patrilocal and patrilineal social structure enforces that. Moreover, certain groups of girls will be affected by the *purdah* notions in the family which will plunge them in a disadvantaged position in comparison with their eventual brothers.

At the secondary school level, where boys form 63 per cent and girls 37 per cent of the students, the figures have remained almost the same. At the level of college and above, the male/female ratio is 75 to 25 per cent.

It could be expected that the higher the agrarian class, the higher would be the level of female primary education, but our findings show the opposite. There are percentage-wise more daughters of marginal and small farmers attending primary school in 1992-3 than daughters of medium and large farmers. However, at secondary school level the percentage fluctuates per class, but it is the highest for girls belonging to large-farmer households.

In conclusion we can say that the chapter shows up the disadvantaged position of women in patrilocal and patrilineal social organization, the sex-ratio figures, higher mortality rates of women, bad health, lower literacy, early marriage, a change from bride-price to dowry, no inheritance rights on land, etc.

So, let us now dip in the impact of the Terai project to look if the project has contributed a little to improve the conditions and position of women.

NOTES

1. According to the Census of India 1991 the overall India sex-ratio figures show a steady decline since 1951 indicating a deterioration of living conditions of women and girls: 1951, 946; 1961, 941; 1971, 930; 1981, 934 and 1991, 929. Of the 25 Indian states, West Bengal belongs to the seven states with relatively low sex-ratios: in 1991, 917. The situation is even worse in Uttar Pradesh (882), Sikkim (880), Punjab (888), Nagaland (890), Harayana (874) and Bihar (812). Kerala has the highest sex-ratio of India: 1,040 in 1991.
2. Sanyal (1965, p. 62) remarks that although this looks horrible because of lack of antiseptic measures, puzzling enough, cases of postnatal sepsis are extremely rare. May be the reason is that after the cord is cut, the end attached to the child is sprinkled with ashes prepared by burning the skin of the dry unripe plantain. This supposed to prevent infection.
3. It was amazing to find many similarities in birth customs and beliefs around birth, childhood and puberty of the Rajbansis and the ethnic minority of the Lao Sung studies in Laos by one of the authors. In particular the burial of the placenta in the room of the house to keep the mind of the child attached to the house and prevent him running away was striking (Schenk-Sandbergen 1995a).
4. The identification criterion for a household is: persons living under one roof and cooking in one kitchen (eating from the same stove). A joint household has been defined as a family of father, mother and married sons with their wives and children, or of (married) brothers living in a common household. In an extended household any relative, usually affinal, or relatives of mother, lives together with a nuclear or

joint family. The findings confirm the general pattern regarding the relationship between poverty, the size and composition of families found in sociological research on family types in India (Krishnaji 1980; Kolenda 1989). The sometimes assumed association of high fertility and hence (large families) and poverty does not apply.

5. A food preparation of puffed rice which is very popular in the Terai.

5. General Achievements, Gender-wise Labour Participation and Domestication

5.1 GENERAL SOCIO-ECONOMIC IMPACT OF THE TERAI IRRIGATION PROJECT

To analyse the impact of the project on the life and work of women of various classes and communities, we first have to sketch in brief the socio-economic results of the Terai small-scale irrigation development project at the general level. Are the objectives reached? Are the target groups of marginal and small farmers and the social categories of the Scheduled Castes and Tribes the actual beneficiaries of the project? Has production and income increased as a result of the irrigation water use, and has a more equal income distribution been achieved?

5.1.1 Is the target group reached?

Our research reveals the very positive result that the target groups (marginal and small farmers) are reached in all schemes, except in the commonly managed 'privatized' ones of the shallow tube wells and pump dug wells. The selection of beneficiaries and sites for the handpumps, river lifts and deep tube wells was carried out in accordance with the social objectives of the project. The sample survey research (1,524 households) proves that 80 per cent of the selected handpump beneficiaries belong to the class of marginal farmers.[1] Only 20 per cent has been selected from a category not entitled: small, and even some big, farmers. In some cases panchayat members apologized to members of the research team that some poor households who were actually entitled did not get a handpump, since the allotment was too small to fulfil the demand.

In the river lifts and deep tube wells the target groups were reached in line with the stipulated criteria (65 per cent of land in the command area).[2] The sample survey shows that the marginal and small farmers in the river lift and deep tube well schemes constitute respectively 88 per cent and 92 per cent of the beneficiaries, owning 76 per cent of the land in both cases.

These figures warrant the conclusion that the social awareness of the implementing officers and local leaders in the selection of sites was high. The fact that there is still a very uneven land-ownership in the command areas of the larger irrigation devices, which has serious consequences for the future planned privatization, will be discussed below.

It is in this context that the project's effectiveness in reaching the target group of marginal and small farmers needs to be put in perspective, as the official classification of the Government of West Bengal is so wide that it becomes almost impossible not to reach the target group (see Section 1.7). This wide classification was discussed in meetings of the Advisory Committee in Jalpaiguri as it was found that these landholding sizes do not reflect the reality of the agrarian Terai stratification. The sample survey and the in-depth study show that the average cultivable landholding for marginal farmers amounts only to 1 acre for marginal farmers, instead of 1 hectare as defined by the government classification, 3 acres for small farmers and not 2 hectares, 5.5 acres for medium farmers and not 2 to 4 hectares, and 10 acres for large farmers and not more than 4 hectares.

The research unit emphasised from the start of Phase II that according to the field findings, the identification of the marginal target groups for the HTW schemes could be dramatically enhanced, if, instead of 1 hectare as the optimum land holding for a marginal farmer, the selection criterion could be changed to one acre (see Coordination Report No. 8) which is the criterion used by the All India National Sample Survey (NSS). The land size standards of the NSS used in other states of India will allow for more refined categories and consequently a better identification of target groups.[3]

Table 5.1 shows that when the NSS classification is applied instead of the official West Bengal classification to identify the

TABLE 5.1: NUMBER OF FARM HOUSEHOLDS IN HTW SCHEME IN TWO VILLAGES ACCORDING TO PROJECT LAND SIZE CLASSIFICATION AND NSS STANDARDS

Categories	Bagjan village		Bhangi II village	
	Project standards	NSS	Project standards	NSS
Marginal farmers	22	9	21	11
Small farmers	2	13	3	10
Medium farmers	1	2	1	3
Large farmers	–	1	–	1
Total	25	25	25	25

handpump target group, the marginal farmers are insufficiently reached in two selected villages.

In view of these outcomes an adjustment in the selection criteria was proposed for Phase III in the HTW scheme to select 50 per cent of the handpump beneficiaries owning 1 acre instead of 1 hectare of land, in order to achieve a better selection of the poorest target groups in the project.

The poverty focus of the project could definitely be sharpened, and dramatically enhanced, if provisions were made to address these very small farmers. The most 'deviant' device is the shallow tube well, which benefits mainly the middle and large farmers. This is a logical consequence of the fact that 25 per cent of the cost has to be paid by the beneficiaries (around Rs 6,000), which marginal and small farmers can ill afford. Moreover, the shallow tube wells enable owners to increase their income by selling water to other farmers, which even enlarges the scope for a 'betting on the strong' effect. To say this is a healthy entrepreneurial initiative is dubious as it might reaffirm unequal power-, and dehumanized patron-client relations. The technology may be 'privately owned, but commonly managed', at least on paper, but during field visits it was observed that there are substantial status and power differences between the 'main' owner of the pump and his co-user/owners. What is relevant here is that in the debate on 'privatization' the shallow tube well management is often perceived as one of the ideal technology choices to make irrigation devices financially sustainable in the future, and therefore it should be promoted. The lesson learned from our impact research is that in the socio-economic reality of the Terai area, the shallow tube well approach subordinates the social endeavour to promote equal income distribution. The same is roughly the case in the pump dug well scheme.

Field visits also reveal that the easy suspicion that panchayats will only select their Communist Party members as handpump beneficiaries, and not members supporting the opposition Congress party, is untrue. The political conditions at village level have an in-built mechanism that ensures that local politicians not give preference only to members of their party. They are interested in gaining votes, and therefore they are careful not to oppose the recommendations of the village extension workers (KPS) who are supposed to be politically neutral and with whom they have to identify potential beneficiaries. Comparison of proposed KPS lists with the final panchayat lists reveal that exactly the same beneficiaries have been proposed. The following field notes illustrate that we have no reason to suspect that potential beneficiaries are not reached as a result of political exclusion:

> The visit to the next house reveals that seven handpump beneficiaries were former landless labourers who got 2 *bighas* of land under the land reform programme Operation Barga. This land was first confiscated under the land ceiling act, which determined a ceiling at 14 acres of land for landowners. It is revealing that, although the panchayat as usual in the area is supported by Communist voters, the handpump beneficiaries are all Congress voters. This shows that the selection of beneficiaries is not determined by local party politics in the sense that only party members of the CPM get the benefits. On the contrary, the ruling party wants to attract voters from the opposition. We meet a woman and to our surprise we come to know that in land reforms a gender sensitive policy is followed by the government as the 'Barga' [land reform] land is put in her name, and consequently the handpump. Her father-in-law states that he has two sons and that he does not want that she works in the fields. Previously they had a ring well, now they use the handpump for all purposes.

We will come back to the special gender aspects related to handpumps again in Chapter 9.

In line with national policies, the project incorporated a focus to give preference to Scheduled Castes (SC) and Scheduled Tribes (ST) in the selection of beneficiaries. The percentage of SC population and ST is substantial in the project area (respectively 57, 48 and 34 per cent in Jalpaiguri, Cooch Behar and Darjeeling). The sample survey shows that 67.6 per cent (1,000 HH) belong to the SC and ST communities. Muslims represent 18 per cent (265 HH) and general Hindu castes 14.4 per cent (213 HH).

5.1.2 Have production and income increased owing to the use of irrigation water?

A few findings showing the successful impact of the North Bengal Terai Project will be presented. For more details we refer to Report No. 15 of the Research and Evaluation Unit.

The in-depth study reveals that there is no question of a growing land polarization in the area as a result of irrigation intervention. On the contrary, there is a slight trend indicating that some marginal farmers could climb up to the status of small farmers. Marginal farmers of the handpump scheme have increased their landholdings by 10 per cent over the three years of study. The increase in leasing-in of land by landless and marginal farmers in the command area (CA) indicates also a betterment in economic conditions. The farm production and farm income of the marginal and small farmers has increased although this is partly counterbalanced by inflation. Income has been differentiated in the in-depth study in three categories: farm-income, non-farm income and income out of services. Farm income is the aggregate of several components and has been estimated by the returns from cash crops and the monetization of subsistence food crops. As food is the main expenditure item in a farmer's household we have standardized for reasons of comparison, the consumption rate.[5] Savings and debts were also investigated. It has to be kept in mind that increases in income in absolute terms are partly neutralized by rising prices (approximately 57 per cent over the period of the in-depth study).[6] However, as food crops form a substantial part of the income of the farmers, and in particular the marginal and small farmers,

TABLE 5.2: ANNUAL PER CAPITA INCOME IN THE DIFFERENT IRRIGATION SYSTEMS IN ABSOLUTE AND (REAL) TERMS

(*in Rs.*)

	1989-90			1992-3		
	Farm income	Non-farm income	Total income	Farm income	Non-farm income	Total income
Landless	75	883	958	177 (113)	1695 (1,080)	1872 (1,193)
HTW	724	767	2,081	1,354 (862)	889 (489)	2,243 (1,351)
PDW	2,527	1,478	4,005	3,753 (2,390)	1,513 (964)	5,266 (3,354)
STW	1,663	585	2,248	2,852 (1,817)	1,471 (937)	4,323 (2,754)
DTW	990	763	1,753	1,701 (1,083)	1,114 (710)	2,815 (1,793)
RLI	997	1,048	2,081	1,311 (835)	2,362 (1,504)	3,672 (2,339)

Source: Base-line/Follow-up study.

the inflation effect is somewhat mitigated. Table 5.2 shows an overview of farm-, and non-farm income and the total income, and the changes (inflation corrected) in it over the years of study.[7]

In comparison with the baseline survey the handpump scheme has had the highest proportional results in terms of increase in farm income: this has almost doubled from Rs 724 to Rs 1,354 per person per year. The deep tube well has had the second best results, although in cash farm income increased more: from Rs 990 to Rs 1,701. It is a positive indicator that the findings show that marginal farmers become increasingly more dependent on farm income for their survival due to the use of irrigation water, as non-farm income opportunities are hardly available in the area.

The overall trend of absolute income gains concerned all categories of farmers, but there is considerable fluctuation in income between the years. In the deep tube well system studied by the Research and Evaluation Unit the most substantial income gains were made by the small and middle farmers. The per capita income of the large farmers had decreased. In the river lift system selected for the in-depth study all farmer categories experienced an increase in absolute income.

Plate 10: Vegetable garden irrigated with handpump water.

The number of marginal farmer households living under the poverty line decreased slightly: from 21 per cent in 1989-90 to 18 per cent in 1992-3. The official definition of the poverty line was scaled upwards in this period from Rs 4,800 to Rs 7,200. According to the Research and Evaluation Unit the number of households just above the poverty line decreased significantly and many households moved to higher income categories. Other indicators, like the ownership of assets and the proportion of income spent on non-food items confirm this upward economic mobility.

The number of families living under the poverty line (adjusted over the follow-up years from Rs 4,800 to Rs 7,200 per year), came down slightly. A real vegetable revolution has been initiated in the region which has had a broad macro-economic impact (see Plate 10). Tomatoes, cabbages, cauliflowers and other vegetables are transported to distant cities such as Delhi, Madras and Hyderabad. However, it has also caused personal tragedies for the poor, since the prices fall dramatically as supply increases.

5.1.3 Is irrigation water available and used?

Although the use of the river lifts and deep tube wells is slowly increasing, the figures remain below expectations. The sample survey shows that when all schemes are taken together, about 33.5 per cent of the CA was irrigated from the scheme source in 1992-3. We shall not go into a debate on wrong 'guesstimations' that actual CA's turns out to be smaller than targeted, whereas the actually irrigated areas seem to be larger than recorded. Neither shall we deal with the possible impact of lack of adequate knowledge on irrigation water management as a factor of low water use which can be improved by training and extension work.[8] Our main point instead is to detect why farmers do not use the irrigation water, as it is obvious that non-using farmers will not be likely to accept ownership and management of something which is very costly and which they can not use. For marginal farmers in particular it is very important to be assured of a guaranteed water supply when they make investment decisions.

Findings regarding the functioning of the deep tube well/river lift irrigation show that 42 per cent of the river lift irrigation, and 31 per cent of the deep tube well respondents complained that they did not get water on time. About 9 per cent in the river lift irrigation did not answer the question.

There are many technical reasons why marginal farmers cannot be sure that they will receive irrigation water in time (operator not available, breakdown of pump, no electricity/diesel, damaged spout, leakage in pipe-line, capacity of the engine insufficient, diameter and length of pipeline not suitable, power cuts, voltage problems, diesel shortage, bad condition or wrong location of spouts, leakages of pumps, insufficient discharge due to farmers opening, lack of *pukka* channels, etc.). Marginal farmers in one command area were eager to try rice in the first year that the deep tube well was installed in the dry season, which shows their readiness to accept innovations. However, once they lost all their investments in the *boro* crop (rice crop of the dry season), because of technical failures, they are simply not willing to use irrigation water in the dry season. Another aspect that demotivates farmers is that the water seeps away in the low quality channels before it reaches their fields. During field visits requests to construct the so-called '4 hectare *pukka* irrigation canals' were frequent.

The problem of non-availability of electricity and load shedding are problems which have to be settled at the state/national level. Unreliable water supply is also reported due to lack of operators and mechanics.[9] The Department of Minor Irrigation is well aware of these problems and last year training of local marginal farmers started so that they could operate the engines themselves, and not be dependent on the government operator. This is all the more urgent as the farmers expressed their wish for irrigation water at night. Tools for repair are provided. The withdrawal of the government operator will considerably reduce the salary costs to the state government. However, the operating staff as well as the assistant-operator and the night-watch, have to be paid by the farmers themselves. The Block Development Officer has estimated that the farmers will have to contribute more than Rs 5,500 per month to cover the salaries. Middle and large farmers can afford to use the water and to pay for it, but they are less interested and motivated. If there is no water supply from the scheme they can afford to rent shallow tube wells and irrigate their land in the command area, as the sample survey shows. This study also shows that they can even afford to leave land fallow in the command area.

The gender-focus and the effort to implement the gender activities as part of a gender-strategy were relatively new components in the management and implementation of the project. The commitment which with these aspects were carried out and the considerable increase in gender awareness among the entire staff needs to be recorded. The Executive Engineer proudly told me that he always speaks nowadays of 'person-days', instead of 'man-days'! The attitudinal changes in awareness can be proved by the many tangible achievements of the project in the field of gender which will be discussed in detail below. But let us now examine if, and what, changes in types of women's work have occurred due to the use of irrigation water over a time span of four years.

5.2 CHANGES IN THE OCCUPATIONAL PATTERN OF WOMEN IN THE IN-DEPTH STUDY

The labour pattern has been classified in the following categories of types of work: household work, work on the family farm, agricultural labour, gainful labour as for example maid-servant's work, *bidi* (local cigarette) and *muri* (puffed rice) making, and begging.

Let us first have a look at the potential women's workforce in

TABLE 5.3: DISTRIBUTION OF POTENTIAL WOMEN WORKERS

Class	Marginal		Small		Middle		Large		Total	
	89-90	92-3	89-90	92-3	89-90	92-3	89-9	92-3	89-90	92-3
RLI	46	46	18	24	31	37	9	8	104	115
DTW	54	56	33	43	26	27	7	11	120	137
HTW	101	83	28	36	7	5	0	0	136	124
STW	12	11	6	6	8	5	2	2	28	24
PDW	2	0	3	5	1	5	7	8	13	18
Landless	0	0	0	0	0	0	0	0	33	29
Total	215	196	88	114	73	79	25	29	434	447

the in-depth study for the four categories, and the changes in the number of women participating in the categories over the four years the in-depth study was conducted.

Table 5.3 reveals that the female population of the river lift irrigation, deep tube well and handpump beneficiary households, which can be counted as the potential women work-force, has somewhat increased among marginal farmers over the three years and (201 to 226), slightly decreased in the category of small farmers women (79 to 67). But if we consider that the total number of households has decreased from 273 to 261 there has been in general an increase in the potential women workforce from 434 to 447 women in the last year of the in-depth study (1992-3).

Table 5.4 gives an overview of the findings of the in-depth study regarding the occupational pattern of women and girls per irrigation scheme and the changes in numbers of participating in the types of work.

Almost all the adult women in all the schemes have answered that they do household work. A large number of girls between

TABLE 5.4: CHANGES IN OCCUPATIONAL PATTERN OF WOMEN AND GIRLS (5-15 YEARS) IN FOUR CATEGORIES OF LABOUR

Occupation	Year	RLI		DTW		HTW		STW/ PDW		Landless	
		A	C	A	C	A	C	A	C	A	C
Household work	89-90	103	22	119	47	132	28	39	15	33	7
	92-93	107	22	126	27	116	26	40	10	24	3
Work in family farm	89-90	74	9	99	3	108	7	27	4	0	0
	92-93	80	8	108	10	109	12	31	5	2	0
Agriculture wage labour	89-90	4	0	20	0	11	2	0	0	17	0
	92-93	2	0	9	0	10	0	0	0	9	0
Other gainful occupations	89-90	4	2	4	0	14	7	0	0	0	0
	92-93	2	0	3	0	9	2	0	0	0	0
Others	89-90	3	1	0	0	0	0	0	0	5	0
	92-3	10	3	0	0	2	0	0	0	3	0
Working female population	89-90	104	45	120	70	136	67	41	19	33	17
	92-3	115	51	137	27	124	65	42	12	29	4

Source: In-depth study.
Notes: A = adult (15+); C = child (girls 5-15).
'Others' include maid servants, *bidi* making, begging.

the ages of 5 to 15 years help the mother in domestic work. In the deep tube well all the girls are involved in household work while this is only 34 per cent in the handpump beneficiary households. Some girls also work on the family farm. In the shallow tube well/pump dug well scheme it has remarkably increased up to 42 per cent of the girls.

The figures show that a substantial number of women in the schemes work in the family farm. It is highest in the handpump beneficiary households scheme, and has slightly increased from 108 women out of 136 (80 per cent) to 109 out of 124 (88 per cent) over the period 1989-90 to 1992-3. In the river lift irrigation it is around 70 per cent and in the deep tube well even higher, almost 80 per cent. Wage labour by the land owning women is less: only 8 per cent of the women of the handpump beneficiary households target group, 2 per cent of the river lift irrigation and 7 per cent of the women in the deep tube well do wage labour. In the deep tube well the percentage of women doing wage labour has come down from 17 to 7 per cent. In the following a profile is presented of a marginal farmers household in which both husband and wife work on their own land but also are wage-labourers to supplement their income:

We visit Mrs Mazumdar in the village Bandar Ganj in Gram Panchayat Bidhan Nagar. Some women have got the handpump in this village in their name under the special allocation of handpump beneficiary households programme for female headed households.

The location of the house is near the banks of the river where they were washed away a year and half ago due to a flood. They are from Bangladesh and had settled on the river bank. There are two small houses in which 13 people live surrounded by a very neat vegetable garden which surrounds the house, bordered by a pineapple field on one side. Long beans, potato and wheat are cultivated. Mr Mazumdar and his wife own 2 *bighas* of land but also earn as agricultural wage labourers. They have two sons and two daughters. His brother has seven members in the family and does not own any land. The Mazumdars have irrigated 2 *bighas* of land by using a rubber tube which can reach very far in the field. They both work very hard in the vegetable garden [I see their small son also helping] but they also employ wage labour [his brother] at a wage of Rs 15 daily.

It is remarkable that of the women of the landless labourers only 17 went for wage labour at the time of the base-line survey and three years later it has reduced to 9 women. The causes for this decline will be discussed in Chapter 7. The strong preference for employment of men over women by the landowners, resulting during the past three years in a rise of 18 per cent more days of employment for male labourers in agricultural work in 1992-3 (when compared to 1989-90 situation) will be revealed. This means that male labourers got more days of work at the cost of women. On the other hand as we shall see, more land could be leased-in by landless households which is mainly cultivated by the women.

There are a few women engaged in 'other gainful employment' as *bidi* binding, *muri* making, husking, etc. The highest percentage can be found among women of the handpump beneficiary households (10 per cent). It is interesting to note that seven daughters of the handpump beneficiary households were involved in 'other gainful employment' during the base-line survey but that in 1992-3 only two daughters do some side-line work. Perhaps the increase in vegetable production and consequently income is changing the multiple- earning survival strategy of households in which all members contribute. This might point to a positive trend in which girls become more released of labour responsibilities, but it is also possible that the girls help in vegetable production on the own field of the house-hold and that makes their labour contribution invisible. The total number of girls working in the various occupation specified has fallen from 201 to 155 over a timespan of four years. The figures do not show that more girls are probably doing more household work now their mothers have more work because of irrigation in agriculture.

5.2.1 *Are there signs of withdrawal (domestication) from farm work?*

We have mentioned that in other studies on gender impact of irrigation (Sharma 1980; Stanbury 1992) a trend was indicated that in case economic conditions of families improve, women are withdrawn from farm-, wage-, and other gainful labour and for status reasons confined within the walls of the house. Can we trace such a potential trend over the years in our study? Are there indications that in certain classes, or communities, of farm households, or more likely in certain types of irrigation schemes the process of 'domestication', as this withdrawal is named in women's studies, will emerge? First, we will analyse the changes in labour pattern over the four years of study by community.

Table 5.5 shows that a high proportion of adult women and girls of all communities work on their family farms. The number of Rajbansi women working on their own family farm has slightly decreased which may be due to the families which have moved out. In the other Scheduled Castes and general Hindu category, the number of participating women has increased during the period of the follow-up study. It is notable that the number of Muslim women in their own land has proportionally increased the most (from 33 to 51 women) and that the number of tribal women participating in family farm labour (30 in the base-line and 20 in 1992-3) and in wage agricultural labour has come down from 17 to 6 women over the same years. But this is due to the reduction in the number of tribal households. The figures do not point in the direction of a withdrawal of women of certain

TABLE 5.5: CHANGE IN OCCUPATION OF WOMEN AND GIRLS (5-15) BY COMMUNITIES

Occupation	Year	Rajbansi SC		Other SC		General Hindus		Muslims		ST	
		A*	C**	A	C	A	C	A	C	A	C
Household	89-90	190	51	50	13	69	17	78	24	39	14
work	92 3	174	25	59	17	75	13	72	27	33	6
Work in	89-90	157	13	38	4	50	1	33	4	30	1
family farm	92-3	149	16	45	4	65	6	51	7	20	2
Agricultural	89-90	14	2	1	0	7	0	13	0	17	0
Labourers	92-3	11	0	0	0	3	0	10	0	6	0
Other gainful	89-90	8	4	2	0	10	4	0	1	2	0
occupations	92-3	5	0	1	0	7	2	1	0	0	0
Others	89-90	3	1	0	0	0	0	4	0	1	0
	92-3	6	0	6	2	0	0	2	1	1	0

Note: *A = adult ** C = child (girl).

communities out of production and a shift to more household work.

The class factor in women's work pattern and class notions on proper behaviour of women regarding working outside the house have also been analysed. Therefore we present in Table 5.6 only the data from the river lift irrigation and deep tube well beneficiary household as more women of small and middle farmers are represented among them. The number of shallow tube well/deep tube well beneficiaries are too small for any valid conclusion.

The number of women of all classes doing household work, and the number of women doing work on their own family farm, have *both* increased (from 224 to 233, and 173 to 188 over the years 1989-90 and 1992-3), despite the fact that the number of river lift irrigation/deep tube well households in 1992-3 has decreased to 133 (135 in 1989-90). The number of land owning women of all classes doing agricultural wage labour has fallen from 22 to 11. This does not mean that de 'domestication' process is imposed, but these women say that, as they have more work on their own farm, wage labour is not longer necessary to

TABLE 5.6: CHANGE IN OCCUPATION OF WOMEN AND GIRLS (5-15) BY AGRARIAN CLASSES (RLI/DTW households)

Occupation	Year	Marginal		Small		Middle		Big	
		A	C	A	C	A	C	A	C
Household work	89-90	99	28	50	17	57	20	16	4
	92-3	96	19	64	18	55	11	18	1
Work in family farm	89-90	87	8	35	1	41	1	10	2
	92-3	75	10	56	6	44	2	13	0
Agricultural labourers	89-90	15	0	3	0	6	0	0	0
	92-3	10	0	1	0	0	0	0	0
Other gainful occupations	89-90	6	1	2	1	0	0	0	0
	92-3	4	0	1	0	0	0	0	0
Others	89-90	0	0	2	0	1	1	0	0
	92-3	9	2	1	1	0	0	0	0

Notes: A = adult; C = child (girl).

'Others'—*bidi*-making, maid-servant, selling of milk, fuel or vegetables.

supplement their household income. The interesting trend is that the number of women of marginal farmers participating in family labour has decreased from 87 to 75 women, while the number of women of small farmers has increased from 36 to 56 women. There is also a slight increase in participating women in the middle farmers category. This could reflect a trend that in the river lift irrigation/deep tube well some households of marginal farmers have managed to go through a process of economic mobility and become small farmers. Anyhow, this trend and the above findings do not point to a tendency that women are withdrawn from productive labour and confined to household work over the years of study or, to express it in more women's studies terminology, there is no evidence that a process of 'domestication' is taking place.

To our view this finding has its background in the weak development caste-structure and notions of Sanskritization in the North Bengal Terai districts, the strong political class ideology, and perhaps the historical dimensions in which women fulfilled an equal role with men in the peasant movement. This outcome shows that gender impact assessments of irrigation intervention have always to be contextualised and that no generalizations can be made regarding the trend of withdrawal of women.

5.2.2 Types of labour of women in the sample survey

What are the findings in the sample survey regarding the labour participation of women's work? Unfortunately only 66 women respondents have furnished information as head of household. We may accept these households as women headed households. Agriculture as their primary occupation has been declared by 46 women (70 per cent). The majority of women come from the handpump sample. Table 5.7 gives the distribution of primary/ secondary occupation of these women respondents. It indicates that women's involvement in agriculture as primary occupation is gradually increasing—it is much more than what we found in 1989-90 when the base-line survey of the in-depth study was conducted.

TABLE 5.7: PRIMARY/SECONDARY OCCUPATION OF FEMALE HEADED HOUSEHOLDS RESPONDENTS

Scheme	Primary	No.	Subsidiary	No.
DTW	Agriculture	2	No-subsidiary occupation	1
			Non-agricultural labour	1
	Agricultural labour	9	Agricultural labour	10
	Any other	3	Any other	3
HTW	Agriculture	38	Agriculture	15
	Household industry	2	No-subsidiary occupation	18
	Profession/service	1	Non-agricultural labour	4
	Trade & business	2	Trade & business	5
RLI	Agricultural labour	1	Agricultural labour	1
	Agriculture	5	Agriculture	3
	Non-agricultural labour	2	Non-agricultural labour	1
			No-subsidiary occupation	2
			Trade & business	1
STW	Agriculture	1	No-subsidiary occupation	1
Total		66		66

5.3 PARTICIPATION OF WOMEN IN OWN FARM PRODUCTION IN THE SAMPLE SURVEY

5.3.1 Gender participation according to age group

The sample survey gives an interesting overview of the participation of family labour in cultivating their own farm per scheme. In order to find out the contribution of children and old people in family labour we have collected data according to three age groups: below 15 years, 15 to 60 years, and 60 years and over.

The data show that about 55 per cent of the work force are men, and 45 per cent are women. Most of the workers are adults but quite a few are children: about 5.7 per cent of the work force (boys 3.1 per cent, girls 2.6 per cent). The percentage of women in the work force is highest in pump dug well, followed by deep tube well, handpump beneficiary households, shallow tube well, and river lift irrigation in that order.

The sample survey data has also been examined from the class point of view, to know whether the women of poorer agrarian categories work more on their own farm than the women in more affluent households (see Annexure 5.1 percentage of households that provides household labour in agriculture in 1992-3 according to class, crop and irrigation scheme).

The figures show that there is not much difference in the participation rate of male and female workers belonging to different classes and schemes except that in some instances women of marginal and small farms work more on their family farm; for instance in all the schemes the marginal and small farm womens' participation rate varies from 86 to 100 per cent, which for middle and big farmers ranges from 70 to 93 per cent. Generally women of middle and large farmers households work less in their family farm than women of other two classes. Child labour in big households is almost non-existent and nominally present among middle farmers. According to the outcomes of the survey the children of marginal farmers contribute to the labour force (5-9 per cent for boys and 5-15 per cent for girls). It can be assumed that qualitative data collection on the subject will give better insight in the scope and nature of their participation.

5.3.2 Gender participation according to crop

The rate of household labour employment in domestic agriculture varies also according to the crop and the extent to which it is cultivated. Some crops like *amon* (winter rice), jute and vegetables (*rabi* crops) being universally cultivated, require the participation of the larger part of the household work force. The high yielding varieties (HYV) of paddy and wheat are now also being widely cultivated and so the participation rate of the household workforce is high. The Annexures 5.2 (Rate of participation in farm agriculture by household male workers force [15-59 years] in 1992-3) and 5.3 (Rate of participation in farm agriculture by household women workers force [15-59 years] in 1992-3) show the rate of participation of male/female household workforce in their farm agriculture.

Gender labour participation in own farm work is directly proportional to the extent of cultivation of a crop (see Annexure 5.1). The acreage under almost all crops is more for small, middle and big farmers than that for marginal farmers. Consequently proportionately more households belonging to these classes have provided labour in growing crops like amon, HYV paddy, jute, oilseeds, vegetables and wheat. Only in the case of cultivation of vegetables in *rabi* and wheat, is the proportion of participating marginal households somewhat comparable to that of other classes. Despite the problem of lower cultivable area, a sizeable proportion of marginal households in the river lift irrigation/ deep tube well schemes (24-57 per cent) have grown HYV paddy of both the varieties. The marginal and small farmers constitute the bulk of handpump beneficiary households but here also the small farmers' households have provided comparatively more labour in growing almost all the major crops.

Though there is some variation in the rate of participation in different crops, generally speaking the rates as shown in Table 5.8 are as follows for the two genders. Only the participation rates in the cultivation of major crops (*amon*, *aus*, HYV paddy, jute, oilseeds, vegetables, tobacco, wheat) are considered here.

Table 5.8 shows that in almost all schemes the participation rate of women workers of the household is equal to that of men in all classes, if not higher in some schemes/classes. Only among the big farmers (river lift irrigation, deep tube well, shallow tube well) is the rate somewhat lower than that of men. Between the three schemes (river lift irrigation, deep tube well, handpump beneficiary households) the handpump beneficiary households household workers of both genders generally show a little more participation in their own agricultural work.

TABLE 5.8: PARTICIPATION RATES OF MEN AND WOMEN ACCORDING TO CLASS AND SCHEME (MAJOR CROPS ONLY)

(*in %*)

Class	RLI/DTW		HTW		STW		PDW	
	M	F	M	F	M	F	M	F
Marginal	82-100	80-100	89-96	91-95	50-100	94-100	94-100	94-100
Small	73-100	77-100	92-98	78-98	80-100	92-100	87-100	100
Middle	44-89	68-100	84-100	86-100	92-100	91-100	60-100	100
Large	71-100	50-100	50-100	75-100	50-100	40-90	0-0	0-0

5.4 PERCEPTION OF WOMEN OF THEIR AGRICULTURAL ACTIVITIES IN COMPARISON WITH MEN

Besides the actual participation rate of women in agricultural activities, it is important to know their own assessment of their agricultural activities in terms of 'more than men', 'equally with men', 'less than men' and 'no participation at all'. The women's assessment in the following table is based on the total number of women in the in-depth study in all the schemes estimated in percentages.

We have specified 20 different types of agricultural work. The following table reflects the answers of 243 land owning women included in the in-depth study.

Table 5.9 shows that almost all women (99.5 per cent) have stated that they do not participate in ploughing and marketing.

TABLE 5.9: WOMENS' ASSESSMENT OF THEIR AGRICULTURAL ACTIVITIES (1992-3) N=243

(*in %*)

Activity	More than men	Equally with men	Less than men	None at all	Undecided
1. Ploughing	0.0	0.5	0.0	99.5	0.0
2. Land preparation	9.4	10.3	33.0	47.3	0.0
3. Purchase of seeds	1.4	0.9	17.9	79.8	0.0
4. Seed selection	0.9	1.4	36.7	60.6	0.4
5. Seedbed preparation	0.9	28.3	22.6	48.2	0.0
6. Fertilizer selection	0.9	0.4	18.3	80.4	0.0
7. Manure application	3.7	26.8	45.7	23.8	0.0
8. Fertilizer application	0.0	3.7	25.9	70.0	0.4
9. Sowing	0.0	3.7	34.9	61.4	0.0
10. Transplanting	1.4	20.8	34.9	42.9	0.0
11. Weeding	5.1	17.4	38.2	39.3	0.0
12. Pesticide application	0.0	1.8	14.6	83.2	0.4
13. Protecting crops	16.9	34.9	32.5	15.7	0.0
14. Irrigating field	1.8	19.8	39.6	38.8	0.0
15. Cleaning and maintaining channel	0.9	12.2	33.0	53.9	0.0
16. Harvesting	2.8	30.1	44.8	22.3	0.0
17. Threshing	4.2	32.0	37.7	26.1	0.0
18. Storing	39.1	35.8	16.5	8.6	0.0
19. Marketing	0.9	1.4	1.4	95.6	0.4
20. Repairing bunds	0.9	6.6	25.4	67.1	0.0

Only one widow stated that she ploughs herself. This is in line with the division of labour in patriarchal/patrilineal societies in which ploughing is considered as an exclusive male activity as it gives a monopoly position on the basic work on which all other operations are dependent. Observing the Bengal peasants standing on their wooden ploughs while their two bullocks (or cows) do the work, it cannot be said that the work is so heavy that women will not be able to do it. The dirtiness of the work is also limited and it struck us that we saw many peasants in 'middle-class style' dress (pants and not the characteristic *dhoti*, and sleeveless pullovers) behind the plough. A monopoly on marketing as a traditional male domain also guarantees that women have no access and control over the local economy. That makes them dependent on the men. This is reality, but, as we have seen poverty modifies this male power and in the marginal farmers households women sometimes also sell their vegetables in the market.

The findings show that women feel that harvesting, threshing and storing are typical female activities but manure application, land and seed preparation, transplantation of paddy, weeding and in particular protection of crops are jobs to which women assess that they contribute to a high degree.

Let us have a closer look at the assessment of women in their role in irrigation. Only 38 per cent of women state that they are not engaged in irrigation activities. That implies that 62 per cent of the women participate in irrigation work. Around 40 per cent of them said that they do less work in irrigation compared with their men of the household, but 19 per cent say that irrigating the fields is carried out equally with men. Regarding the cleaning and maintaining of irrigation channels 54 per cent claimed not to be involved, 33 per cent less than men, 12 per cent equally with men and 1 per cent more than men. These warrant the conclusion that the far majority of the women in our study can be considered as water users although they have only indirect access to the water through their husbands, fathers and brothers.

Of the twenty agricultural activities, three can be mentioned where quite a number of women assess that they participate more than men. These are land preparation (9.4 per cent), protection of crops (16.9 per cent) and storing of crops (39.1 per cent).

5.5 OTHER CASH EARNING WORK OF WOMEN

Before discussing other female income-generating activities, the point should be made that as the labour participation figures above show, most women contribute substantially to the family income. However, that share is invisible as the agricultural crop is sold by the males of the household. Selling crops in the market is an almost exclusively male undertaking: few women are involved. The fruits of the labour of the women are thus monetized by the men. In some instances, however, we found that the money earned by selling agricultural crops was kept and controlled by the women of the household.

The in-depth study shows that the number of land-owning women involved in agricultural wage labour elsewhere, has declined in all farm classes, mainly as a result of increased workload on their own farm and therefore a lower necessity to supplement the cash income of the household. Most women in the sample survey said that they preferred not to work for wages outside their home, yet economic conditions compel a substantial number of women to do so. It was found that of the women in the marginal farmer class, between 20 and 28 per cent (depending on scheme) actually work outside their home for wages, whereas in the small farmer households between 6 and 11 per cent of women work outside for wages. The respondents gave several reasons in support of the low prestige of external employment, such as: 'young women should not go out on their own'; 'children are neglected when their mother works elsewhere'; 'it is not good that domestic work suffers'. Furthermore, social and religious restrictions impede the free movement of women. In spite of these views, those women who worked outside the home said that they liked working outdoors, and faced no problem. It appeared that many women have no objection to work for wages, but cannot say so, because of cultural norms. Only in poor families is economic necessity so obvious that social barriers play no role.

There are a few women involved in non-farm labour, in particular *bidi* binding, *muri* making, husking, selling of milk, selling of fuel, brick-kiln work, basket/mat making. The highest percentage is found among women of the handpump beneficiary households: 10 per cent. Similarly 10 per cent of the daughters of the handpump households were involved in non-farm labour during the base-line survey, a figure that had decreased in 1992-3 to only 3 per cent.

In the three scheme types, river lift irrigation, deep tube well and handpump beneficiary households, it is noticed that 26 per cent of the female work force amomg marginal farmers and 10 per cent among small farmers were engaged in these occupations in 1992-3. Women of the other two classes are seldom engaged in wage-earning jobs.

Some idea of the various occupations in which the women interviewed in the sample survey are engaged can be obtained from the analysis of occupations of 66 women key informants. Table 5.10 shows the non-farm occupations of women (15-60 yrs) in the total workforce. A remark on the figures in the table seems to be in place. The collection of data was done mainly by male field workers who interviewed 1,412 male respondents and only 66 female respondents. This may have caused an under-reporting of cash earning activities in combination with a slight *purdah* hesitation that it is not proper to mention cash earning by women outside the house.

Respectively 13, 12 and 10 per cent of the adult female work-force belonging to marginal class of river lift irrigation, deep tube well and handpump beneficiary households schemes work as wage labourers. The proportion of such wage workers is very insignificant among the small farmers and nil in the other two classes. Besides working as wage labourers, some women of the two poorer classes of farmers work in a variety of occupations—selling of milk, making of parched rice, binding *bidi*, husking paddy, spinning and weaving, and basket/mat making. Table 5.10 shows that only 290 women of marginal farmers out of the total of 1,424 women of marginal farmers households work in non-farm occupations: that is not more than 20 per cent.

In this context we want to point to the subtle way in which richer women hire poor women in helping them to make these preparations. We have the impression that this labour relation plays an important function in keeping good relations, and functions as a kind of distribution mechanism of spreading a

TABLE 5.10: WOMEN (15-60 YEARS) IN NON-FARM OCCUPATIONS

	RLI			DTW			HTW		STW		PDW
Type of Work	1*	2**	3***	1	2	3	1	2	1	2	2
Selling of milk	4	2	0	0	0	0	13	0	0	0	0
Bidi-binding	2	0	0	0	0	0	22	5	0	0	0
Muri/Chira making	3	3	0	4	1	0	21	2	0	0	0
Husking of paddy	0	5	0	3	2	0	7	0	0	0	0
Working as wage labourer	37	2	0	20	0	0	92	7	0	2	2
Spinning and Weaving	11	4	0	0	0	0	0	0	0	0	0
Selling of fuel	0	0	0	0	0	0	0	0	0	0	0
Basket/Broomstick making	5	0	1	0	0	0	0	0	0	0	0
Mat making	2	0	0	2	0	0	9	0	1	1	0
Selling in the market	3	1	0	2	0	0	16	3	0	0	0
Stitching & embroidery work	0	0	0	2	0	1	0	0	0	0	0
Tailoring/Knitting	0	0	0	1	1	1	1	0	0	0	0
Total Non-farming Women's workforce	289	145	62	163	61	16	922	234	18	50	18
Total women in non-farm occupations	68 (24%)	19 (13%)	4 (6%)	35 (21%)	6 (10%)	5 (31%)	182 (20%)	19 (8%)	2 (1%)	5 (10%)	4 (22%)

Source: Sample Survey.

Note: *1 = Marginal Farmer; **2 = Small Farmer; ***3 = Middle Farmer

scarce resource. Making *muri* is an activity whose product can be used for home consumption but also used to sell. A few women, particularly among handpump beneficiary households, go regularly to markets to sell vegetables and other home grown crops. The income from these jobs help them augment their family income, particularly welcome in marginal households.

All the data indicate that the possibilities for women to earn an income are very limited in the project area of the small-scale irrigation project. For reasons of 'autonomy' of women and certainly in view of the planned 'privatization', it will be an urgent requirement that the scope for women's employment be considerably enhanced.

NOTES

1. Selection has been carried out by the village extension worker (KPS) and his boss, the agricultural development officer (ADO) in cooperation with the village panchayat members. The size of the landholdings is checked at the landcadastre. In some cases a general meeting was held to inform the villagers that they could apply.
2. The Panchayat Samiti members can decide that applications to instal a DTW or RLI can be made. It should consist of mass petition, the name of potential beneficiaries, the size and plot numbers of their landholdings and a map of the location. These documents should be sent to the Assistant Engineers of Agri-I or Agri-M. Staff of the respective departments checks the overall feasibility. Reports on the sites are judged by the District Site Selection Committee, consisting of higher government officials and panchayat members. A proposal is sent to the chief Engineer and the Steering Committee in Calcutta who decide on the final sanctioning. After sanctioning a preliminary design is made by the staff of Agri-I and Agri-M. After estimating the costs based on the design by the Executive Engineer, contractors are asked to submit their estimations. Land surveying personnel will mark the locations where spouts will be constructed. At the time of control by the Assistant Engineer adaptions can be made according to the conditions of the field or the desires of the people. For the construction of the pump-house land should be donated by (one of) the villagers. The panchayat has an active role in finding a farmer who will donate a place. In one case they even found a marginal farmer who became the Secretary of the BC and got a lot of power in decision making. In another case no farmer would be found to donate land free of cost, and compensation was paid. In case of

failure and final removal of the scheme the plot is to be returned to the previous owner(s). This is contractually determined.

3. The official agrarian class classification according to the All India National Sample Survey is as follows:

Marginal farmers	*0.1-3 bighas*	0-1 acre	0-0.4 ha
Small farmers	3-7.5 *bighas*	1-2.5 acres	0.4-1 ha
Middle farmers	7.5-15 *bighas*	2.5-5 acres	1-2 ha
Large farmers	5-30 *bighas*	5-10 acres	2-4 ha

4. Field notes reveal that a dug well costs Rs 9,591 and the pumpset Rs 10,200, which makes the costs altogether Rs 19,791. According to the main beneficiary, the government was Rs 14,843 and their contribution Rs 4,947.75. From the logbook it appears that one farmer has contributed the main share and the other four farmers Rs 500 each. The five beneficiaries are of Hindu and tribal communities. The Hindu beneficiaries are relatives. There is a considerable social heirarchy among the farmers in the cluster.
5. We have assumed the consumption rate of rice as 750 g per adult and 500 g per child per day for 360 days a year.
6. The inflation rate in India has fluctuated during the past around 12 per cent, per year. The inflation correction can be illustrated by the fact that the official 'poverty line' standard was Rs 4,800 in the base-line year 1989-90 and was adjusted to Rs 7,200 in the final year of the data collection. Poverty line adjustments are of course also influenced by political decisions.
7. For reasons of simplification the income of service (government employment) is included in the non-farm income.
8. The KPS (extension worker) has to contact 1,200 HH and to visit the villages 4 days per week. According to the ADO it is impossible to contact all the households. The Contact Farmers System is developed to solve the problem. Once a week (once in a fortnight in Siliguri) the KPS staff meets at the ADO office to be informed on policy and activities.
9. For example, the technical staff of Agri-I of Jalpaiguri sub-division consists of 1 senior mechanic, 2 mechanics and 1 electrician. They have to look after all minor irrigation schemes in 7 blocks (DTW).

6. Impact of Irrigation on Workload, Division of Household Labour and Gender-wise Demand for Wage Labour

6.1 IS THERE MORE WORK FOR WOMEN?

In the earlier chapter it was indicated in Table 4.4 that over the four years of study the labour participation of women and girls in family farm work has increased. The problem of increasing workload for women as a consequence of the implementation of new irrigation technology in development projects is a central one. When agricultural work mounts up, other work will suffer. It is not acceptable that production and income increase result in much heavy burdens on women. In such circumstances the identification of labour reducing devices will be necessary as part of the gender planning in the project.

To asses the question as to what extent the increase in irrigation water use increases the workload of women is not easy, and requires painstaking, detailed research. We did our best, and investigated the participation of women in 16 agricultural activities over the three years of study to investigate the changes in workload. As it is well known that the participation of women in different activities depends on the crops to be cultivated, data was collected crop-wise per season (see Annexures 6.1 Participation of women in family farm activities, pre-*kharif*; 6.2 Participation of women in family farm activities, *kharif*; 6.3 Participation of women in family farm activities, *rabi*).

The findings of the collected data have a common feature. We have estimated the participation rate as the percentage of the female workforce of the households growing the crop. The findings show that irrespective of crop or season, in certain types of agricultural activities, the participation of women has been traditionally quite high, and the rate has gone up since the inception of the irrigation devices. These activities are: sowing and transplanting, weeding, protecting crops, harvesting, drying of crops, threshing, winnowing and storing. In some cases the participation rate has gone upto 90-5 per cent. However the participation rate of these activities varies from scheme to scheme, according to the availability of adult women relatively free to attend to the work in question. However, a few notable changes in the pattern of their activities could be observed over the years that the irrigation devices were operational.

1. Increasingly more women have participated in activities like land preparation, seed selection and the preparation of seedbeds, manure and fertilizer application, irrigating fields, preparation and re-pair of bunds particularly for vegetables and tobacco growing in comparison with the base-line survey.
2. Among the schemes, vegetables seem to be one of the important crops for handpump beneficiary households, and their women are taking more part in almost all the activities, though in varying degrees of participation.
3. Compared to the base-line study in 1989-90, in the year 1992-3 a greater number of women have participated in various activities in growing HYV paddy, wheat and tobacco in all schemes.

The general conclusion that can be drawn is that irrigation has brought economic relief to the households, but at the same time has increased the workload of women (as well as men). Field visits reveal that in the better-off households women have to prepare more meals for the wage labourers they engage. The following field notes illustrate this point:

The very articulate, smart woman of the house tells that they have 7 *bighas* of land. Her husband gives all money of sold crops to her and she keeps it. They rent a pumpset to irrigate the land. She works in the fields. When they hire wage labourers she has to cook for them and stays at home. Wages for male labourers are Rs 10, tea, *muri*, rice and half kg. *dhan* (rice in husk); wages for the females are Rs 8, tea, *muri*, rice (*bhat*, cooked rice). There are only four people in the house

TABLE 6.1: PARTICIPATION RATE OF WOMEN WORKERS IN GROWING SELECTED CROPS, 1989-90 (A) AND 1992-3 (B) (RLI/DTW households)

Crops	Marginal				Small				Middle				Big			
	RLI		DTW		RLI		DTW		RLI		DTW		RLI		DTW	
	(a)	(b)	(a)	(b)	(a)	(b)	(a)	(b)	(a)	(b)	(a)	(b)	(a)	(b)	(a)	(b)
Summer paddy (*aus*)	64	82	59	93	82	100	58	77	85	77	92	95	57	83	86	100
Winter paddy (*amon*)	79	94	91	95	100	100	72	92	95	89	89	93	43	75	86	91
HYV paddy (*kharif*)	60	94	100	87	89	100	81	90	67	87	86	89	0	75	100	100
HYV paddy (pre-*kharif*)	0	83	100	0	0	100	0	80	0	70	88	87	0	50	0	0
Jute	58	74	83	85	100	78	44	59	67	71	9	67	43	75	0	38
Vegetables (pre-*kharif*)	0	89	100	100	0	100	33	100	0	92	0	93	0	75	100	0
Vegetables (*kharif*)	81	86	0	0	85	100	0	0	80	0	0	100	100	0	100	0
Vegetables (*rabi*)	0	94	83	100	0	77	67	96	0	84	100	96	0	62	100	100
Tobacco	89	92	93	96	71	7	66	88	53	62	68	93	57	75	71	80
Wheat	75	96	85	95	44	13	43	92	50	67	100	91	33	75	75	80
Oilseeds	100	86	0	0	0	10	67	0	0	71	50	75	0	75	100	100
Potato	0	0	100	0	0	0	40	0	0	0	85	0	0	0	100	0
Pulses	0	0	0	0	0	0	25	75	0	0	75	75	0	0	0	0

Note: Participation rate is the percentage of female workforce of the households growing the crop.

(she, her husband, one son of two years and her old mother-in-law). She studied up to class four.

When we look at the participation rates of women workers per class for selected crops in the river lift irrigation and deep tube well in Table 6.1 the following outcome can be presented.

The figures do not give a clear picture in which it can be traced that women participate more, or less, in the growing of certain crops, or that women of a certain class are more engaged in certain crops. All classes of women participate in growing of *aus, amon*, HYV paddy (*kharif*), jute, HYV paddy (pre-*kharif*), vegetables (*pre-kharif, kharif, rabi*), tobacco, wheat, oilseeds, potato and pulses, but the rates fluctuate per scheme and year.

Over all the classes the participation rates in growing *aus, amon* and HYV paddy (*kharif*) are very high and show a slight tendency that the participation rate has increased. In the river lift irrigation scheme even 100 per cent of the women of small farmers' household participated in growing these three varieties of rice, as women of marginal farmers' households participated to the extent of 82 to 94 per cent.

The participation of women in growing jute fluctuates, which can also be said for tobacco growing. Only participation of women in potato growing is reported at the time of the base-line study but during field visits we observed many times landless women busy with harvesting potato.

6.1.1 Perception of workload

In the sample survey data have been collected of 653 women from an equal number of households belonging to river lift irrigation, deep tube well, pump dug well, and shallow tube well schemes. It was asked, 'has the irrigation facility caused more work for household women?' Most of the women (83 per cent) answered that it had. Only 13 per cent respondents thought otherwise, i.e. gave 'no' to the question, and the rest did not reply.

To know how the workload has increased four alternative answers were provided in the questionnaire and the respondents were asked to choose one or more of these answers. The result is presented in Table 6.2.

TABLE 6.2: PERCEPTION, HOW THE WORKLOAD HAS INCREASED?

Answers	RLI N=354	DTW N=176	STW N=74	PDW N=49	Total N=653
More direct participation in agricultural work	244	158	62	32	496 (76%)
Increase in domestic work (cooking, fetching water, fuel etc.)	167	48	42	25	282 (43%)
Feeding of more labourers	98	37	15	3	153 (23%)
Increase in other off-farm work	29	18	1	0	48 (7%)

It is apparent that 76 per cent of the respondents think that the agricultural work load has increased for women due to irrigation because of increased agricultural activity. Forty-three per cent of the women said that there was also an increase in their domestic workload: feeding more labourers (23 per cent) and 7 per cent perceived an increase in their off-farm work like working as wage earners for some women. The women, however, stated that they do not mind the extra work as they now also have more food and more income. Nevertheless, improvement in post-harvest technology, which is entirely a woman's job, will be very helpful as this work is tedious and time consuming. Introduction of better and easier post-harvest technologies is recommended to reduce the workload of farm women. In view of these findings, we may recall that the handpumps were highly recommended by the gender experts in the formulation mission of Phase II with exactly the argument that they contribute substantially to the relief of women's domestic labour.

6.2 CHANGES IN THE GENDER DIVISION OF HOUSEHOLD LABOUR?

So far we have seen that agricultural work has increased but what about the changes in the division of labour in non-agricultural and domestic work? We investigated 18 different domestic tasks and household related tasks to get an insight into the existing sexual division of labour at the start of the North Bengal Terai Project, and to reveal the change in the division of labour as a consequence of the implementation of small-scale irrigation interventions since the base-line study in the years 1989-90.

Table 6.3 shows that fetching of water is mainly done by women although in the river lift irrigation, 25 per cent of the males are assisting with water fetching. This might be due to the relative high proportion of Muslim households in the river lift

TABLE 6.3: GENDER PROPORTION OF PARTICIPATION IN NON-FARM AND HOUSEHOLD RELATED ACTIVITIES (RLI, DTW and HTW households) *Participation rate (%)*

Activity	RLI				DTW				HTW			
	89 90		92-3		89-90		92-3		89-90		92-3	
	M	F	M	F	M	F	M	F	M	F	M	F
1. Fetching water	14	86	25	75	0	100	2	98	25	75	15	85
2. Collecting fuel	25	75	47	53	0	100	16	84	32	68	63	37
3. Drying/boiling paddy	0	100	0	100	0	100	0	100	0	100	0	100
4. Husking paddy	0	100	34	66	0	100	0	100	0	100	0	100
5. Milking	69	31	69	31	54	46	53	47	70	30	88	12
6. Grazing livestock	68	32	65	35	65	35	67	33	68	32	65	35
7. Gathering fodder/ watering, feeding livestock	76	24	58	42	64	36	67	33	56	44	73	29
8. Buying/selling livestock	100	0	100	0	100	0	100	0	100	0	100	0
9. Buying/selling Crops	100	0	100	0	100	0	100	0	100	0	97	3
10. Making parched rice	0	100	0	100	0	100	0	100	0	100	27	73
11. Making dung cakes/dung sticks	0	100	0	100	0	100	0	100	0	100	0	100
12. Selling Milk	45	55	60	40	48	52	56	44	50	50	100	0
13. Marketing	97	3	85	15	95	5	92	8	73	27	97	3
14. Repair/thatching huts	100	0	92	8	98	2	90	10	100	0	92	8
15. Religious activities	50	50	25	75	3	97	85	15	11	89	47	53
16. Household industry	20	80	25	75	100	0	100	0	50	50	33	67
17. Child care	10	90	7	93	5	95	8	92	20	80	45	55
18. Cooking/serving meals	20	80	13	87	0	100	2	98	1	99	5	95

Source: In-depth Study.

beneficiary households in the in-depth study. The collecting of fuel is also mainly done by women but there is a trend in the river lift irrigation and hand pump beneficiary households for the years 1992-3 for more men to participate in the fuel collection, respectively: male/female, 47 and 53 per cent for river lift irrigation, and male/female 63 and 37 per cent for hand pump beneficiary households. Drying and boiling of paddy and making dung cakes and dung sticks are exclusively women's activities. The same can be said for the husking of paddy, although in 1992-3 in the river lift irrigation some men were engaged in it. Milking of livestock is carried out by men and women, but men have a larger share in the milking. The selling of milk, however, is almost equally done by men and women. The grazing, gathering of fodder, watering and feeding is done more by men than by women. Buying and selling of livestock and crops is again a totally male activity as well as repair and thatching of huts. The vital activity of marketing seems to be mainly dominated by men. However during field visits we came across women who also stated that they are involved in marketing. Religious activities, household industry and cooking are female activities. Detailed information on domestic tasks and the division of labour follow in the next paragraph.

6.3 DOMESTIC LABOUR AND DIVISION OF LABOUR

6.3.1 Child care

Child care is mainly a mother's activity. Mothers will within the reach of their possibilities look after their children. In particular bathing of small children and washing hair can be observed often. In several places we observed that the baby is bathed in cold water and then liberally smeared with mustard oil and exposed to the sun for about two hours in the morning. The mothers say that the sun's rays do not burn the skin of the child due to the oil. The bathing and basking in the sun starts from the second day of the birth. In modern families bathing is done with the water warmed in the sun. When the sun is hot a screen of cotton cloth is hung to prevent the delicate skin of the child from being scorched. The child is then wrapped in old cloth and laid on the floor inside or outside the room. The sunshine is believed to be conducive to the health of the child.

The anthropologist Sanyal mentions a rich culture of 'bathing the child songs' (1965, p. 70). One has the following text: 'let the well water go back into the well and make my child bigger'. Also 'oil smearing songs', and 'massaging the child songs' are popular. During oil smearing the legs and hands of the child are flexed and extended as a little exercise for the child and the following song is sung, 'let the bones grow bigger, let the body grow up, if not I cut the ears of your son'.

If the economic condition allows, the hair of girls will be oiled, combed and plaited by the mother. In particular tribal women have developed skills to combine motherhood with other productive labour they have to do. They carry their babies and small children in a cloth on their backs which keeps them mobile. It is our impression that non-tribal mothers transfer the responsibility of carrying small children more easily to their older children, in particular girls.

A surprising positive outcome from our in-depth study is that in the handpump scheme there is a remarkable change in the share men take in child care over the years of study. The figures in the base-line were, male/female, ratio 20:80 but in the years 1992-3, the male/female ratio is more equal and 45:55. This can be considered a positive outcome which might indicate that men become more aware that they should share responsibilities in the domestic sphere, as their women do the same in the agricultural.

6.3.2 Water fetching for ritual, irrigation and drinking use

Water can mean more rice, more food, less poverty. No water might mean landlessness, indebtness, undernourishment. Therefore it is obvious that as everywhere in India the religious notions related to water are very strong. Nothing in the world is to believed as more purifying than the water in the river Ganga. The Ganga-god, and in our three Terai districts, the Teesta-god, the Water-god, is worshipped by many women in the morning. Some water purified with some *tulsi* leaves is sprinkled in the compound, and they lightly touch their face to be pure that day. Holy water is indispensable in daily life in the fulfilment of pujas. *Dharma* will be in danger if no holy water is used. Water and food are the commom yardstick in the whole complex of untouchability notions. Wells, and touching wells are subject to many customs, believes and prescriptions related to notions of untouchability. Charu Chandra Sanayal has given a unique description of customs around touching wells and water, and the meaning of water as a vital necessity for mother and child in Rajbansi households around 1965. Sanyal (1965, p. 63) writes that after the birth of a child.

> She [the mother] gets up and cleanses the room herself by pouring an emulsion of cow dung and water on the floor and sweeping it with a broom made of straw. The cow dung is held in great esteem by the common people. It is regarded as a purifier. No other person does the cleaning business. She then retires to a secluded corner outside the room and washes herself clean with hot water. She cleanses her own blood-stained clothing with water. She is not allowed to touch the well and hence the water is drawn by some other women of the house. In modern Rajbansi families the cleaning works are done by the '*dhai*' [midwife] or by any other woman of the house.

It would be interesting to conduct participant anthropological research thirty years after Sanyal documented the 'water well' customs of the Rajbansis, and to observe the changes as a result of the introduction of new water technology of handpumps.

Traditionally for irrigation in certain parts of Jalpaiguri where the water table allows (even at some places in the *rabi* season at 3 m), *katcha* wells were dug and the water is lifted in a bucket on a long flexible bamboo stick in the old way. Women are involved to irrigate crops in this way. There are traditionally not many ponds and tanks for irrigation in the districts as the soil is too porous and the water easily seeps away. Water from rivers was also used for irrigation and fetched with a half-boat like vessel. According to the observation of the executive engineer of the project, men and women work together to apply this irrigation system.

In some places Muslim men assist in fetching domestic water, in other places Muslim women stated that their husbands will not fetch water, as the fieldnotes illustrate,

She has two *saris* [the one she is wearing full with holes] and one *sari* and blouse her husband got as wages from a landowner. For marriages she borrows a *sari* from a richer neighbour. For fuel she and her children collect leaves and twigs on the way home from work. She is also fetching water as her husband gets cramps in his stomach when fetching water. But this alleged illness is not the only reason—other women are categoric in their statements that no men will collect fuel and water; it will lower their status.

Discussions with very poor Muslim women reveal that nuances have to be made when it comes to the degree to which *purdah* ideology is observed. In this case it seems to be subordinated to the 'male status protection'. Fathers even agree that marriageable Muslim girls of 14, 15 and 16 years draw water from the public well, instead as in other places happens, of fetching water themselves.

However, in some situations there is no choice:

20 May 1992, visit to river lift irrigation Pataram Jodh, block Kharibari Phansidewa.

We speak with a woman, Maloti of the Pahan [tribal] community. The family have ¼ of a *bigha* and she has to do wage labour. She earns at this time 8 rupees a day and some bread and curry. In the season she gets 10 rupees [minimum wage is 18 rupees in Bengal]. She has two goats and grows some chillies, brinjal and tomatoes around her house. For drinking water she has to cross the river to a *gua* [*katcha* well] on the other side. She has to make 5 to 6 trips a day. In the monsoon the water is so high that the men have to fetch water by swimming, with the pots on their heads. Pumps will be implemented under the project but she is not entitled because their landholding is too small.

6.3.3 Irrigation technology and domestic use of water

In fact the women of the handpump scheme get the most relief from the drudgery of water fetching. As will be shown below they use the handpump water for everyday purposes. The women in the river lift and deep tube well schemes are still fetching water from public or private wells which requires much more time and energy, and often causes bad health. However, the women living in river lift schemes are very happy when the spouts are opened to irrigate the land as they use the water also for bathing and washing clothes, but they admitted that it feels like stealing the water.

We arrive. Good to be in the village again. Muslim women living around the spout, of all classes, are washing clothes in the water of the opened spout. They stand in the concrete structure and can use the walls and floor as a place to shrub the cloth with soap. Such places are not available elsewhere. Release of irrigation water is of great help to them in their domestic labour. Males only use spout water to wash their feet. They also fetch water for bathing and drinking of cattle. They have public dugwells for drinking water. This is a Muslim ward and 42 households live here.

In our talk at the spout, women stated to be glad that the river lift irrigation came for domestic use. But when the spouts are closed the women have to fetch the water for the cattle again from the wells. The data show that the supply of water to livestock is still done by the majority of women from the well in the river lift scheme (57 out of 61 women) and by a substantial number of women in the deep tube well scheme (18 out of 72 women). However, in the handpump scheme the water for the cattle is fetched from the handpump only by all 34 women respondents interviewed in the in-depth study.

On our question, 'are there any problems with water supply?' only 19 women out of 148 interviewed in the handpump, river lift and deep tube well sample admitted facing problems. The nature of the problems vary from too low water tables, being too old to fetch water, and the high iron content of the water.

6.3.4 Irrigation and the kitchen garden

In the river lift irrigation 53 out of 61, in the handpump cluster 31 out of 34 and in the deep tube well scheme 63 out of 72 households responded to the question 'who cares for the kitchen garden?'.

The main pattern is that husband and wife work together in the kitchen garden (94 households out of 147); however more women than men have stated to look alone after the garden (23 women and 10 men). In the handpump beneficiary households no man is stated to alone look after the kitchen garden.

Plate 11: Tobacco, irrigated with handpump water.

We asked in what way the kitchen garden is irrigated, what tools are used to get the water in the right place. In Cooch Behar we saw a farmer irrigating his tobacco fields with handpump water. He had a special way of bringing a bucket with water to a certain place and then to beat the water with his hand, so that it spread in small drops around him (see Plate 11). Of the 147 interviewed households, only two used a spray bucket, 13 made use of channelling the water, and the far majority, 132, made just use of a bucket to irrigate the plants in the kitchen garden. We inquired about the price of a spray bucket in the local market: it is Rs 40. Many families declared they were not to be able to make the extra cost for a spray-bucket although they know the irrigation is better. They can use a bucket in a multiple-purpose way. To channel the water to a distance they make use of a rubber tube or from inventive bamboo constructions.

Often the question in the project is raised, 'who is pumping' the water out of the implemented handpumps by swinging the handle. Some people were of the opinion that this is heavy and exhausting work and that therefore a better design of the pump

TABLE 6.4: NUMBER OF TIMES IN A WEEK AND DURATION TO FETCH WATER FOR KITCHEN GARDEN

RLI				HTW				DTW			
No. of times	No. of HH	Duration in min.	No. of HH	No. of times	No. of HH	Duration in min.	No. of HH	No. of times	No. of HH	Duration in min.	No. of HH
1	17	15	10	1	4	15	9	1	21	15	27
2	11	20	2	2	4	20	8	2	16	20	5
3	15	30	9	3	2	30	10	3	11	30	14
4	1	35	4	4	11	35	1	4	5	35	6
5	8	40	23	5	7	40	2	5	3	40	9
6	1	45	5	6	3	45	1	6	7	45	2
Total	53		52		31		31		63		63

should be introduced with makes the drawing of water easier. Our data show that in the far majority of cases men and women both pump the water (114 households out of 147 households interviewed). Those men and women who declared they look after the kitchen garden alone are also the only 'pumpers'. To have an impression of the times in a week and the duration that water for the kitchen garden is fetched, we present the Table 6.4.

The maximum time spent swinging the handle of the pump is 45 minutes, and 14 families do that 6 times a week which comes to 4.5 hours a week. The modal value however is around 3 times irrigation of 30 minutes each time a week.

6.3.5 Fuel collection

The same concern with 'male status' counts in the collection of fuel, and as a consequence is mainly done by women. A landless woman said that she and her children search for dry leaves, cow droppings and twigs on their way home from work. Even when her husband has no labour that day he will not collect fuel to relieve his working wife. But there is a remarkable and positive trend in the river lift irrigation and hand pump beneficiary households for the year 1992-3: more men are participating in the fuel collection in comparison with the base-line survey: from 25 to 47 per cent for river lift irrigation, and even from 32 to 63 per cent in the hand pump beneficiary households which means that women's shares came down from 68 to 37 per cent. It is difficult to say if this is the effect of the awareness of men that women can spend more time looking after the vegetable garden. The data on the fuel used in the households for boiling water and cooking reveal the following. Firewood and dry leaves are used in any season (respectively 95 and 83 households out of 167), dung cakes are used by 102 families out of 167), but less in the rainy season. Jute sticks used the most (149 out of 167) are in particular used after pre-*kharif* and kerosene by the better off households (22 out of 167). It has to be noted that handpump beneficiary households have the lowest firewood fuel consumption. This might be due to poverty or lack of land to grow trees.

Women stated that they collect fuel on their own from their own land and from public land (respectively 17 and 27 out of 167 total households). In the majority of cases men and women fetch fuel together from their own land (150) and public land (78). Forty-three households do not fetch fuel at all from public land.

In the river lift irrigation 9 out of 61 families buy fire wood (4,260 kg in the *rabi* season 1992-3); only one family out of 34 in the handpump scheme can afford to buy fire wood (240 kg) and 6 households out of 72 in the deep tube well scheme (Rs 1,600). Concerning the gender-wise collection of fuel our data show a slight *purdah* effect in particular in the collecting of fuel from public land: 19 males fetch fuel from public land but no male fetches fuel from his own land on his own.

6.3.6 Looking after cattle

Milking and grazing of livestock is carried out by men and women, but men have a larger share in it. The selling of milk, however, is almost equally done by men and women. Gathering of fodder, watering and feeding is done more by men than by women. In many places people told us that with the introduction of irrigation the grazing and gathering of fodder is becoming more difficult. On the other hand it seems to be a customary right that poor households are allowed to cut grass in wheat fields of richer farmers. The benefit is two way: they have grass and the landowner has his land weeded. Buying and selling of livestock and crops is again a 100 per cent male activity as well as repair and thatching of huts.

6.4 CHANGING PERCEPTIONS OF TYPES OF WORK?

Table 6.5 gives an interesting insight in the perceptions of the women of their own work in terms of what type of work they feel they participate the most, or equal with men.

Forty-nine per cent of the women respondents felt in the base-line year 1989-90, that they did mostly household work. In 1992-3 the percentage came down to 42. In line with this perception, 47 per cent of the women felt at the time of the base-line study

TABLE 6.5: WOMEN'S PERCEPTION OF THEIR OWN WORK
(89-90) = 240 N(92-3) = 234

Description of work	No.		%	
	1989-90	1992-3	1989-90	1992-3
Mostly housework	118	97	49	42
Mostly agricultural work	9	3	4	1
Both equally	112	130	47	55
Other works	1	4	0.4	2

that they participated equally with men in the agricultural work but in 1992-3 this has increased to 55 per cent. This means that more women in all the schemes perceive themselves more as workers, equally participating with their husbands in their own farm, than as being only housewives doing household work. It is interesting that 4 per cent of the women stated at the time of the base-line survey that according to their perception they do mostly agricultural work and this percentage has come down to one per cent in the final year of study. This interesting finding also supports our conclusion in the previous chapter regarding the non-withdrawal of women from productive labour.

6.5 DEMAND FOR WAGE LABOUR ACCORDING TO GENDER

A high degree of participation of household members in family farm activities does not necessarily meet the labour requirement of agriculture. The data of the sample survey show that many households hire labour of both sexes. The small overview in Table 6.6 compiles the enormous load of data that has been collected on the actual demand for wage labour in the project area, and to know which class of farmers in which schemes make use of wage labour the most. This knowledge might be useful in

TABLE 6.6: HIRED LABOUR, MALE/FEMALE EMPLOYMENT AND WAGE RATE

Sex	Total number of households	Number of Labour-employing households	wage-generated labour days	wage rates (Rs)	
				Minimum	Maximum
Male	1,478	961	71,278	4	40
Female	1,478	609	30,220	4	30

developing policies to support the weakest categories of people dependent on wage-labour.

Of the total of 1,478 households in the sample survey of all classes in the five irrigation schemes, 961 have employed male wage labourers and 609 female labourers. It is surprising that, of the 1,053 marginal farmers households, 589 have hired additional male, and 306 households female wage labour. The data reveal that the marginal households have generated a substantial employment opportunity for agricultural wage work. The number of days that employment has been provided is impressive. In total 71,278 days are reported for male, and 30,220 days for women labourers. That means that 961 families hired male agricultural labourers for, on average, 74 days per year and, on average 50 days a year for women. Only 517 families relied exclusively on family labour and did not hire male workers from outside. Of this 517, 464 belong to the marginal farmers category. The daily minimum wage was Rs 4 for men and women and the highest wage for men Rs 40 and women Rs 30. Apart from the differences in wage rates, it also varies from one area to another. The median value is probably between Rs 15 and 20 for men and Rs 12 and 16 for women. Generally the wage rate is higher in the *kharif* season and low at the end of pre-*kharif* and *rabi* seasons.

Obviously, men are preferred to women as workers and the employment ratio of the latter is half, or less than half in all the schemes.

The figures show the demand for wage labour of the farm households and it should be kept in mind that this wage labour has to be shared between the members of the landless families, as will be described in the next chapter, but also with the members of land-owning marginal, and small farmers' households.

Table 6.7 shows the proportion of households in different agrarian class and schemes which had employed hired labourers in the last year of the in-depth study in 1992-3.

It may be observed that the proportion of households employing hired labour generally goes up with the increase in the agrarian classification of the household. The small, middle,

TABLE 6.7: HOUSEHOLDS EMPLOYING HIRED LABOUR IN 1992-3

(in %)

Class	Households employing hired labourers									
	RLI		DTW		HTW		STW		PDW	
	M	F	M	F	M	F	M	F	M	F
Marginal	60	44	71	36	52	22	80	67	46	35
Small	94	77	89	76	79	57	79	74	88	81
Middle	94	71	100	100	93	67	93	93	100	100
Big	88	75	100	100	100	100	83	83	0	0

and large farmers' households, in greater proportion, employ hired labour of both genders than what the marginal farmers' households can do. But, the farmers of deep tube well scheme have employed more hired labour in more households that in the river lift irrigation households.

Table 6.8 deals with the average number of persondays of employment per household in different schemes. Though the marginal farmers account for a sizeable proportion of total persondays of employment in a scheme, as the tables show, in some cases they have given employment to more persondays (e.g. in deep tube well, hand pump beneficiary households schemes) but the average days of employment per household is lower than that in other schemes. This is because the number of marginal farm households (except in shallow tube well and pump dug well schemes), is much higher than the number of the households of the other three classes. This consequently reduces

TABLE 6.8: AVERAGE PERSONDAYS OF HIRED LABOUR PER HOUSEHOLD IN 1992-3

Class	Average persondays hired labour per household									
	RLI		DTW		HTW		STW		PDW	
	M	F	M	F	M	F	M	F	M	F
Marginal	34	20	61	37	30	20	81	34	70	49
Small	74	52	134	65	72	35	147	100	149	72
Middle	132	79	198	76	159	79	359	226	201	86
Large	290	175	579	115	326	51	596	336	0	0

the employment rate per household. Table 6.8 presents the comparative employment rate of hired labourers per household.

The figures show that the employment of male workers has increased in small, middle and large farmers' households in all the schemes. Generally the middle and large farmers, though their numbers are few, have given more persondays of employment per household than other categories of farmers. This is obvious because the size of their cultivable land is so much that it can not be cultivated by household labour alone.

The average days of employment of female workers in each household is usually half or slightly more than half the employment rate of male workers. However a few households belonging to middle and large farmers have given more employment to women than other classes of farmers. It is not because they have less prejudice against female workers, but because their dependence on hired labour is more, and as they employ large numbers of workers the number of women workers also increases.

In the next chapter the spotlight will be on the members, and particular the women, of landless households. What did they gain from the interventions of the North Bengal Development Project? Did the irrigation water generate more wage-labour for them, and in particular for the women?

7. Irrigation and its Impact on Landless Women

7.1 THE MEANING OF BEING LANDLESS

Being landless means dependency and vulnerability. It means hunger and a constant fight against rising prices of basic food, constant weakness, indebtness, illness. Being landless means endless suffering, waiting and searching for work, longing for the day that a small piece of land, or a cow, can be bought, hoping that the landowner will give one blouse and a cheap *sari*, hoping that the small bamboo hut will not collapse during the next monsoon. For women it means also very few days that some money can be earned in comparison with the men of the family. It means lower wages for being a woman. It means giving birth on the floor of the hut and starting hard physical labour one week after that. And, dreaming that the children can be sent to school and that the daughter can get a nice dowry with golden earrings and may be a small calf. And, it means seeing the wealth of others, their houses with tin roofs, their nice dresses, their good meals. Around 30 per cent of the households in the Terai are landless. The definition of landless used in the area is households with less than 1 *bigha* agricultural land.

The in-depth and sample survey studies also tried to assess the impact of the project on the livelihood of the non-target groups in the districts: the members of landless households. In the in-depth study 30 rural landless households were followed for a period of three years, whereas 46 more households were interviewed in the sample survey.

The landless households derived a major proportion of their income from wage labour (75 per cent according to the sample survey), mainly as farmhands. Other sources of income were of less importance and concerned agricultural production (17 per cent) and self-employment in for instance diary and fuel trade, in brokerage or in stone quarrying. On average, landless men were employed in the sample survey for 200 days (in-depth study 234 days) in a year and landless women for 80 (in depth study 109) days. There is a clear seasonality in labour demand in the area, with peaks in the pre-*kharif* season (during the cultivation of *boro* rice) and the *rabi* season (in potato cultivation).

The overall findings are that the proportion of women earning wages with agricultural labour has come down from 17 to 9. Whether this is a positive or negative development has to be seen. More landless families could acquire land for cultivation mostly by the woman of the house. Only in the handpump scheme can landless women obtain more employment in the *rabi* season.

7.2 THE LANDLESS WOMEN IN THE IN-DEPTH STUDY

As a fall-out of the installation of various irrigation schemes in the North Bengal Terai Development Project area it is assumed that the landless labourers will also be benefitted indirectly from the schemes, by way of increased employment opportunities. The benefit was anticipated in two ways, first by way of a rise in person-days of employment in farms, and in off-farm employment while the irrigation facilities are being constructed. To test this assumption we selected two clusters of 15 landless households each, one in the river lift scheme village (Paschim Harmati in Jalpaiguri district) and the other in the deep tube well village (Jamadarerbos in Cooch Behar district). These households were studied in 1989-90 to ascertain their socio-economic position 'before' the irrigation schemes were installed. It provided us with the bench-mark data. In the next three years the progress of these families was followed up and the social and economic changes noted. The main findings 'before' and 'after' installation will be shown.

7.2.1 Social and economic profile of the landless labourers (1992-3)

There has been a reduction in the number of household from 30 in 1989-90 to 26 in 1992-3. Four households in deep tube well area (Jamadarerbos) have been taken off from the sample as three of them have migrated elsewhere, and one family has joined its parents and stopped working as labourers. Because of this reason the demography of these households cannot be compared between 1989-90 and 1992-3. The total adult population of 26 households in 1992-3 was 109: 58 males and 51 females (of which 26 boys and 22 girls).

The size of the landless households is very small and has slightly increased from 4.16 in 1989-90 to 4.19 in 1992-3. Muslim households are somewhat bigger than others—about 4.7. Marriageable girls (2) of Rajbansi (SC) community were also married out of the village in 1992-3. In the sample Muslims constitute half of the landless, and mostly come from Paschim Harmati village (river lift irrigation). They are followed by the Rajbansis: one-third of the landless households. The size of the work force (15-60 years) in 1992-3 was 32 men and 28 women. There have been eight live births (5 boys, 3 girls) and two death cases (male) in three years. There were three marriages, in which one girl came in as a bride and two girls (less than 15 years), one Muslim and one Rajbansi, were married out.

7.2.2 Literacy and education

The general literacy rate (excluding 0-5 yrs) shows some improvement in three years. It was about 35 per cent in 1989-90 which has gone up to 42 per cent in 1992-3. Even so, the rate is much below the rates among the participants of various schemes (55 to 72 per cent). Except the Muslims and Rajbansis the sample size of other communities is too small to comment upon. Among the Rajbansis the literacy rate has gone up from 13 to 16 people due to increase in the number of literate women. Among the Muslims also it has gone up, but here the gainers are men. The literacy rate among Muslim women does not show any marked improvement. In general the literacy rate of the women is less than half of that of men. Of the 40 literates in the sample 31 have read upto primary level and the rest upto secondary level. There is no women literate who has read beyond the primary level. There is no doubt that the landless labourers are the most educationally backward section (particularly the women) of the population in a village. There has been some progress in their rate of literacy over the years but that may be due to incidental demographic circumstances of having more girls than boys in the total 30 households of the sample.

7.2.3 Landholding: own and leased land

In the 1992-3 survey it was found that 22 out of 26 households have homestead land (1 acre); the other four households live in someone else's land with the permission of the owner. It was also found that 8 households owned together about 3.32 acres of cultivable land, which was 1.87 acres owned by the same households in 1989-90. Between the two years it appears that at least some landless labourers have improved their ownership of land by way of acquiring a few acres of cultivable land. Two families in 1992-3 have taken 3.66 acres of land on lease; it was four acres taken by four households in 1989-90. At the same time one family has given out 0.83 acre of land on lease because it had no plough/bullock to do the work.

7.2.4 Occupation

About 60 per cent of the work force of the landless labourers households is engaged as wage labourers in agriculture. The rest work in different types of occupation, non-agricultural labour, *bidi*-making, work in their own small plot, rickshaw/van pulling, hair-cutting, etc. About 70 per cent of women in the work force work as agricultural wage labourers either on a regular or casual basis. The occupational distribution of work force as found during the 1992-3 survey is given in Table 7.1. The majority of the labourers work in their own villages (particularly the women), but during the lean months males also seek employment in adjoining villages. This conforms with gender ideological restrictions, viz., that it is considered undesirable for women to work outside the village.

Of the 28 female respondents 17 declared domestic work as their main occupation though 9 of them work subsidiarily in other generating occupations and 4 engaged in their family farm. Muslim women generally refrain from working as a wage labourers, particularly when young. Older women may take up

TABLE 7.1: OCCUPATIONAL DISTRIBUTION OF THE WORK FORCE (1992-3)
N = M-32

Occupation	Main		Subsidiary	
	M	F	M	F
Agriculture labour	19	6	3	7
Non-agriculture labour	4	1	8	1
Cultivation (own farm)	4	1	8	4
Bidi-making	1	0	8	4
Business	0	0	1	1
Domestic work	0	17	0	0
Others*	4	3	1	0

Note: *Others include- maid servant 1, female beggar 1, van-rickshaw pulling 2 (M), hair cutting 1 (M), fuel collection 1 (M).

employment as maid servants in houses of their employer landowners.

7.2.5 Wage labour

What is the division of labour between male and female agricultural labourers? Table 7.2 gives the findings of the in-depth study.

TABLE 7.2: PERCENTAGE OF LANDLESS LABOURERS WORK FORCE ENGAGED IN DIFFERENT AGRICULTURAL ACTIVITIES (1992-3)
N = M-25 F = 12

Agricultural activities	% of work force	
	M	F
1. Land preparation	51	0
2. Seed selection/seed preparation	20	3
3. Fertilizer/manure application	11	3
4. Sowing/transplanting	68	13
5. Weeding	75	16
6. Pesticide application	3	0
7. Protecting/caring crops	4	0
8. Irrigating fields	12	0
9. Preparation/making of bunds	14	5
10. Harvesting	77	15
11. Threshing/winnowing	30	16
12. Washing of jute	22	6
13. Drying of tobacco pleaves	10	1
14. Storing	8	4

The table shows clearly that landless male agricultural labourers are preferred for all kinds of agricultural work. Sowing transplanting, weeding, harvesting and threshing and winnowing are the activities in which women get some share in comparison with men.

7.3 IS THERE MORE EMPLOYMENT FOR LANDLESS WOMEN DUE TO IRRIGATION?

It was assumed that irrigation use would create more wage labour for landless men and women. As we have seen particularly male landless labourers benefitted from higher demand. Let us look more in detail into the findings of the in-depth study on the number of days of work women said they could get in the baseline year when the irrigation devices were not in operation (1989), and after four years.

In Table 7.3 the ratio is presented of the female agricultural labourers hired (in percentage of total person days) per season per scheme as well as the number of days of their employment.

The table shows a mixed picture. In some schemes, deep tube well, handpump beneficiary households, and STW, the total days of employment of women workers in 1992-3 have increased. The increase varies from 1 to 7 per cent of total persondays of employment in the year. In the other two schemes, river lift irrigation and pump dug well the women's days of employment per year has decreased by 2 to 5 per cent. The highest increase in women's employment has been among the handpump beneficiaries. It has increased from 10 per cent in 1989-90 to 17 per cent in 1992-3. The increase can be noticed in all the seasons of the year but particularly in the *kharif* and *rabi* seasons. The phenomenon is not only indicative of better economic condition of the handpump beneficiary households but also as most of them are vegetable/tobacco growers, women labourers are considered as good as men in the tending of small vegetable/tobacco plots. In most other cases the strong preference given to men labourers is evident. The following field notes may give an impression of the improvement in employment opportunities for female labourers in *rabi* season.

TABLE 7.3: FEMALE HIRED LABOUR IN AGRICULTURE

Scheme	Year	Pre-*kharif*			*Kharif*			*Rabi*			Total F (%)
		M	F	(%)	M	F	(%)	M	F	(%)	
RLI	1990-1	1,454	306	17	1,981	102	5	794	54	6	10
	1992-3	1,212	128	10	2,831	118	4	874	167	16	8
DTW	1990-1	1,373	319	19	1,671	416	20	1,229	88	7	16
	1992-3	1,225	283	19	1,909	510	21	1,391	126	8	17
HTW	1990-1	1,056	133	11	426	34	7	532	47	8	10
	1992-3	1,179	205	15	1,094	274	20	867	177	17	17
STW	1990-1	723	77	10	336	25	7	443	196	31	9
	1992-3	514	44	8	737	116	14	48	15	24	11
PDW	1990-1	1,051	172	14	651	60	8	653	90	12	12
	1992-3	768	187	20	1,252	0	0	492	0	0	7

(%) = Percentage of female persondays to the total days of employment in the season.

Note: In the base-line reports of RLI/DTW the persondays of hired labour appear to be exaggerated, hence the figures of 1990-1 have been given here.

At the roadside I have a talk with a group of female landless labourers. They state that they have equal wage as men and that they will not work for less. Before the river lift irrigation there was no scope for 6 months agricultural labour but now there is. Before they could only get work as household servants to pound rice, make *muri*, etc. The wage for that type of work is very low and they just do not do that any more. So, it is difficult for 'landowners women' to get help for this type of post-harvest paddy activities.

But taking all schemes together the proportion of women's person days of employment to the total days of employment in a season has remained more or less constant as is shown in Table 7.4.

This means that despite the rise in the persondays of employment in two seasons of 1992-3 (*kharif* and *rabi*) their share has remained the same. The male labourers have benefitted more by securing more days of employment than the women labourers. In the pre-*kharif* season, compared with 1989-90 or 1990-1 there has been a general decline in the persondays of employment for both the sexes, but this has not affected the proportion of male/female employment ratio.

The in-depth study shows that there is a net increase in employment opportunities for wage labourers. The average persondays of employment of a wage labourer went up from 198 days in 1989-90 to 234 days in 1992-3 for male workers. For female workers, on the other hand, opportunities appear to have stagnated: the average number of working days per year decreased slightly from 113 to 109 days.

TABLE 7.4: MALE AND FEMALE HIRED LABOUR IN AGRICULTURE

(all schemes combined)

Year	Total persondays of employment					
	Pre-*kharif*		*Kharif*		*Rabi*	
	M	F	M	F	M	F
1989-90	5,657	1007	5,065	637	3,651	475
1990-1		(15)		(11)		(11.5)
1992-3	4,898	847	7,823	1,018	3,672	485
		(15)		(11.5)		(11.6)

Note: Percentage of women's person days of employment.

In the same period landless incomes went up as well: from Rs 958 annually per capita to Rs 1,872,[1] which—accounting for the effect of inflation—is a 39 per cent rise. Still the in-depth study found that 35 per cent of the landless households were living below the poverty line of Rs 7,200.

7.4 GENDER IDEOLOGY IN EMPLOYMENT

The lower labour utilization of landless women was already noted above (234 days a year for a male labourer against 109 for a woman). The number of landless women participating in the labour market is less, and as a result women account for only 8-17 per cent of the agricultural labour in the schemes studied in the in-depth study. Men are hired for ploughing and land preparation, sowing, transplanting, weeding, harvesting and threshing. Women are hired for sowing, transplanting (see Plate 12), weeding, harvesting and threshing, tasks undertaken by male labourers as well, who in addition are also employed for ploughing, land preparation and drying of tobacco leaves.

Plate 12: Female landless labourer.

As indicated, landless female labour participation has fallen over the years of study. On the other hand several of the landless households studied in the in-depth survey were able to take small plots of land on lease or mortgage, to be cultivated by female household members. Still many women complained of remaining idle for most of the year. The general opinion among male and female landless alike was that though irrigation has provided more labour opportunities, it is still insufficient to keep them employed throughout the year, and that counts the more for women.

Daily wages for male and female labourers differ as well. For men they range between Rs 11 and 16 and for women between Rs 6 and 15. In addition a tiffin and a meal is usually provided. In the pre-*kharif* and *kharif* season the wages are slightly higher (Rs 1 to 2) than in the *rabi* season. Adolescent children are also employed during the agricultural peak season for wages, which are considerably lower than these of adults: Rs 11 to 16 for boys and little as Rs 2 to 4 for girls.

The wages for labourers hardly increased in the three years of the in-depth study: by Rs 2, indicating that despite the development of irrigated agriculture there is still no shortage of agricultural labour. The wages paid to farm workers are far below the official minimum prescribed by the government for unskilled workers in 1992, i.e. Rs 20 per day. Increase in wages and work days of in particular of the men have helped them to take small plots of land on lease/mortgage. However, the women have no land rights or control over the land: they have only access to the land of their husbands to produce food for the family. Those who have some land wished to have regular supply of water from the scheme (river lift irrigation/deep tube well) so that they could get a good yield, but were often excluded as the location of their land is mostly outside the command area. A technical design that includes their land will require huge changes in the world of standard designs.

7.5 LANDLESS LABOURERS OF THE SAMPLE SURVEY

As a part of the Sample Survey a small number of landless labourers living in the site village of river lift irrigation and deep tube well were also investigated to ascertain how far the irrigation schemes could generate employment for the wage labourers and in particular for women. The other purpose of the survey was to compare the findings of the small sample of the in-depth study (30 landless households) with the findings of the sample survey (46 landless households) and to match the two sets of data.

The river lift irrigation scheme in Paschim Chepani village and deep tube well scheme in Madhya Boragari village are two of the better performing schemes according to reports published by the NBTDP authority. As such it is expected that due to increase of water use more persondays of employment for landless labourers of the village will be created. Both the villages are quite big, and landless households living in a section of the village near to the pump site were selected. Thus in Paschim Chepani 20 and in Madhya Boragari 26, landless labourers' households were included in the investigation. The survey was conducted in May-June 1993.

7.5.1 Social background

The population of 46 households is 199, with 4.3 members as the average size of a household which is slightly higher as in the in-depth study, 4.1 members. While the Muslims predominate the sample from Madhya Boragari (79 per cent) the Rajbansis are the dominant community in Paschim Chapani (84 per cent). The distribution of various communities is as follows:

Although the numbers are small, it is tempting to compare two interesting communities: the Muslim in which the position of women is subordinated, and the Rajbansis, with a tribal background, where the gender relations can be expected as more equal. The general sex ratio is 913 per 1,000 males, which is below the rural average of 947. But, as we expected in Madhya Boragari, the Muslim village, the proportion male/female is alarmingly low, 770, while it is extremely high, 1,116, in Paschim Chepani. It is striking in Table 7.5 that in the Muslim case there are substantially fewer girls than boys. We cannot give any interpretation to this fact as the numbers are too small, but we leave the option open that under-reporting of girls can be an explanation. The adult population (15+ years) is evenly balanced between two sexes at 52 each. This is the main work force, but all of them do not work as labourers for daily wages as the table

TABLE 7.5: COMMUNITY-WISE DISTRIBUTION OF LANDLESS POPULATION IN THE SAMPLE SURVEY

Community	Village	Household	Adult 15+		Child 0-15		Total		Total
			M	F	Boys	Girls	M	F	
Muslim	MB	21	23	24	25	13	48	37	85
	PC	0	0	0	0	0	0	0	0
Rajbansi (SC)	MB	4	4	4	8	2	12	6	18
	PC	16	20	17	16	23	36	40	76
General Hindu	MB	1	1	1	0	3	1	4	5
	PC	4	4	6	3	2	7	8	15
Total	MB	26	28	29	33	18	61	47	108
	PC	20	24	23	19	25	43	48	91

Note: MB = Madhya Boragari; PC = Paschim Chepani.

on occupation will show. A number of adolescent boys and girls also work from time to time and contribute to the family income.

The average literacy rate of the population (excluding 0-5 years) in the sample survey is about 35 per cent, but it considerably varies between communities and sexes. Looked at this way the literacy rate of the sample population is quite lower than the national literacy rate (52 per cent). The landless labourers of the in-depth study, have a 42 per cent literacy. Muslim and Rajbansi men have higher literacy rates than their women who are overwhelmingly illiterate. Community difference in literacy rates among men and women shows that 48 per cent of men are literates, among Muslims the percentage is higher, and only 22 per cent of women are literate. Muslim women have the lowest literacy rate in the three communities: 22 per cent, while Muslim men are 58 per cent literate. Almost all the literates have education only upto primary level, that means they can read Bengali and sign their name. Only one male person from the 46 landless households in the sample survey went to secondary school.

7.5.2 Economic activities

Though most of the male work force is engaged in daily wage labour a few of them work as brokers, van pullers and petty traders. Forty-five men out of 57; and 26 women of landless households out of a total of 46 earn their livelihood from agricultural labour work. Twenty-six women work regularly as wage labourers, others from time to time, as and when work is available. In the in-depth study we found that only one/third of the women was engaged in agricultural labour.

The average working days of adult workers is about 197 days for men and 84 days for women in a year which is much lower than we found in the in-depth study: respectively 234 and 109 days. Subsidiary to the main occupations listed above a number of persons also work in their own land to grow some crops. This is particularly evident in the sample we conducted in the Rajbansi village Paschim Chepani. About 58 per cent of men, and 28 per cent of women workers work on their own farms in addition to working as wage labourers. As we shall see the women interviewed in the sample survey also find it hard to find employment, because the employers prefer to engage men. But the men of the village (21 out of 24) work subsidiarily as non-agricultural labourers in the nearby railway yard as and when they find work there.

Besides the adult population about 10 children between the ages of 10 and 15 (3 boys, 7 girls) work as agricultural labourers, as and when called for, particularly during peak agricultural activities. All the adolescent girls do not belong to the Muslim community.

7.5.3 Land holding and leased-in land

Very little cultivable land is owned by the landless labourers in either of the villages. All of them do not even possess homestead land. To augment their income about half of the households have taken land on mortgage or seasonal lease. The leased-in land has been taken on 50:50 crop sharing basis after paying equally the cost of cultivation (fertilizer, manure and seeds). This mode of land transaction was more evident in Paschim Chepani than in the other village. The land ownership situation including the mortgaged and leased-in land at the time of survey was is shown in Table 7.6.

Respectively three households in Paschim Chepani and six in

TABLE 7.6: OWN AND MORTGAGED/LEASED-IN LAND

Type of land	No. of household		Area (acres)	
	PC	MB	PC	MB
Homestead	17	20	1.55	0.88
Cultivable land (own)	3	7	0.24	0.50
Kitchen garden	10	5	0.29	0.15
Mortgaged land	7	4	5.92	0.63
Leased-in land	11	1	3.58	0.16
Leased out land	0	1	0.00	0.08
Total household	20	26	–	–

Madhya Boragari households have no own homestead land. A very negligible amount of land (1.18 acres) which includes both the cultivable land and kitchen garden is owned by less than half of the households. But about half of the households have taken land on mortgage or lease (some households have taken both) in 1992-3—the total of such land amounted to a little over 10 acres. Most of the households come from Paschim Chepani. The martgage arrangement is that the mortgager produces crop(s) on this land and keeps the produce, until the debt is paid-off. But in leased-in land either a fixed amount or half of the share of the produce is paid to the lessor. The cost of cultivation (manure, fertilizer, seeds) is shared only when the crops are shared. The following fieldnotes give an impression of the economic activities of a landless labourer in Paschim Chepani:

We make a long walk in the fields to reach a cluster of 60 landless families next to the railway: they are all Rajbansis. Six years ago they came to this place. We sit in the compound of one family and the man tells us that there is much more labour now with the river lift irrigation than before: he makes the comparison 25 per cent to 75 per cent. In former days they survived with earth cutting in this lean season but now they get work preparing fields for *boro*. He earns Rs 10, two heavy meals and 0.5 kg of rice. He has 180 days wage-work in a year. He has four sons and two daughters so he cannot smoothly run the household. His wife works an equal number of days for wage labour. He leases 1 *bigha* of land for growing paddy [*boro*]. He has to invest Rs 700 as inputs. The share-cropper arrangement is on 50-50 basis. He expects 22 *maunds* [40 kg]. One *maund* can be sold for Rs 120. He estimates that he has around 6 months food from 1 *bigha*.

7.5.4 Crop production

The produce from the field in their own or mortgaged/leased land has given the landless households about 17 per cent of their annual income in 1992-3. The Paschim Chepani households have grown HYV paddy (*boro*), jute, HYV paddy (*kharif*), wheat, oilseeds and some vegetables. The Madhya Boragari households have grown primarily vegetables (potato), HYV paddy (*kharif*) and jute. Both the households have followed the cropping pattern of their respective regions as Table 7.7 shows.

The intensity of agricultural activities can be gauged from the fact that about 14.5 acres of land were under different crops grown by the Paschim Chepani labourers' households. In Madhya Boragari the corresponding area was only 4 acres in 1992-3. It appears that the labourers are good farmers but resource constraints do not allow them to go beyond the above limit. In the two samples of labourers studied during the in-depth study the per capita farm income was 9 per cent of the annual income, but these labourers found more days of employment on a daily wage basis.

TABLE 7.7: CROP OUTPUT OF THE LANDLESS LABOURERS (1992-3)

Crops	Village	HHs	Area (acres)	Output (100 kg)
HYV paddy (pre-*kharif*)	PC	16	5.93	58.00
Summer paddy (pre-*kharif*) (*aus*)	PC	4	0.99	9.00
Jute (pre-*kharif*)	MB	8	0.69	9.00
	PC	1	0.16	6.00
HYV paddy (*kharif*)	MB	8	0.64	7.00
	PC	9	2.82	29.00
Winter paddy (*kharif*)	PC	1	0.50	2.00
Vegetables (pre-*kharif*)	MB	1	0.02	0.25
	PC	5	0.42	17.00
Vegetables (*rabi*)	MB	14	2.69	167.00
	PC	2	0.50	6.00
Wheat (*rabi*)	PC	3	1.34	3.00
Oilseeds (*rabi*)	PC	4	1.34	2 .00
Pulses (*rabi*)	PC	1	0.50	0.20

7.5.5 Wage labour

The major income of a household comes from wage labour. About 75 per cent of the income is earned from this source. Most of wage labour is in agriculture, but 7 to 21 per cent of earning (depending on the village) is obtained from non-agricultural labour.

Table 7.8 shows that the three seasons, the labourers get most work in pre-*kharif* in Paschim Chepani, primarily because of HYV paddy (*boro*) cultivation which was started during the last few years after the river lift irrigation scheme was established. But in Madhya Boragari potato cultivation in *rabi* season is quite extensive (started after the irrigation was available) and as such the labourers get the maximum days of employment in this season. Potato cultivation is known in the area for a long time, and indigenous storage methods with air circulation have been developed as our fieldnotes show:

On our way back we saw an example of indigenous potato storing. The potato owner had stored 80 tons of potatoes from 22 *bighas* own land and 7 *bighas* rented land. He and five family members, and 7 to 8 labourers work in the land. He has a private shallow tube well. According to the official qualifications he may be classified as a rich peasant. From his jutestick house rises a TV antenna. Women of the house are busy drying stacks for fuel and making walls. His wife does not work in the fields. He came from Bangladesh in 1971 and could buy this property because he could sell his house and land in Bangladesh before migration.

TABLE 7.8: SEASONAL VARIATION IN EMPLOYMENT AS WAGE LABOURERS (1992-3)

Seasons	Village	Work force		No. of work days				Avg. days of work/person	
				AGL		NAGL			
		M	F	M	F	M	F	M	F
Pre-*kharif*	MB	28	29	1,685	626	153	0	66	22
	PC	24	23	1,483	951	293	19	74	42
Kharif	MB	28	29	1,304	589	205	0	54	20
	PC	24	23	1,218	497	245	17	61	22
Rabi	MB	28	29	1,962	1,177	222	0	78	41
	PC	24	23	768	476	706	10	61	21
Total		52	52	8,420	4,316	1,824	46	197	84

Note: AGL = agricultural labour; NAGL = non-agricultural labourer.

On the whole the labourers (both sexes) get, on average, the same number of days of employment in the two areas. In Madhya Boragari we had a talk with a female agricultural labourer engaged in potato harvesting:

Several women of poor and small farmers stated that they work also in the field in the command area. A talk with a female agricultural labourer revealed that she expects more wage labour because of the irrigation facility. Today she was called for work and she is harvesting potatoes; she started at 8 o'clock in the morning and takes her small children to the field. She belongs to a poor Muslim caste and earns 7 to 8 rupees a day. Her husband is also an agricultural labourer and earns 12 to 14 rupees a day. She has a small boy and a daughter. Her main problem is to survive because the daily wages earned are not at all sufficient for their daily basic needs.

Another feature of employment pattern is that a woman labourer gets less than half of the days a man is employed. The chances of their securing employment against competition of men is about 100:42, i.e. for every 100 days of employment of a man, a woman gets only 42 days. Moreover, the table shows that men could obtain 1,824 days, and women only 46 days of non-agricultural wage labour. These findings urge us the more to

TABLE 7.9: NUMBER OF DAYS OF WORK IN DIFFERENT SEASONS (1992-3)

(*no. of persons*)

Days of work	Pre-*kharif*				*Kharif*				*Rabi*			
	AGL		NAGL		AGL		NAGL		AGL		NAGL	
	M	F	M	F	M	F	M	F	M	F	M	F
Below 40	5	7	12	1	11	17	11	1	9	11	11	1
40-50	3	4	4	0	5	2	0	0	7	5	1	0
50-60	3	4	0	0	8	7	1	0	4	6	1	0
60-70	2	3	0	0	8	1	1	0	1	2	3	0
70-80	12	1	2	0	5	1	0	0	4	4	2	0
80-90	6	4	0	0	3	0	2	0	6	3	1	0
90-100	7	1	0	0	3	1	0	0	7	1	1	0
100+	5	3	0	0	1	0	0	0	4	2	1	0
Total	43	27	18	1	44	29	15	1	42	34	21	1

Note: AGL = agricultural labour; NAGL = non-agricultural labour.

initiate income generating activities and credit facilities for women in the area.

Table 7.9 shows how the labour force is distributed according to number of days of work a person gets in different seasons of the year (1992-3). As there is not much variation in average days of work of a person in the two samples of the villages, we have combined them in the table.

The table shows the difference in the employment pattern of men and women workers. The percentage of women getting employment for 60 days or more in a season is: pre-*kharif*—45 per cent; *kharif*—10 per cent; *rabi*—35 per cent. The corresponding employment rate for men is: pre-*kharif*—75 per cent; *kharif*—45 per cent; *rabi*—52 per cent. In the non-agricultural labour the share of the women workers is negligible.

From the preceding two tables, Tables 7.8 and 7.9, it becomes apparent that the agricultural labourers do not get work for about five and a half months for a male workers and nine months for a female worker. About 70 per cent of the respondents said that August to October are the most lean months. It is because transplantation of paddy seedlings and jute harvest have been completed by August/September and the harvesting of paddy starts only in November. Some respondents (40 per cent) said they have difficulty in finding work in the months of January-February. The paucity of work makes the life in a labourer's household difficult. The gap in the wage income and expenditure is partially met from the produce of the family farm for those who have it. Other means adopted are: to secure small loans from villagers, to buy goods on credit from grocers, to sell livestock or a tree or make an advance sale of labour.

Is the problem of unemployment realized by the landowning employers? Talks during field visits revealed that women-employers showed an awareness of the problem and stated to give alternative employment to labourers working for them in the peak season.

7.5.6 *Wage structure*

The wage structure in both the villages is much better than that prevailed in 1992-3 in the two village studied in the in-depth study. The minimum wage of Rs 10 per day was paid only to four women in *rabi* season. Most of the rest of labourers received wages ranging from Rs 15 to 30 for male workers and from Rs 10 to 20 for female workers. These figures correspond with the data we collected from the landowners side of wages given by them as described in Section 5.5. The mentioned wage includes the cost of a meal/tiffin or cash in lieu of it. The seasonal variation in wages is shown below in Table 7.10.

There is not any notable seasonal variation in wages. It appears that most of the male workers (50 per cent) have received wages between Rs 15-25 and women between Rs 10-20. The factors which determine the daily rate of wages of a worker are: the age of the worker—elderly persons get less wages; nature of work—ploughing demands higher wages and contract work which usually pays a worker more in a day than on daily rate basis.

While discussing the occupation of the landless labourers we have mentioned that in Paschim Chepani the male workers often find employment in the nearby railway yard (loading/unloading stone in wagons). The wage rate is often high, Rs 25 to 30+, depending on the nature of the contract. Under the contract system a labourer, who works under a contractor, works for longer hours to complete the work and this earns him double the normal wages for day. This is a lucrative job but such jobs do not come on a regular basis. In Paschim Chepani in the *rabi* season of 1992-3 about 500 such persondays of work were available.

As the wage rate fluctuates on the basis of work and season

TABLE 7.10: DAILY WAGE RATE (1992-3)
N = M-52; F-52

(no. of persons)

Daily wage rate (Rs)	Pre-*kharif*		*Kharif*		*Rabi*	
	M	F	M	F	M	F
Below 10	0	0	0	0	0	4
10-15	2	19	6	15	1	24
15-20	11	8	28	11	22	4
20-5	19	0	7	4	15	2
25-30	7	0	3	0	5	0
30+	4	0	1	0	3	0
Total	43	27	45	30	46	34

TABLE 7.11: AGRICULTURAL WORK PERFORMED BY THE LABOURERS
N = M-52; F-52

Sl. no.	Activities	Participation rate (%) M	F
1.	Land preparation (ploughing, levelling, etc.)	67	4
2.	Making bunds	58	25
3.	Seedbed preparation	12	0
4.	Plucking of seedlings	12	37
5.	Sowing/transplanting	77	60
6.	Weeding	80	48
7.	Washing/drying of jute	46	27
8.	Application of fertilizer/manure	56	19
9.	Application of insecticide/pesticide	42	0
10.	Irrigating field	15	4
11.	Protecting crops	6	0
12.	Harvesting	75	63
13.	Transplanting crops from field	35	8
14.	Threshing/winnowing	46	6
15.	Storing	27	19

some discussion on the work performed by the labourers will not be out of place. There is no migrant labour for the peak seasons; therefore the question of demand and supply affecting the wage rate does not seem to apply so far in the Terai project area. Looking at the list of tasks performed by the labourers of both sexes it becomes clear that the men usually perform what is perceived as 'the heavier tasks' and get paid more.

Table 7.11 shows the nature of agricultural activities performed by labourers in the two villages during 1992-3.

The differences between the nature of work of the two sexes are quite clear from the above table. Proportionately few women have been engaged who mostly worked to make bunds, plucked seedlings and did sowing, transplanting, weeding and harvesting. For application of fertilizer/manure and storing of crops very few of them were hired.

7.5.7 Child labour

We have earlier studied that a number of adolescent boys and girls are also engaged for work that requires to be completed in a short time. While in Madhya Boragari Muslim households six

TABLE 7.12: CHILD LABOUR EMPLOYMENT (1992-3)

Village	HHs	No. of child labourers		No. of days worked		Wages received (Rs)	
		M	F	M	F	M	F
MB	26	6	2	289	287	3,162	534
PC	20	2	6	274	110	4,478	440

boys and two girls were employed in 1992-3 from time to time, in Paschim Chepani from Rajbansi households two boys and six girls were employed during the same year.

Table 7.12 shows that the average daily wages for boys in Madhya Boragari comes to Rs 11 and Rs 16 in Paschim Chepani; the corresponding wages for girls is Rs 2 and Rs 4 per day. This shows the low value given to the work girls do. When we have a closer look at the activities carried out by boys and girls we see that this wage discrimination is very unwarranted.

–Activities of children

(1) Boys: potato sowing, weeding, transplanting, making channels, harvesting and storing potato (Madhya Boragari); ploughing, plucking of seedlings and transplanting, harvesting, tending cattle (Paschim Chepani).
(2) Girls: cutting of potato seeds for sowing, weeding, drying of jute, plucking of seedlings, sowing and harvesting potato (Madhya Boragari); transporting, plucking of paddyseedlings and transplantation, washing of jute, harvesting of pulses (Paschim Chepani).

Sometimes a family takes a job on contract, particularly transplanting and harvesting a particular plot of land. In that case the children of the household also work along with their parents. The days of work in Table 7.12 include such contract labour. Child labour of young boys and girls, usually between 10 and 15 years, is very common in landless labourer's household. Their earnings go to the maintenance of the family, at least its major share. They receive lower wages and also find work for far fewer days than the adult workers. Sometimes even much younger boys/girls are engaged for picking a harvest which requires many hands. In one such event in Paschim Chapani village we found at least 20-5 young children along with adults harvesting chillies. The remuneration paid was Rs 3 per bag of chillies (40 kg). A young child of 10 years could pick one bag in a day. The work was for only one day as the entire harvest had to be sent to the market as fresh as possible. Child labour is often engaged on such occasions. A child becomes a bread earner from his/her very young days. This to a large extent deters him/her from going to school and even if they are sent, absenteeism and dropping out from school is common.

7.5.8 Income, savings, debts and assets

The income of the landless labourers, per capita and annual household income, compares favourably with that of the sample labourers studied during the three-year period of the in-depth study. Let us first look at the per capita income of the labourers in 1992-3 according to the findings of the Sample Survey.

Table 7.13 shows that there is a marginal difference in the overall per capita income of labourers of two villages, but notable difference exists in the proportion of farm income: 15 per cent in Madhya Boragari, and 19 per cent in Paschim Chepani. There is also a difference in the contribution of agricultural labour to the total income of a person. It is higher, by 13 per cent, in the Madhya Boragari sample. The income from non-agricultural labour is quite

TABLE 7.13: PER CAPITA INCOME OF THE LABOURERS (1992-3)

Area	HHs	Population	Per capita income (Rs)	% of per capita income from			
				Wages		Farm	Others
				AGL	NAGL		
MB	26	108	2,001	67	7	15	11
PC	20	91	2,063	54	21	19	6
Total	46	199	2,029	61	14	17	8

Notes: AGL = agricultural labour; NAGL = non-agricultural labour.
'Others' include cart pulling, broker, stone breaking, selling of parched grains, fuel, milk, bamboo, etc.

high, 21 per cent in Paschim Chepani as against 7 per cent in Madhya Boragari. This is because of the availability of work in the railway yard explained earlier.

The per capita income of these two groups of labourers compares favourably with the per capita income of one group of labourers of the in-depth study. In one group of such labourers (river lift irrigation site in Paschim Harmati village) this income was Rs 2,028 in 1992-3; however, in the deep tube well site in Jamadarerbos the income was only Rs 1,586 in the year. The average per capita income of these two groups of labourers was Rs 1,871 (92-3) while the average in the sample survey is Rs 2,029. However there exists some difference in the amount of per capita income among labourers of different communities. The Muslims have Rs 2,047, Rajbansis Rs 2,042 and Hindus Rs 1,511. The higher incomes in these two samples (as compared with the in-depth samples) are possibly because of higher wages and extensive cultivation of at least two crops—HYV paddy, *boro*, in Paschim Chapani and potato in Madhya Boragari which provide more days of employment. The per capita income mentioned above is the average income of a person in a year including non-working population. There is some difference in this income from person to person as the Table 7.14 shows.

The conclusion that can be made from the above table is that the higher the income (except for five persons in the income range of Rs 3,000-35,000) of a person, the greater his share of

TABLE 7.14: DISTRIBUTION OF POPULATION ACCORDING TO PER CAPITA INCOME (1992-3)

Per capita income range (Rs)	Population		Per capita income (Rs)	% of per capita income from		
	No.	%		Wages	Farm	Others
1,000-1,500	51	(26)	1,224	81	9	10
1,500-2,000	57	(29)	1,688	79	11	10
2,000-2,500	48	(24)	2,252	74	16	10
2,500-3,000	25	(12)	2,682	67	23	10
3,000-3,500	5	(2.5)	3,172	98	11	1
3,500+	13	(6.5)	4,156	60	36	4
Avg. per capita	199		2,029	75	17	8

income from farm. About 55 per cent of the population have an income below the average per capita income.

A household's annual income from all sources has been taken in all our studies to determine the proportion of households that fall below the poverty line (below Rs 7,200 in a year with 1992 as base). It appears from Table 7.15 that 16 out of 46 households (35 per cent) were below the poverty line in 1992-3, some of them are even poorer than others in this group.

The proportion of households below the poverty line is evenly distributed among the two village groups (35 per cent), but there are more poor families in Paschim Chepani (Rs 4,000-6,000) than in Madhya Boragari. 61 per cent of Madhya Boragari and 50 per cent of Paschim Chepani households have an income between Rs 7,200 and 13,000. There are three households in the Paschim Chepani group which have incomes between Rs 13,000 and 23,000; only one such household exists in the Madhya Boragari group. We may infer that the economic condition of the landless

TABLE 7.15: DISTRIBUTION OF HOUSEHOLDS IN ANNUAL INCOME RANGES (1992-3)

Ranges (Rs)	Village	HHs	Pop.	% of HHs	% of income from Wages	Farm	Others
4,800-6,000	MB	4	14	16	95	3.70	1.30
	PC	5	19	25	85	11.00	4.00
6,000-7,200	MB	5	19	19	74	2.00	24.00
	PC	2	8	10	50	32.00	18.00
7,200-10,000	MB	11	51	42	80	9.00	11.00
	PC	6	26	30	78	20.00	2.00
10,000-13,000	MB	5	21	19	76	17.00	7.00
	PC	4	20	20	66	25.00	9.00
13,000-16,000	MB	0	0	0	0	0.00	0.00
	PC	2	10	10	79	12.00	9.00
16,000-20,000	MB	1	3	4	11	84.00	5.00
	PC	0	0	0	0	0.00	0.00
20,000-23,000	MB	0	0	0	0	0.00	0.00
	PC	1	8	5	79	14.00	7.00
Total	MB	26	108	100	74	15.00	11.00
	PC	20	91	100	75	19.00	6.00
Average	—	46	199	0	75	17.00	8.00

labourers in Paschim Chepani is a shade better than their counterpart in Madhya Boragari.

Despite the comparatively better economic condition of the landless households in the sample survey, about 80 per cent of the respondents in Paschim Chepani and 38 per cent in Madhya Boragari said they did not have enough to sustain their family through the year (1992-3).

Unlike the situation prevailing among the landless labourers of the in-depth study, the savings position of some of the households in these two village samples looks somewhat better. The majority of the households do not have any savings worth mentioning, but some have as Table 7.16 shows. Even some households have given money on loan or have taken tiny plots of cultivable land on mortgage.

There are some households who have given cash loans and mortgaged-in some land. So at best we can say about 25-30 per cent of households have some savings. Cash at home amounts to Rs 50-900. The notable feature of the above table is that seven households had sufficient savings to invest in mortgaging of land. The amount of savings is slightly higher among the Madhya Boragari group of labourers.

A far bigger amount of debt than what could be saved, exists among the landless households. The larger part of this debts is due of taking 'development loans' from the bank to buy cattle or to set up small business. The details are shown in Table 7.17.

TABLE 7.16: SAVINGS POSITION OF THE LANDLESS LABOURERS (1992-3) (Rs)

Village	Cash at home		Cash given on loan		Cash given to mortgage land	Total savings
	Amount	HHs	Amount	HHs		
MB	2,120	8	3,100	2	2,800 (4) (.60 acres)	8,020
PC	1,834	5	505	2	5,000 (3) (.50 acres)	7,339
Total	3,954	13	3,605	4	7,800 (7)	15,359

Note: ( ) = No. of HHs.

TABLE 7.17: DEBT SITUATION OF THE LANDLESS LABOURERS (1992-3)

Village	Source	Amount (Rs)	HHs	Purpose	Utilization
MB	Private	1,800	3	Domestic needs and marriage, medical treatment	Same as purpose
PC	Private	600	1	Medical treatment	Same as purpose
PC	Temple fund	700	2	Cultivation	Same as purpose
MB	Bank	4,700	1	To purchase cow and goat	Purchased cow and balance used at home
PC	Bank	25,500	6	Business of parched grains	Mortgaged-in land, Cultivation, repayment of old loans, marriage and home consumption.
PC	Bank	18,000	3	Home crafts	Mortgaged-in land, repayment of old loans, funeral expenses.

The total amount of debt of Paschim Chepani labourers is about Rs 45,000, but Rs 5,500 only among the Madhya Boragari labourers. Bank loan was possible as the debtors belong to the Scheduled Caste community who have mostly spent the money on land and other purposes. Only one person in the Madhya Boragari group has utilized the money to purchase a cow for which the loan was taken. In addition to the above instances of debt one labourer in Madhya Boragari has mortgaged out a small piece of land (0.07 acre) to a neighbour for Rs 150. The amount was spent to meet domestic needs.

The asset position of the 46 households in this sample does not vary much from that of the landless labourers studied during the in-depth study (Report no. 11, Part II). Table 7.18 gives a general idea about the state of their living condition.

Apart from having a small living room, some households do not even have a separate place to cook their meal. Furniture consisting of a wooden bed and/or a table-chair is owned by only half of the households. To have a cycle, a common mode of transport in village, is rare; only one out of 46 households has one. Milch cows and bullocks are possessed by only very few

TABLE 7.18: ASSET POSITION OF THE LANDLESS LABOURERS (1992-3)
N = 46 (HHs)

Asset	No.	No. of owning HHs	% of owning HHs
Milch cow	8	8	17
Bullock	4	2	4
Goat	43	16	35
Calves	19	14	30
Fowl	116	22	48
Ducks	23	2	4
Furniture	23	23	50
Brass utensils	22	7	15
Stainless steel utensils	344	46	100
Cycle	1	1	2
Radio	4	4	8
Watch (male)	5	5	11
Petromax	1	1	2
Living condition			
Living room	49	46	100
Kitchen	35	35	76
Cattle shed	13	13	28

houses; even goats, very common animals and an important investment for difficult times are owned by less than half the households. The poor living condition of the landless labourers are reflected in the above description.

Summarizing the above we can say that irrigation has undoubtedly given the men of landless households more work, as also the results of in-depth study shows, but still a lot more needs to be done. Schemes to benefit them directly, securing employment throughout the year, particularly for the economically disadvantaged women, need to be devised. Agricultural development through small-scale irrigation can only partly solve the problems as the employment generated is seasonal.

7.6 MANAGING A HOUSEHOLD

After the detailed statistical presentation of the socio-economic conditions of landless households in the project area this part of the report deals with domestic labour and the status of landless women. What is her decision making power in the household?

Whether a woman works for wages or not, she has to do the

cooking, fetch water and collect the fuel. It may be sometimes her husband or grown up son who helps her to fetch fuel, but if it has to be collected from the field generally the woman and her daughters do the job. Other heavy domestic chores of the woman include—fetching water, washing clothes, preparing meals, pounding of rice, making parched grains. The jobs in which the husband or a son may give a helping hand are—selling milk, fruits and vegetables (occasional), looking after the cattle or other animals, irrigating the kitchen garden, grazing animals (usually the task of small boys and sometimes girls).

The main source of drinking water is a *pukka* well, located 10-20 m from the house. These wells are mostly owned by others; 13 households (30 per cent) collect water from handpumps, also two of which are owned by them. Almost anything dry is used for fuel—leaves, jute sticks, dung cake, dry plants, bamboo roots, twigs. About 65 per cent of households reported that they buy fuel particularly in the rainy months when field collection yields poor results.

Child care is a woman's responsibility. She is often assisted by her grown up daughters or other female members of the household. But as the landless labourer's family is small, she has often to look for a neighbour to take care of the child during her absence, if there is no one else in the house.

We have seen, that compared to a man, a woman's chance of finding work for wages is less than half (Table 7.8). The average employment in a year is 84 days for a woman, so most of them are desperately searching work for the greater part of year. About 80 per cent of the adult women said they have no hesitation to work outside the home. Those few who said 'no' to the question offered a host of reasons—'husband/mother-in-law did not like her to work outside', 'nursing a child', 'no one else to look after children when she was away', 'working outside being below the prestige of the family' and 'physical weakness'. But more than half of those who normally work for wages (as and when work is available) said that working outside clashes with domestic responsibilities.

A wage earning woman does not have full freedom to spend her earnings the way she likes. Only about 27 per cent of such earners said that they can spend their wages in whatever way they like; the others offered a variety of reasons to explain the lack of this freedom as 'husband does not approve', 'quarrel may break out between husband and wife', 'neighbours may abuse such free spending women', 'it is a social custom to hand over the earning to the husband' or, 'the fear of being cheated in the market if anything is purchased alone'. The outcome is that 31 out of 37 respondent women hand over their money to their husbands or sons. This included a few women who said that they could spend the money as per their desire. A woman's earning are spent on food, clothing for members of the family and home improvement. A little money that is left may be spent on toilet articles.

It has been stated earlier that most of the women labourers do (when available) farm labour, very few of them find work in non-agricultural jobs. Wage discrimination is notorious even if they are engaged in the same type of jobs. The stereotype explanation of the employer that 'a woman cannot do heavy jobs', or 'their output is low and so they must be paid less' ignores the fact that women do heavy labour (transplanting of rice) and work for long hours.

Though women in matters of spending depend heavily on their husbands' consent there are a few occasions when in family matters the husband or wife takes a decision ignoring the other partner. Usually they jointly take the decision. In our sample survey we asked one adult woman from each of the 46 households to express her views on a number of household matters. We asked who takes the decision: men, women, or both about food purchase; purchase/sale of livestock; purchase of clothing; purchase of fodder; sale of harvest; house repair/improvement; securing loans; repaying loans; general household expenses.

It seems in some matters the women in landless households have a slight edge over their husbands (purchasing of food and cloth), though most of the decisions are jointly taken, except perhaps in matters regarding sale of harvest and securing/repayment of loans. In this sense these women are better placed than their counterpart in a farmer's household. The plausible explanation is that women as wage earners enjoy a better status vis-a-vis other women. The family being nuclear also contributes to a survival strategy in which husband, wife and children are dependent on each other. The economic contribution that a woman makes to the landless family perhaps allows her to move more freely than other women. This is reflected in the fact that about half the women we interviewed (N = 46) said that they often visit the weekly market in company with other women whenever the need arises. The other half of the respondents (particularly the Muslims) said they never go to market though they go to work whenever the occasion arises.

In both the villages a Beneficiary Committee has been elected to manage the water. It seems that there is one male landless labourer representative in the BC of Paschim Chepani. Landless women have no opportunity to make their voice heard and do not have any control on the management of the water, while that is a matter of survival for them, perhaps more for them than any other category of women in the project area. Therefore the suggestion to elect at least two women (a wife of a marginal/small farmer and a landless woman) in the water-users' committee to defend the needs and interests of women seems valid and useful. In practice this will be a problem as the assumption that 'women keep silent in public meetings' is firmly rooted in circles of male decision makers. However, during visits we came across landless women who were very vocal and could articulate their interests very well.

7.7 PERCEPTION OF LANDLESS LABOURERS OF EFFECTS OF IRRIGATION

The questionnaire contains a very specific question to the landless labourers to ascertain what, in their view, has been the consequence of irrigation. Has it helped them to improve their economic condition? Did they find more work? The overwhelming response was 'yes' (90 per cent). As to how it has affected their livelihood, a variety of answers were given, which are tabulated in Table 7.19 according to the frequency of the answer.

There is no doubt that the opinion of the landless labourers is very positive with regard to the benefit they have received

TABLE 7.19: PERCEPTION OF EFFECTS OF IRRIGATION
N = 46

No.	Nature of answer	No.	%
1.	No. of work days increased	33	72
2.	Rate of wages increased	28	61
3.	Water available to cultivate own crops	18	39
4.	More wages give us more food	9	20
5.	Agricultural labourers' condition has improved	6	13
6.	With increased wages livestock can be purchased	5	11
7.	More women are getting employment	4	9
8.	Increase in wages helped us to take land on lease/ mortgage	3	7
9.	Potato cultivation possible on large scale	3	7
10.	Multiple crops can be produced	2	4
11.	Additional hut could be constructed with increased wage	2	4
12.	Irrigation has benefitted land owners	2	4
13.	Increase in output rate of crops	1	2
14.	More potato production has given me good income	1	2

Note: A person may have given more than one answer.

from irrigation. Seventy-two per cent stated that their work days increased, and 61 per cent that the wage rate increased. Unfortunately, these perceptions can not be presented in a gender specific way. We could also not substantiate those perceptions in the in-depth study.

7.8 LOOKING AT THE FUTURE

In view of the hard survival strategy we were curious to know more about the vision of the landless labourers of the future. We made a little probing in this direction, armed with the questionnaire and open-ended discussions, both among men and women. It transpires that all their hopes and aspirations centre around improvement of their immediate economic condition by getting regular work in the fields. Next in order of priority are—to purchase livestock, to lease/mortgage/purchase a little land in the command area and to get a loan from the government to set up a small business. No one said anything about educating their children.

In this sample no couple was found to practise any family planning although we spoke with landless labourers who went on their own initiative to the hospital for a sterilization. More than half of the married young women wanted to have information on family planning, child care, nutrition and home improvement. They wished to have wooden beds, an additional hut with a tin roof and some utensils. Certainly not very high expectations by any standard!

The economic condition of the landless labourers as reflected in the above study has partially improved with the introduction of irrigation in the area. But their social condition has not much changed. Children lack education, child labour exists, girls are married early, to name a few things. It calls for a concerted effort of social action.

NOTE

1. Average landless household income in the sample survey was of comparable magnitude: Rs 2,029 per capita annually.

8. Irrigation and Empowerment

8.1 OPERATIONALIZATION OF EMPOWERMENT

In this chapter, we will deal with the impact of the irrigation project on gender relations and gender ideological aspects. So far we have analysed the material impact on the lives and work of women, but what of the unequal power relations between men and women. The underlying question as mentioned in Chapter 1 is, is it possible to pursue empowerment, or autonomy, of women through irrigation development? Or, to reflect on the historical chapter, is it possible to strengthen the heroines of the past who became the beneficiaries of the Terai project so that they can themselves struggle against patriarchal forces and fight for better living conditions? This is not only a matter of social justice and the right of gender equality, but if achieved, it will highly contribute to the development of households, the village, the state and India in general. Women have many capacities and skills which cannot develop as they are curtailed and restricted by male prejudices and assumptions and perpetuated by all kinds of associative notions on the inferiority of women.

'Autonomy' and 'empowerment' are ambitious theoretical concepts of development cooperation policies. It is our view that as long societies are patrilocal, patrilineal and, in particular, patriarchal these concepts are very difficult to realize in practice. Male dominance in decision making is an almost universal characteristic of patriarchal societies. In view of that we have assessed how far a small-scale irrigation project can contribute to the process of empowerment by reducing this male dominance. The assumed underlying links are that because of irrigation, the participation of women in agricultural operations and productive labour will increase, which in the long run will make her role in the economic sphere stronger and consequently her decision making power in the household. The questions on decision making are included in the in-depth study to gain some indication of the character and extent of inequality in gender relations, and as parameters to indicate possible changes over time. We are fully aware that the period of study is too short to expect a fundamental change in attitudes, norms and values in prevailing gender relations and ideology. Nevertheless, we can be alert to trace a worsening of the gender power relations in time.

The sample survey questionnaire contains a special section on women of the interviewed households. The purpose of these to get the women's perceptions of non-farm work, decision making, control over income, consequence of having a handpump and freedom in the general. However, we have to keep in mind that these replies have been filled in by male interviewers. In other words we wanted to know to what extent the project irrigation intervention has initiated a process of potential strengthening of women in earning cash outside the home, more decision making, more control over the fruits of their labour, and more independence in a general way.

Let us first consider the group of wage earning women, and analyse whether change has occurred in perception of going out of the home to work.

The findings of the in-depth study showed that over the years women have participated more in agriculture on the family farm, the exception being the women of the handpump beneficiaries. In this category we assume a slight adaptation of *purdah* norms to keep women in the house as soon as circumstances allow: a process that is called domestication in women's studies.

We have found that very few women are also engaged in non-farm occupations which give them cash. Only 13, 12 and 10 per cent of adult women belonging to the marginal class of river lift irrigation, deep tube well and handpump beneficiary household schemes respectively work as wage labourers. The proportion of such wage workers is very insignificant among the small farmers, and nil in the other two classes. Besides working as wage labourers, some women of the two lower classes of farmers work in a variety of occupations which can be characterized as self-employment and trade: as selling of milk, *muri/chira* making,

TABLE 8.1: DO THE WOMEN OF THE HOUSEHOLD WORK OUTSIDE? *(in %)*

Class	RLI Yes	DTW Yes	HTW Yes	STW Yes	PDW Yes	Total
Marginal	28	23	20	0	8	79
	(222)	(124)	(666)	(15)	(26)	(1,053)
Small	6	8	10	11	0	35
	(90)	(38)	(120)	(37)	(16)	(301)
Middle	0	1	0	0	0	1
	(34)	(10)	(27)	(15)	(7)	(93)
Large	0	0	0	0	0	0
	(8)	(4)	(2)	(7)	(0)	(21)

Note: Only the 'Yes' answers have been computed in the table. The rest are 'negative' answers. Figures in the ( ) denote the N value of the respondents.

husking of paddy, spinning and weaving, selling of fuel, *bidi*-binding, basket/broom-stick making, mat making, selling in the market, stitching and embroidery work, tailoring/knitting.

In the sample survey the percentage of women doing wage-labour outside the home was more than in the in-depth study. Interesting percentage variation was observed in the answers from women of different classes as Table 8.1 shows.

It is seen that only 7.5 per cent of the women of the marginal class households actually work outside their home for wages. In the small farmers' households, 8.6 per cent women work outside for wages. In the middle and big farmers' households there is hardly any woman who works outside for wages. This is understandable. Economic condition of the family and women working for wages are directly correlated in an economic and social way. In this sense women of the poorer households not only provide economic support to the family but also are more free to accept wage earning jobs.

A question was asked to the women of the households in the sample survey: 'do the women of your household work outside the home/village? If "no" state the reasons'. Most of the women respondents answered, 'no'. The respondents gave four reasons (pre-set in the questionnaire), which arranged according to weightage, are: 'it is below the prestige of the family', 'young women should not go outside the home freely', 'social/religious restriction on movement of women', or 'any other cause' namely, 'it clashes with domestic work', 'children are not properly cared for', 'health does not permit', etc. A respondent often gave more than one reason to explain her attitude. Besides the more practical considerations, the answers reveal that the *purdah* restrictions play an important role.

There is hardly any difference in the response among women of different classes. To the question, 'if you work outside the home for wages what are the problems you face', most of the women wage earners said that they face no problems, and they enjoy working outside in a team. But others said that when women go outside to work the esteem of the family will come down, and it creates domestic problems particularly in regard to looking after the children. It is for this reason that women with very small children rarely go to work unless there is someone in the house to take care of the children. It was clear from the discussion with the women that notwithstanding the social and familial constraints women like to work for wages, at least a good section of them, as it gives them some freedom and economic independence.

The implementation of the small-scale irrigation devices has created more job opportunities for members of landless households. Though the men have cornered the larger share of additional persondays of employment (as the in-depth study shows) the women have also found somewhat more employment in this type of work. To reduce the empowerment problem for landless we could consider the handing over of suitable adjusted irrigation devices to groups of landless women to enable them to sell irrigation water (van Koppen 1995, 1997).

8.2 CHANGING ATTITUDES TO WAGE LABOUR

Although these findings show that a small group of women enjoys a relative economic independence, the general attitude of women towards working outside the house for wages remains negative as the following data collected in the in-depth study will show.

Table 8.2 reveals that in 1992-3, 69 per cent of the women have a negative attitude towards wage labour outside the home, and 31 per cent have a positive attitude. However there is a clear

TABLE 8.2: ATTITUDE OF WOMEN TOWARDS WORKING OUTSIDE FOR WAGES

Scheme	Year	Respondents	Positive attitude		Negative attitude	
			No.	%	No.	%
RLI	89-90	60	17	28	43	72
	92-3	61	29	48	32	52
DTW	89-90	74	13	18	61	82
	92-3	72	25	35	47	65
HTW	89-90	83	20	24	63	76
	92-3	80	13	16	67	84
Total	89-90	217	50	23	167	77
	92-3	213	67	32	146	69

trend that the positive attitude is increasing over the years of the in-depth study. In particular in the river lift irrigation and deep tube well schemes, more women are positive than three years ago. Only in the handpump scheme do women show a less positive attitude over the years of study. Complementarily the negative attitude came down in river lift irrigation and deep tube well areas but increased among handpump beneficiary household women.

The negative trend in the opinion of marginal farm women in the handpump schemes is difficult to explain, when the general trend is towards more freedom of movement of women. The only plausible explanation is that the handtube respondents are influenced by the Hindu upper-caste gender ideology, and assume that it will give more status to state that women should not work outside the home for wages. Perhaps a mild form of Sanskritization and even a slight acceptation of domestication values might be traced here. Consequently, adoption of *purdah* notions among them might have influenced their replies. Moreover, the respondents come from three disparate areas and the local customs vary from one area to another. It is these customs which finally influence the attitude of women towards working for wages outside the home.

On the other hand in the same target group of handpump households in the Terai project we met women who are free and independent, and do not all accept the Hindu behaviour rules.

On the contrary they earn money by smuggling goods as torches, pants and shirts from Nepal. They know that the customs officers have to be bribed. As carriers they get ten per cent of the value of smuggled goods.

8.3 CONTROL OF WOMEN'S EARNED MONEY

8.3.1 Male permission

To know more about the independence of money earning women, we asked, 'how far they had control over their own earned money'. Could they spend it independently?

The figures in Table 8.3 indicate that the majority of women can spend money independently, and their percentage has increased over the years (86 to 91 per cent). 71 per cent of the women in 1989-90 and 80 per cent of the women in 1992-3 replied

TABLE 8.3: INDEPENDENCE/CONTROL OVER ONE'S OWN MONEY

Questions	Year	YES							
		RLI		DTW		HTW		Total	
		N=9 (89-90) N=12 (92-3)		N=15 (89-90) N=12 (92-3)		N=25 (89-90) N=21 (92-3		N=49 (89-90) N=45 (92-3)	
		No.	%	No.	%	No.	%	No.	%
1. Can you spend the money you earn or your own money independently?	89-90	6	67	11	73	25	100	42	86
	92-3	9	75	11	92	21	200	41	91
2. If you want to spend some of money for personal use can you spend it independently?	89-90	6	67	11	73	18	72	35	71
	92-3	9	75	10	83	17	81	36	80
3. Do you have to ask your husband or any other person for personal use of your earning?	89-90	3	33	4	27	7	28	14	29
	92-3	3	25	2	17	4	19	9	20

that they can also spend money independently for their personal use. Only 20 per cent (29 per cent in 89-90) of them state that they have to seek permission of their husband, or any other person for spending earned money for their personal use. This indicates that wage earning women have a reasonably independent position. However, we have to consider for what purposes the women spend their wages.

8.3.2 Type of spending

When we look at Table 8.4 at the forms of how the women spend their own earned money we find in line with outcome of many other empirical women's studies that 84 per cent spend on daily food; 69 per cent purchase also cloth and 62 per cent on home improvements.

There is an increase over the three years of study in the percentage of women who purchase also toilet articles from their own earnings (35 per cent in 1989-90 and 47 per cent in 1992-3. Also the spending on education of children paid from the earnings of the mother has gone up. These two last items show that it is possible to meet some expenses beyond direct survival.

TABLE 8.4: FORMS OF SPENDING ONE'S OWN INCOME

Expenditure on	Year	YES							
		RLI		DTW		HTW		Total	
		N=9 (89-90) N=12 (92-3)		N=15 (89-90) N=12 (92-3)		N=25 (89-90) N=21 (92-3		N=49 (89-90) N=45 (92-3)	
		No.	%	No.	%	No.	%	No.	%
Purchase of	89-90	7	78	10	67	25	100	42	86
food items	92-3	11	92	10	83	17	81	38	84
Purchase of	89-90	8	89	10	67	15	60	33	67
clothing	92-3	11	92	9	75	11	52	31	69
Home improve-	89-90	7	78	6	40	18	72	31	63
ment	92-3	8	67	8	67	12	57	28	62
Purchase of	89-90	2	22	5	33	10	40	17	35
toilet articles	92-3	5	42	9	75	7	33	21	47
Education of	89-90	2	22	3	20	5	20	10	20
children	92-3	3	25	5	42	4	19	12	27
Any	89-90	3	33	0	0	9	36	12	24
other	92-3	2	17	3	25	1	5	6	13

TABLE 8.5: VISIT TO WEEKLY MARKETS

Scheme	Year	Frequency of visits									
		Regularly		Sometimes		Seldom		Never		Total	
		No.	%	No	.%	No.	%	No.	%	No.	%
RLI	89-90	2	3	25	42	25	42	8	13	60	100
	92-3	6	10	20	32	12	20	23	38	61	100
DTW	89-90	7	10	19	26	46	62	2	2	74	100
	92-3	5	7	27	38	39	55	0	0	71	100
HTW	89-90	5	6	54	65	19	23	5	6	83	100
	92-3	3	4	55	69	20	25	2	2	80	100
Total	89-90	14	6	98	46	90	41	15	7	217	100
	92-3	14	7	102	48	71	33	25	12	212	100

8.4 WHO IS GOING TO THE MARKET?

Another indicator to assess the independence of women was data on their freedom of movement. Therefore it was asked if they frequently visit the weekly markets; 7 per cent replied that they go regularly to weekly markets, 48 per cent go sometimes, and 33 per cent seldom; 12 per cent of the women never attend weekly markets.

Table 8.5 shows that in the river lift irrigation scheme a high percentage of women (38) never go to weekly markets. This may be due to the relatively high number of Muslim women among the river lift irrigation beneficiaries. The findings on the purpose of visiting weekly markets in Table 8.6 show that selling of agricultural crops is only 8 per cent of the women. The majority (68 per cent) just go to the market for recreation and to buy things (62 per cent); 24 per cent of the women state that they go to the market to meet friends.

8.5 WHO DECIDES IN AGRICULTURAL MATTERS?

We included several questions on the decision making in the household regarding agricultural activities, and family matters in the questionnaires to have a better insight in the prevailing gender power relations and gender ideology in the project area.

We shall examine first the data collected on agricultural decision making by the women in the river lift irrigation, deep

TABLE 8.6: PURPOSE OF VISIT TO WEEKLY MARKETS

Scheme	Year	Purpose of visit								
		Selling		Buying		Meeting friends		Recreation		
		No.	%	No.	%	No.	%	No.	%	
RLI	89-90	5	10	46	89	10	19	23	44	N=52
	92-3	5	9	27	47	8	14	17	30	N=57
DTW	89-90	1	1	40	56	7	10	55	76	N=72
	92-3	4	6	36	51	25	35	65	92	N=71
HTW	89-90	15	19	46	58	21	27	54	88	N=79
	92-3	7	9	66	83	16	20	59	74	N=80
Total	89-90	21	10	132	65	38	19	132	65	N=203
	92-3	16	8	129	62	49	24	141	68	N=208

Note: Most respondents have stated more than one purpose of visit to weekly market.

tube well and handpump beneficiary household combined, and second the decision making on family matters in the same schemes.

Table 8.7 shows that men are dominant in agricultural decision making. Only nine per cent, at the maximum of the agricultural decisions are exclusively taken by women. Almost 90 per cent of the agricultural decisions is taken by men for which they consult their women 'often', 'sometimes' or 'not at all'. Decisions exclusively taken by men can be traced in the column in which women have stated that they are not consulted at all. The figures fluctuate from 70 per cent in decisions on application of pesticide and application of fertilizers. The corresponding figures in the base-line study for application of fertilizer was 60 per cent which has changed to 51 per cent in 1992-3. These decisions, which are connected with the use of new technologies in agriculture are obviously dominated by men. It is therefore surprising that the application of pesticide is also a decision which scores nearest to the highest in the row of decisions exclusively taken by women, and shows an increase in comparison with the base-line study.

Nine per cent of the women decide exclusively at what time the harvesting should be done. Here we can also trace an increase in decision making power compared with the base-line study. However, a remarkable decline of decision making by exclusively

TABLE 8.7: AGRICULTURAL DECISION MAKING BY WOMEN (RLI, DTW AND HTW HOUSEHOLDS) N (89-90) = 217 N(92-93) = 212

Decisions on	Exclusively by women		Men consult with women: Often		Sometimes		not at all		Undecided	
	(a)	(b)	(a)	(b)	(a)	(b)	(a)	(b)	(a)	(b)
1. Time of ploughing	3	5	10	8	40	46	46	41	1	0
2. Time of planting	3	1	18	10	53	47	26	42	0	0
3. Time of transplanting	4	2	23	19	46	50	26	29	1	0
4. Area to be cultivated (paddy)	3	2	12	11	43	49	42	38	0	0
5. Area to be cultivated (other crops)	12	3	16	12	46	57	26	28	0	0
6. Type of seed to be used	4	4	10	8	39	40	47	48	0	0
7. Application of pesticide	2	8	4	1	24	20	70	70	1	0
8. Cleaning of channels	2	2	5	12	33	41	59	45	1	0
9. Time of weeding	3	3	25	25	49	45	23	27	0	0
10. Time of harvesting	4	9	17	23	49	54	30	14	0	0
11. Application of fertilizer	2	6	9	6	28	36	60	51	1	0
12. Time of irrigation	2	3	14	23	48	44	35	30	1	0
13. Marketing the harvest	5	3	13	25	39	42	42	30	1	0

Note: All decimals rounded off (a) = 89-90; (b) = 92-3

women can be traced in decisions as what crop to grow on what area of land. Decisions on marketing of the harvest, time of irrigation, time of weeding, time of transplantation are 'often taken in consultation' with the women.

Generally speaking there is a slight tendency that women are 'somewhat' more consulted on agricultural decisions in 1992-3 than during the time of the base-line. The Table 8.8 shows that the agricultural decision making has not much changed since the base-line. Concluding, we can state that the unequal gender relations have not worsened during the period of study, and that there is a slight trend that women are 'sometimes' more consulted. These outcomes more or less hide that it is likely that women, although not the formal decision makers in agricultural activities, exert their social influence in a more informal way.

TABLE 8.8: DECISION MAKING IN FAMILY MATTERS

Decisions	RLI/DTW/HTW households								Landless labourers							
	N = 217 (89-90)				N = 212 (92-3)				N = 30 (89-90)				N = 26 (92-3)			
	Men		Women		Both		Undecided		Men		Women		Both		Undecided	
	(a)	(b)	(a)	(b)	(a)	(b)	(a)	(b)	(a)	(b)	(a)	(b)	(a)	(b)	(a)	(b)
1. Food to purchase	7.	1	10	3	82	95	1	1	43	7	13	19	43	73	0	0
2. House repair/ improvement	17	5	4	2	79	93	1	0	43	12	10	15	47	73	0	0
3. Purchase/sale of livestock	29	26	5	2	61	60	5	12	36	27	0	8	37	38	27	27
4. Purchasing clothing	10	15	7	4	82	81	1	0	30	8	17	19	50	73	3	0
5. Purchasing fodder	22	12	8	2	60	79	10	7	23	12	7	19	37	38	33	31
6. Harvest to be sold	33	19	6	2	60	73	1	6	33	27	7	11	37	46	23	16
7. Securing bank loan	31	33	3	2	55	38	11	27	17	27	13	4	27	31	43	38
8. Repayment of loan	26	32	5	2	43	37	26	29	23	27	10	4	23	35	44	34
9. Other household expenditure	14	4	4	4	81	88	1	4	43	8	13	19	37	73	7	0

Note: (a) = 89-90; (b) = 92-3.

The following field notes illustrate the informal decision making power women have when conditions allow.

RLI, Paschim Chapani.

The research assistant Narayan Ghosh, who is conducting the sample survey in a village, stays in the village with a family and we had a talk with the mother of the house. In the enormous compound four brothers and one son of a brother live, each in nuclear families: they have separate household economies. The host family of Mr Ghosh has improved their economic condition in a remarkable way due to the use of irrigation water and the entrepreneurial skills of the wife of the household. The man of the household came in 1955 from Bangladesh and his wife was brought from there to marry him. They have three children. They got a handpump under the Dutch Programme 5 to 6 years ago when they possessed 7 *bighas* of land. With the profits of selling vegetables they bought another 3 *bighas* in the command area of the River Lift Irrigation. They used irrigation water from the River Lift Irrigation and with the surplus profits of the 10 *bighas* they could buy another 5 *bighas* of land. Now they have 15 *bighas*, that is 5 acres of which 3.3 is cultivable [the rest is homestead, bamboo-bush, pond, waterland] and are obviously well-off. The cropping intensity has gone up from two to three crops. New crops they grow are *boro* and mustard oil. They have invested 50 per cent of their profits in agricultural inputs and 50 per cent in social/domestic assets like cloth, food and education of children. They have shifted the handpump from their land, and use it only for drinking water and other domestic purposes. The father of the household earns an additional Rs 50 per month as health guide at a Primary Health Centre. It is obvious that the wife of the house runs the farm. She decides what crops are to be grown, and when to be planted. She approaches the Secretary of the Water Users Committee to release the water for her land. She pays the water rate to him in case her husband is not there and does not go to the Block Development Officer's office. She states that her workload has increased for two reasons: she has to supervise the work of the wage labourers and to cook for them; and she has more crops to store, clean, and sell. She states that the wage for male and female labourers is the same, because the female agricultural labourers demand Rs 10, two heavy meals, and 0.5 kg rice. She cooks one rice and one *chapati* meal for the labourers. At the moment she has hired five men harvest labourers for 0.7 acre wheat. She ensures that certain landless families will come in peak time, by giving labour in lean times [contract system]. She has her own money and savings account. She sells cabbage, potato and rice from the land 'in the absence of her husband'. She enjoys the fact that she can support the economy of the household, and can contribute to a good education of her daughter. She does not know if there is a Mahila Mandal in the village, but it is a surprise that her son of ten years tells us that he knows that there is a Mahila Samity of the Left Party. They have no TV or newspaper: they listen to the radio of one of the brothers for world news [she is illiterate and her husband studied to Class IV]. They went to Bihar and Assam on a pilgrimage.

8.6 WHO DECIDES IN FAMILY MATTERS?

Most of the decisions in family matters are made by men and women together. There is a trend that over the three years of the in-depth study the decisions taken by both have increased, except those that relate to the securing and repayment of loans. When we look at the decisions taken exclusively by women we see that the percentage of women who did so in 1989-90 came down, a trend which is also shown in the decisions exclusively taken by men, except again the matters that relate to bank affairs. We could cautiously conclude that there is more consultation and communication between men and women in the household on relevant family decisions to be taken. The separate gender fields of decision making are eroding somewhat, but may be replaced by new ones like the securing of bank loans.

What does the sample survey show on decision making in family matters?

In a strong patriarchal society as in the project area we expected that men would dominate over women in the decision making process. But in reality it is not quite so. The women take decisions in many matters, particularly in regard to running of the household. The dominant trend is clear that in almost all matters concerning home and finance decisions are taken jointly by men and women. This observation also supports the findings of the in-depth study.

Table 8.9 shows that according to the women respondents, except in matters of securing/repayment of loans, which are frequently decided by men, men and women join together and take decisions in all other matters.

In sum it cannot be said that irrigation has empowered women

TABLE 8.9: DECISION MAKING IN THE HOUSEHOLD IN THE SAMPLE SURVEY N=1,478

Decisions in the Households	Taken by			
	Men	Women	Both	No reply
Foods to purchase	126	278	1,038	36
House repair/improvement	213	125	1,106	34
Purchase/Sale of livestock	325	45	966	142
Purchase of clothing	148	83	1,189	58
Purchase of fodder for livestock	380	25	617	456
Harvest to be sold	482	31	889	76
Securing loans	506	16	448	508
Repayment of loans	436	16	519	507
Daily household expenditure	147	284	952	95
Arranging for marriage of son/daughter	46	14	772	646
Expenditure on marriage feast	53	13	758	654
Expenditure on other purchases during marriage for bride/bridegroom	61	13	742	662

to achieve a partnership role in the decision making process. The economic contribution that a woman makes by way of her increased labour participation on own farm have perhaps contributed to a better status. Increased irrigation has enlarged the workload for both men and women but also raised the production and income level. And it is in this sense it may be said that irrigation has strengthened women, at least some of them, to secure a more prominent role in agriculture, which in turn might enhance their participation in the decision making process.

8.7 CHANGING PERCEPTIONS OF AGRICULTURAL PROBLEMS

In the previous it is shown that there is a higher participation of women in agriculture, and that their formal and informal influence in the agricultural decision making has somewhat improved as men tend to consult them more.

The base-line data point to the fact that women have also a high awareness of agricultural problems and how to overcome them. It is therefore interesting that over the three years of study there is a change in perception of the women regarding the weightage given to choices for increasing agricultural production.

TABLE 8.10: WEIGHTAGE GIVEN TO CHOICES FOR INCREASING AGRICULTURAL PRODUCTION*

Scheme	Year	Choices							
		1		2		3		4	
		No.	%	No.	%	No.	%	No.	%
RLI	89-90	47	78	23	47	6	10	5	8
	92-3	40	66	39	64	42	69	45	74
DTW	89-90	70	95	65	88	59	80	70	95
	92-3	46	65	44	62	68	96	65	92
HTW	89-90	65	78	69	83	35	42	30	36
	92-3	64	80	68	85	67	84	40	50

Notes: N (89-90) - RLI = 60, DTW = 74, HTW = 83.
N (92-93) - RLI = 61, DTW = 71, HTW = 80.
*a respondent has given more than one choice according to priority.
1 = By irrigation.
2 = By having more land.
3 = By using improved seeds/fertilizer.
4 = By getting assistance from government.

Table 8.10 shows that in 1989-90 they emphasised that irrigation and more land were the first choice. In 1992-3 this perception has changed to using improved seeds and fertilizers and to get more assistance from government. Obviously the women arc eager to adopt new agricultural inputs as the irrigation water is available to improve their living conditions.

That we have to be happy with this change in thinking over how to improve their lives, can be questioned. It is a well-known fact that the higher production and increase of income by implementation of the *boro* crop requires a lot of inputs like chemical fertilisers, pesticides and herbicides. In the long run this may be detrimental from an ecological point of view. In this respect it is interesting to look more in detail at figures we collected in the riverlift scheme of a total of 61 households in the *rabi* season in 1992-3. The river lift scheme is in operation now for around five years. 16 women told that they worry about the loss of fertility of the land they have noticed over the years: they had all used agricultural inputs during those years for the *rabi* crop. They noticed that production of the *kharif* rice harvest came down.

No irrigation or insufficient irrigation was mentioned by

women of 43 households. Many complained that their land could not be reached by the irrigation water due to a wrong positioning of the spouts and a lack of *pukka* 4 hectare channels. Other problems mentioned were that they need bullocks but cannot afford to buy them (20 out of 61); 31 women complained that fertilizing the land is a problem as there is a lack of cattle. Non-agricultural problems were bad health (22 out of 61), education of children (48 out of 61) and dowries (15). Alcoholism of men was only a problem in one household out of 61. Lack of money (43), bad health (39), no bullocks (27) and education of children (52) were the main problems mentioned by women of 72 handpump households. It is notable that they did not mention the loss of fertility of the soil: so far they all use compost for fertilizing the vegetable garden around the house.

Woman's double role is evident from the analysis presented so far. Although her role in production is substantial she remains responsible for the nutritional status, health and child care in the family, although, luckily, we have found that in the handpump beneficiary household scheme more men are also involved in looking after their children. Information on family planning, health and child care and nutrition have been relegated to lower priority than home improvement. In view of this it is interesting to examine the outcome of the question in which women were asked to give weightage to choices on home improvement information.

Table 8.11 shows that in the base-line study women gave the highest weightage to information on nutrition and health and child care. Three years later their interest has shifted in that sense that by far the majority (84 per cent) wants to know more on home improvement in the first place. Family planning information has the lowest priority. This may be partly because television, radio and other forms of mass media provide ample information on these topics.

8.8 POLITICS AND ROLE OF WOMEN PANCHAYAT MEMBERS

There are no NGOs in the Terai project districts which can give a substantial contribution to rural development or water manage-

TABLE 8.11: WEIGHTAGE GIVEN TO CHOICES ON HOME IMPROVEMENT INFORMATION

Scheme	Year	Information on							
		1		2		3		4	
		No.	%	No.	%	No.	%	No.	%
RLI	89-90	19	32	50	83	50	83	40	67
	92-3	60	100	25	42	23	38	22	37
DTW	89-90	36	49	48	65	48	65	31	42
	92-3	48	68	58	82	50	70	35	49
HTW	89-90	52	63	57	69	62	75	62	75
	92-3	67	84	44	55	48	60	31	39

Notes: N (89-90) - RLI = 60, DTW = 74, HTW = 83.
N (92-93) - RLI = 60, DTW = 71, HTW = 80.
1 = Home improvement.
2 = Health and child care.
3 = Nutrition.
4 = Family planning.

ment, let alone NGOs pursuing the improvement of living conditions of women. Political parties claim that their women's mass organizations fulfil this role in the area. The districts are very politicised and the Communist Left Front is in power at all levels. It is true that they are committed to improve the lives of the poorest households in the area, and evidence shows that they are to a large extent successful (Lieten 1992, 1995). We have asked the farm women if they belong to any political party, and 'if yes, to which party'. Only 4 women out of 72 households investigated on this point in the in-depth study claimed to be members of the CPI(M) and Congress I parties. However, other women emphasized that they were sympathizers of political parties.

During field visits we noticed many times that recent world-political issues were discussed by political leaders with the poor farmers in the village. In line with the 73rd Constitutional Amendment women have been elected as representatives in the panchayats at the three administrative levels of the state of West Bengal. The 73rd Constitutional Amendment 1992, gives panchayat institutions power for local self-government. Regarding the reservation of seats it is stated that:

(1) Seats shall be reserved for (a) the Scheduled Castes; and (b) the Scheduled Tribes, in every Panchayat and the number of seats so reserved shall bear, as nearly as may be, the same proportion to the total number of seats to be filled by direct election in that Panchayat as the population of the SC in that Panchayat or of the ST in that Panchayat area bears to the population of that area and such seats may be allotted by rotation to different constituencies in a Panchayat.

(2) Not less than one-third of the total number of seats reserved under clause (1) shall be reserved for women belonging to the SC or, as the case may be, the ST.

(3) Not less than one-third [including the number of seats reserved for women belonging to the SC and the ST] of the total number of seats to be filled by direst election in every Panchayat shall be reserved for women and such seats may be allotted by rotation to different constituencies in a Panchayat.

(4) The offices of the Chairpersons in the Panchayats at the village or any other level shall be reserved for the SC, ST and women in such manner as the Legislature of a State may, by law, provide. [The Constitution Amendment Act, 1992, 20 April 1993]

In the two main districts of the Terai project the move to elect women as representatives in the panchayats has made good progress in 1994/5. The gender representation over the two locations, Siliguri and Jalpaiguri, was as follows:

Siliguri	Nr	Men	Women
Parishad	1	8	4
Block Level	4	61	21
Gram Panchayat	21	387	138
Jalpaiguri			
Zila Parishad	1	26	9
Samiti	13	354	110
Gram Panchayat	125	2,190	704

Source: Joint-Director of Agriculture, Jalpaiguri.

The figures reveal that in general a third of the members are women which is the national target for women representatives in local bodies. It shows the commitment to give women a platform to voice their interests.

At the local level we collected some data on the political membership of the women panchayat members. Gender aspects are illustrated in the following field notes but the integrated fieldnotes are presented here as it provides the context of the work and problems of a Gram Panchayat in the Terai area faces.

Field visit Velkujote 9 February 1995.

Visit to Gram Panchayat of Biniwada, discussion with members who belong to the richer farmers in this location [one member has 80 *bighas* of land and seems to be a big landowner, another elected representative has 20 *bighas*, he shares the land with two or three brothers and parents].

34 villages lie in this Gram Panchayat [Velkujote village is one of them], and 14 *mouzas* [hamlets or neighbourhoods].

There are 10 UNICEF pumps, 3 are out of order. The repair comes under the Block Development Officer, nobody of the local community knows about repair of handpumps. 12 shallow tube wells of the World Bank Programme are not working as there is no electricity. Nepal [2 km from this place] and Bhutan in contrast have electricity. The water table is deep at 10 m. Drinking water is collected from dug wells with 3 m deep water tables. There are 15 public wells in the Gram Panchayat. What about mother and child care?: there are 14 Anganwadi programmes under the India Child Development Scheme which provide vaccinations against polio. There is a need for more Anganwadis. The Anganwadis have food programmes for nursing mothers and children from 1 to 5 years. 50 to 150 children attend each Anganwadi centre.

There are 16 Gram Panchayat members and three Samiti members of the Karabari block. There are four Gram Panchayats in the Kharibari block and 12 elected members at Samiti level which are distributed over the Gram Panchayats. There are six women members in the panchayat: 30 per cent belongs to the Scheduled Castes and 7 per cent to the Scheduled Tribes. Elections were on 17 April 1994. The gender/political composition is as follows: 4 members are from the Congress party [three men and one woman] and the same number is from the Forward Block; one man is from the Communist Party of India and seven members representing the Communist Party of India [Marxist] [five men and two women]; one woman calls herself independent. The three members from the Samiti level [all men] represent Congress, CPM and Forward Block.

The women elected members are very enthusiastic. They consider women's programmes for education and action to demand minimum wages for female landless labourers as important topics.

In 1986 there was an adult education programme. It was running for ten years and then stopped. They want to revive the adult literacy programme. In one model village in the Gram Panchayat the Land

Development Cooperative Bank has introduced a literacy programme. The whole village is literate now. There is also a youth club [football].

There is only one Primary Health Centre for 34 villages. The Gram Panchayat has 13,000 inhabitants: 300 babies were born last year. The mortality rate is unknown. Family Planning Camps are organized and there is a Family Planning Centre in Kharibari. There are 16 primary schools and one junior high school. 4,000 people are landless and for them there are Food for Work programmes and credit schemes from the Grameen Bank.

The Mahilla Samiti [women's organization] of the Marxist Communist Party marched recently with 250 people [including men] to the police station and reported a dowry murder case. They succeeded in getting the husband, mother-, and sister-in-law arrested.

Their deep wish is to get irrigation [deep tube well], electrification, road construction, higher education. The Pradhan [head of the panchayat] has no land. He was in government service.

The election of women on reserved seats in panchayats has raised a debate how far these women have qualities and capabilities to manage the villages and if they will be able to resist male dominance in decision making. In several states of India special training courses in gender awareness and practical knowledge and skills for elected women panchayat members are organized on a huge scale. In this way it is hoped that they are better prepared for the difficult tasks they have to fulfil. The following interview gives a profile of an elected woman panchayat member which shows her dependence on the political decision making of her husband. Nevertheless, within the context she tries to make the best out of it to do something for the poor women in the village.

Visit 6 February to Paschim Harmati, Mainaguri to elected female Panchayat member.

The people are glad to see us again. Nunnahar Begum is there, she is 24 years and married 12-13 years ago and has 3 children [one son, two daughters, 6, 5 and 2 years] and has studied to the seventh standards.

It was a kind of cross-cousin marriage. Her father-in-law has two wives. Her husband is the eldest son of the first wife. She is brother's daughter of the second wife. No dowry was given but the parties agreed about the amount of money to be paid in case of divorce. Of the 17 panchayat members, five are women: Shanti Rai Rajbongshi,

Koranu Rai Rajbongsi, Maya Rai Rajbongsi [RSP] and Joytsna Rai, Rajbansi. They are CPI[M] members.

Her husband was a Panchayat member, but recently two seats are reserved for women: one for Scheduled Castes and one in the 'general' category. Her husband resigned, and gave his place to her as she had more chance to be elected. In this constituency she went door to door in the whole village with the other candidates. She had a programme of latrines, roads and education. She is a member of the Panchayat now for two years. What are the activities and achievements?

She looks after the Anganwadi: Children from 1 to 5 years are attending, weak children get 75 gram food, and stronger ones 40 gram. (see Plate 13)

95 per cent of the women work in the fields. The women's resolutions are accepted or not accepted, there is no pressure. The sitting arrangement in the Panchayat meeting are as follows: the Pradhan and Vice-Pradhan in front, women in a row to one side and men on the other side.

Achievements: there is a sewing training programme, and informal education [literacy drive]. They purchased one knitting- and two sewing machines: 75 per cent of the costs are subsidized and 25 per cent the contribution of the women. In this part of the village 10 sections of 10 people participate in informal education. There are three women unit teachers: 70 men and 30 women follow the informal education classes. The timing of the education is adjusted to the convenience of the participants and is two to four hours in the afternoon. Teachers receive Rs 50 per month from the government [volunteers]. Seven loans have been given for buying a cow and paper-bag making. One cow costs Rs 2,500. The loan is given by the Grameen Bank of Mainaguri with 10 per cent interest. A loan was also given for three roofless women. They got thatched roofing but no money.

The consequence of being a Panchayat member is that five to six poor women a week come to their house to ask for food. Her father-in-law tells to help them and they give it.

Talks with other women panchayat members revealed that they are inclined to improve mother and child care. In many villages Anganwadi programmes have been introduced under the Integrated Child Development Scheme. They look after vaccinations and polio prevention. The Anganwadi programmes implement also food programmes for nursing mothers and children between 1 to 5 years attending the Anganwadi. Mostly

Plate 13: Anganwadi programme in village Velkujote.

50 to 150 children attend each Anganwadi centre. Women panchayat members are very enthusiastic to take up other gender issues in the future, including pursuit of women's informal education and minium wages for female landless labourers, although landlords have said that will not be possible because of high production costs.

In 1986 the Government of Bengal started an adult education programme, which was running for several years but stopped in many places for several reasons. The women panchayat members want to revive the adult literacy programme.

The women panchayat members emphasise that only small steps forward can be expected in order to change male gender perceptions, or to raise more gender awareness and self-esteem in making women's work and their skills and capabilities more visible in the given context. Therefore, they speak of efforts to strengthen women of various classes in various social contexts (age, marital status, household composition, etc.) to pursue a more equal power position in comparison with men.

9. From Mandays to Persondays: Impact of Gender Activities

9.1 GENDER AWARENESS OF MALE GOVERNMENT STAFF

Many gender recommendations were made at the beginning of Phase II of the Terai project to 'improve the living conditions of marginal and small farm women'. The nature of the recommendations have been briefly described in Chapter 2, and the possible positive and 'empowerment' effects that might be achieved by them anticipated. How these recommendations were finally implemented and worked out over a time span of five years will now be discussed.

To recapitulate, the following overview shows the tangible results of the gender intervention after five years of implementation of Phase II of the NBTDP:

(a) 24,030 handpumps have been sanctioned and are almost all installed in 1993 (planned 13,500 in the prepatory documents: Master Plan Phase II).

(b) Female headed households which belong to the marginal farmers have been given preference to get a handpump, and 10 per cent of these handpumps have been given in the name of the woman of the household. As an unplanned side-effect, husbands transfer land ownership (landrights) in the name of their wives.

(c) The sample survey shows that in 95 per cent of the cases the site of the handpump was selected in consultation with the woman of the house.

(d) Construction works of the project (pumphouses, 4 hectare units, etc.) has provided wage labour to local landless women (and men).

(e) Nine of the planned 27 women extension workers (two per block) are appointed in the Department of Agriculture.
(f) Farm women of marginal and small landholders are trained to improve agricultural management and operations.
(g) In some cases women are members of the water-users committees (Beneficiary Committees).
(h) Substantial research on the impact of the irrigation project on women has been conducted and 15 reports, including a detailed report (no. 12) on 'Women and Irrigation' have been published.

When we compare the intended interventions at the beginning of the project as described in Chapter 2 and the actually achieved ones, we may conclude that only the recommended appointment of a woman in the advisory committee of the project could not be achieved. More important than the tangible list of achievements, however, could be the invisible considerable increase in gender awareness among the whole male staff of the Department of Agriculture and the irrigation line departments. The executive engineer of the agri-mechanics department proudly told me that now he speaks of 'persondays', instead of 'mandays'. The attitudinal changes in awareness can be proved by the many tangible gender achievements of the project. Moreover, this has been accomplished as an integrated process. The emphasis on gender in the impact research has in general stimulated communication and debate and raised gender awareness among the implementing officials and managers at various levels. During the whole period of Phase II briefing meetings were organized for the staff in the office of the Joint-Director of Agriculture in Jalpaiguri. On those occasions the research supervisors and authors of this book presented the findings and asked the staff for comments. The gender focus has played a catalyst role in the total social and gender atmosphere of the project, not in the least to make the role of women in agricultural production visible. Perhaps that is more important than concluding that the representation of women in the water users committee has remained far below target.

Let us now look at each of the components of the achieved gender activities.

9.2 A TRIBUTE TO HANDPUMPS

For the implementation of the handpump programme congratulations should be offered to the staff of the office of the Joint-Director of Agriculture in Jalpaiguri. The programme has been implemented in an admirable effective and certainly low-cost way, but more important with dedication and a great respect for social justice.[1]

The assumption at the formulation of the second phase by the gender experts that handpumps would be extremely useful for women in view of their multi-purpose use, has been fully proven. What could not be foreseen was, that the project regulation that women would get a handpump if the land is in their name, has resulted in an unplanned, but very positive side effect in the sphere of 'empowerment'. Ninety-five per cent of the land is owned by the men and the 'ownership' document in the name of the head of the household. But many men have transferred ownership into the names of their wives, since they understood that this creates a pre-condition for their wives being selected as bene-ficiaries. This transfer might be perceived as just a formality, but it ultimately can work out very positive in case of early death of the husband, divorce and abandonment, or when a collateral to obtain credit is necessary: anyhow the woman is under those conditions the owner of the land. The transfer of the *patta* (land right document) costs only Rs 10. Ten per cent of the handpumps are now registered in the name of women (Schenk-Sandbergen and Choudhury 1994b). In the first batch of 5,000 handpumps implemented under Phase III, 14 per cent of the handpumps were actually given to women.

To understand how far the hand tube wells have helped the women of the household in easing their work a number of questions in the sample-survey were specifically asked to them. The questions ranged from selection of sites to the various uses of a handpump. The general conclusion that can be drawn from these answers is that the hand tube wells have been very useful to women in domestic and in agricultural work. The specific questions and their answers are stated below.

(a) Have women been consulted on the location of the handpump?

Most of the respondents in the sample survey (785 out of 825, i.e. 95 per cent) said that they were consulted on the location of the handpump. Only 4 per cent said they were not. About 97 per cent of them also said they were satisfied with the site of the pump. This point was anticipated as a kind of small catalyst aspect to involve women as the main users in the decision on the location and it was hoped that this would encourage participation in other aspects of decision making. It was a gesture, an example of women as visibly equal partners. How far this 'example-role' has been picked up might be indicated by our findings of the changes of the decision making role of women in agricultural matters. A slightly more powerful position was revealed by the fact that women are 'somewhat more' consulted by their husbands.

(b) Do you use handpump water for drinking, cooking, washing/bathing, irrigation?

A very high proportion of the respondents said that they use the hand tube well for all the purposes as stated in Table 9.1.

The sample survey data show that the hand tube well has indeed multiple uses. 93 per cent of the respondents use the handpump water for drinking, and 97 per cent use it for irrigation.

TABLE 9.1: USE OF HANDPUMP

Class of farmers	Drinking	Cooking	Washing/bathing	Irrigation
Marginal	626	579	573	643
Small	117	122	114	125
Middle	24	25	23	27
Large	2	2	2	2
Total	769	728	712	797
Total HH	93%	88%	86%	97%
Women (N) = 825				

However about 7 per cent of the respondents (56 women) said that they do not drink the handtube water as it gives a bad smell (4 per cent), or there is too much iron in the water (5 per cent) and/or the water is sandy and gritty.[2] Because of too much iron in the water, the milk in tea becomes sour, and hair washed with soap feels 'like ropes'. Some of the respondents had more than one reason for not using the handpump water for drinking. How far earlier cultural notions of purity and impurity of water sources play a role could not be investigated in a one-time survey. That water coming from handpumps has a religious meaning for the people is shown in the small *puja* that is performed for each handpump that will be used for the first time, to pray for plentiful and good water. Though the percentage of non-users of handpumps as the source for drinking water is small, we must make an effort to look into their problem. The dual use of handpump, domestic and agricultural, would make it more acceptable to women, thus increasing its utility value to the beneficiaries.

(c) *Do the women use handpump water throughout the year?*

The question, 'do you use water throughout the year' was asked to check the proper functioning of the handpumps as it is known that in particular in summer water tables come down in India. If the depth of the tube well is not enough it can be difficult to draw water. The other reason was that we wanted to assess differences in gender control over the use of the handpumps. In the monsoon season handpumps are usually not necessary for irrigation in case of sufficient rainfall, and in some places men dismantle the pumps with the argument that they fear their theft. That this dismantling increases the drudgery for their wives to fetch water from elsewhere will be clear. Ninety-three per cent of the women (769 out of 825) said that they use the handpump throughout the year. Only 46 respondent women (6 per cent) said that they did not. To the question whether the handpump remains idle in the monsoon month, only 11 women (1.3 per cent) said 'yes'. The reasons are: men of the household decide to keep it in abeyance, irrigation is not required during monsoon months, fear of it being stolen, so that it is dismantled and stored away. The number of handpumps that are so kept idle is rather insignificant, but as 46 women had said that the handpump is not used throughout the year it is possible that quite a number of them remain idle for some time in all seasons. This period of non-use of handpumps should be minimized because besides irrigation the handpump is the source of drinking water.[3] If it is idle it is the women who suffer most. Only a small fraction of the respondents (18 per cent) have a dug well whose water is used both for domestic and agricultural purposes.

As stated, many children in the project area suffer from severe malnutrition and water-borne diseases. Water-borne diseases are caused mainly by drinking the water of open water resources such as traditional wells. Water tests have proved that handpumps provide safer drinking water. In line with the assumptions 92 per cent of the respondents said that the incidence of diarrhoea among children has decreased since they switched over to drinking handpump water. This reflects the women's awareness of the importance of clean drinking water.

In the perception of the women the handpumps have brought notable changes in their lives. Domestic work has become easier, though the workload of cultivating crops has increased. The women like very much to have more and better vegetables for the family and income has increased particularly from growing vegetables. However, the in-depth study shows that the home-consumption of handpump irrigated grown vegetables varies very much with the crops grown in the location as shown in Table 9.2.

The differences are striking. In Velkujote almost all households have been eating more vegetables, in Bagjan more than 50 per

TABLE 9.2: HAVE YOU EATEN MORE VEGETABLES SINCE YOU HAVE ACQUIRED A PROJECT HANDPUMP?

Schemes handpump	Do you eat vegetables? Yes	No
Bhangni 25 HH	1	24
Bagjan 22 HH	14	8
Velkujote 34 HH	30	4

cent, but in Bhangni only one family. The explanation is that in Bhangni the handpump is mainly used for growing the cash crop, tobacco. In Velkujote the cash crops are vegetables, and in Bagjan it is mixed.

Another spin-off effect of the implementation of handpumps that was brought to our notice is that in some cases of public water sources private handpumps have made women less dependent on neighbours, thus reducing the chances of quarrels. On the other hand it can be questioned if the individualisation of the handpump has not caused a loss of opportunity for women to have a daily chat on village matters together when they are waiting in the queue.

In the following fieldnotes the 'greening' of the environment as a positive side-effect of handpumps will be shown: an aspect that has never been mentioned in official project reports. The greening can contribute to higher income as crops are grown, but it also means the beautification of the surroundings. We observed that waste water from the handpump was used to grow nice flowers. Big orange and yellow marigolds around the handpumps were a pleasure for the eye (see Plate 14). The transformation of the environment is documented before and after the implemen-tation of the handpump, resulting from a dry and yellow land-scape to a fertile and green one.

Saturday, 16 November 1991. Field visit to Muhammed Baks and Bedengarch, Kharibari-Phansidewa.

In February the village Muhammed Baks has been visited [see project report no. 10] to watch the sinking of the hand tube well. At first glance the change around the house is that a fence of bamboo has been made but the invisible change is that their income has doubled. He has got Rs 4,000 of his sweet gourd crop and is expecting another Rs 2,000. He spent Rs 1,200 on constructing the bamboo frame on which the leaves of the gourd are creeping. For 15 to 20 days labour was hired to do the work. Another woman of the next house tells me that she repairs the washer herself but that she needs some tools to do that.

We visit a very poor family where we had been in February. At that time the area around the house was totally barren and brown. Now we see much green and gourd plants are grown in front of the house. The farmer is a sharecropper on 5 *bighas* of land: he got 1 *bigha* waste land

Plate 14: Beautification of the surrounding.

in the framework of the land reforms. Also other poor people got land under the wasteland programme. He sold Rs 2,000 worth of spring beans and Rs 1,000 worth of gourd. His old mother looks after the children. A daughter of ten is responsible for the cooking while the wife of the house is away at her parents'.

One outcome of the handpump programme is that the village extension workers (KPS) are more popular with the local population than before. It is realized that the work of the KPS who has to visit 1,000 families in his area is highly intensified by the handpump instalment. The KPS is the one who supports the selection of potential beneficiaries by making a list. But it can not be said that the increasing popularity relates to the power he has to select beneficiaries. A real change in attitude among the farmers has been noticed. Previously, a KPS would not even be invited to sit down but now they are everywhere invited and called *dada*, brother. The KPS is trained to advice on crops and cultivation methods with the best use of handpump irrigation water.

The sample survey questionnaire contains a special set of questions aimed at finding the state of functioning of handpump at the time of survey in 1992-3. It was found that out of 825 handpumps, 73 (9 per cent) were not functioning. The reasons given by the beneficiaries for the non-function of the handpump were:

Reasons	No.	%
Breakdown of the pump	18	25
Kept in abeyance	8	11
Washer needed change	35	48
Other problem	12	16
Total	73	100

It seems that frequent change of washers and occasional breakdown of pumps requiring major repair are the two most common problems besieging the beneficiaries. As to the question how long it was out of order, in most cases it was found to be one month (53 cases), one to three months, 15 cases and three to six months, 5 cases.

The next question that was asked was how many times in the

Plate 15: Handpump which needs repair.

last one year the handpump had gone out of order. 714 respondents (87 per cent) answered that their pumps had gone out of order 1 to 3 times and the rest said that more than 3 times their pumps had gone out of order in the past year. Most of the cases of short-term disorder is due to worn out washers which require replacement. The survey was conducted when, as we have stated earlier, maximum use of handpumps is made for irrigating the *rabi* crops. So it is natural that in this season fewer pumps will remain idle.

Normally male members of the household attend to the repairs of the handpump. Out of 796 respondents, 705 (89 per cent) said that men of the household do this work (see Plate 15). Only in 4 cases it was found that women also do the work (0.5 per cent). Paid mechanic was engaged in 9 per cent households and in the remaining cases friends/neighbours helped the household restore the pump to working order.

As to the source of knowledge of repair most of the respondents said that they had taught themselves the technique, or learned it from friends/neighbours or by watching a mechanic.

Very few, only 6 out of 788 responses, said that they had acquired the skill from the KPS, or someone from the Agricultural Department. But the following experience in the field shows that in certain locations KPS extension workers certainly demonstrated to the male villagers how to repair the handpump,

The next house we visit of a Rajbansi participant of the project, is living among a whole cluster of *baris* surrounded by a fence and entrance gate of bamboo. The Rajbansi handpump-owner wears the sacred thread of the twice-born caste. He shows his Hinduized attitude by claiming Kshatriya origin. He shares 9 *bighas* of land with his father and two other brothers. The *bari* and *rajanam* [kitchen] is spick and span. The women of the house have made nice decorations of flowers and birds in the walls of the house. It is remarkable that the *chulha* (with three potholes) is made in the floor. The kettle hangs so to say in the fire. The fuel is jute sticks from their own field. The owner of this house is not working in the tea-gardens because as he states he has somewhat more land [3 *bighas*]. His elder brother is working there. He has bought a spanner to repair the handpumps. Till now, three months after implementation, there are not many problems with the maintenance and repair of the pumps. He says that other people will pay him in case of repair. During the installation they were instructed by the KPS on the technical aspects of the pump.

Costs for maintenance and repair have to be born by the owners as the pump is privately owned. The research and survey on the non-functioning of handpumps reveals that in general there is no problem although there are poor female headed households which cannot pay for repair. For these emergency cases there should be a provision in the project to assist very poor (female headed) households financially and technically in repair of handpumps.

The following field notes highlight the necessity of such intervention.

We visit the sister of Bhargavi, Mrs Savitri's house which we have visited also twice before. The family is busy constructing new walls of the house. The handpump of the project is defunct and was out of order 5 to 6 times before. They need not only a washer, but have to replace parts of the pump that will cost Rs 100. According to her husband they have no money for the repair. Later in the discussion their financial problems became more clear. Now Mrs Savitri, who is living at a large distance from the well, has to expand a lot of energy and time to fetch the water for household needs. We ask her husband if he realizes her increase in work if the pump is not repaired, and if he also helps in fetching water. He does not assist in fetching water and states 'that it is her job, she has to do it', but admits that it is more work. Savitri states the following to me, 'Madam take away this pump and give me a well.'

With a well, she explains, she is always assured of access to water, and assured of a reliable quantity. The tornado which roamed around in large parts of the area has completely destroyed their house. The hut collapsed and they had to buy materials for Rs 2,000 to construct a new house. In order to pay this Savitri and her three children went to Siliguri to do domestic servants' work there. As they have relatives in Siliguri, they had connections to find an employer. She got a salary of Rs 250 monthly and did the work for three months. She has to come home now for the construction but she has to leave her two children behind. She prefers to stay in the village. However, agricultural wage labour is hard to get, in particular in this lean season. They have only 2.5 *bighas* of land. After some talk it was also mentioned that they also have to repay a loan for their daughter's marriage and this was another reason why she took up the domestic servant's work. Her husband did not contribute to the family income with off-farm work. The question is raised in what way the pump has helped them to improve their condition? The husband states that instead of one *lungi*, he has two now [one in the house and one for outside]. They eat somewhat more but not in all seasons of the year. The children still get the left-overs of dinner for breakfast. In an ideal situation they buy 3 kg rice a day, which costs Rs 20 but they cannot always afford that because every time they face some new calamities and social obligations which are not incidental but structural aspects of their existence.

Only about 18 per cent of the respondents said that they have a well (148 respondents). But these wells may not be necessarily used as a source for drinking water. They are used for washing, bathing, cooking and other sundry purposes. Only 12 per cent of respondents (97 respondents) said they use well water, either their own or neighbour's well, for drinking. About half of them use the well water for drinking in some seasons, and the rest throughout the year. To 94 per cent of the women respondents (774) it is easier to fetch water from a handpump than from a well. Notwithstanding the advantages of a handpump about

11 per cent (89 respondents) said that given a choice they would use a well. There are many reasons for this. In some cases a well is within the house or very near, which makes it convenient to use. Some women have been in the habit of using a well since their childhood. A well is a part of their tradition. To such women a handpump is a novelty which might take some time to get absorbed in the social usage.

The women were asked a few questions on the effects of pumped drinking water on the health of the children. 92 per cent of the women respondents (out of 825) said that their children do not suffer from diarrhoea since they have started drinking handpump water. But for 37 respondents (4.5 per cent) the handpump water gave no relief. The intention of this question was not to find out the health effects of handpump on the population, but to asses the attitude of women to a handpump's domestic use. The positive answer of the majority of women reflects their awareness about the utility of a handpump. The above response was, albeit partly, corroborated by the answer to the question—did you observe any change in the health of children since drinking of handpump water? Most of the women could not notice any change in the health of the children—only about 25 per cent said that their health improved after using the handpump water for drinking. The two replies of the respondents give some positive indication that the women are realizing that a handpump, besides its utility in irrigation, is a dependable and healthier source of supply of drinking water for the family.

The women of the households were asked what in their view, were the changes in the household since the installation of a handpump. They were given seven choices and each respondent could chose as many answers as she liked.

From the above responses and the data of Table 9.3, we can see the positive changes that had taken place in the household as a direct consequence of the handpump scheme. It has lessened the domestic work of the women, though agricultural work has increased. It has given a little more income and more food to the family and has helped to reduce the health problems of children. It has also helped them to reduce their dependence on others, thus lessening the chances of friction. Some women however

TABLE 9.3: CHANGES THE HANDPUMP HAS BROUGHT IN THE HOUSEHOLD (N = 825)

Sl. no.	Opinion of the household women	No.	%
1.	Domestic work is easier	733	89
2.	More food for the family because of increased vegetable production	508	62
3.	Some assured income from vegetable/crop	565	68
4.	Less health problems with children	244	30
5.	Less dependency/conflict in fetching water from other's well	441	53
6.	Increased workload (for irrigation) for women	418	51
7.	Jealousy of neighbours	142	17

felt that as they own a handpump it has caused envy of neighbours.

The handpump has given considerable relief to women in their domestic work and has increased their agricultural work load, but the changing situation has not yet empowered them to control the vegetables/crops produced by them with the help of a handpump.

To the question—'who controls the money from vegetables/crops grown by women?', 62 per cent of respondents (510 persons) said that it is the men of the household who control the money received from the sale of such vegetables/crops grown by them. But 26 per cent of them said that it is not the men, but they themselves control the money. It seems to be a promising indication that at least some women have assumed control over the produce of their labour. The problem partially lies in the manner in which the produce is marketed. Only 86 women out of 825 interviewed (10 per cent) said that they go to market to sell the produce. The rest, 720 respondents (87 per cent) said that it is the men, or children, who sell the produce in the market. A few women did not answer this question. As the transaction are in most cases in the hands of the men, the women are deprived of the control over the money received from the sale of their home grown produce.

We found that landless women and women of river lift and deep tube well sites who have no, or a few, handpumps, often complain that there is plenty of irrigation water, but no safe drinking water, or not enough water for domestic use for the people. They 'steal' more or less water when the spouts are opened for domestic use. Moreover they use the concrete structure of the spout for washing clothes as there is no other provision in the design of the larger irrigation devices. We recommen the inclusion of washing and bathing places (also for cattle) in the design of the irrigation facilities and to investigate if the deep tube well water is fit for drinking purposes, and if yes, to plan water facilities in the irrigation construction design for domestic use.

In view of the very positive effects of handpump implementation on the lives of women we recommended more hand pumps in the coming phases of the North Bengal Terai Development Project. However, ways and means should be worked out to give women more control over the fruits of their labour. This might be better transport, special women's corners and facilities in markets and women's cooperatives.

It will be a good plan to provide toolkits for the handpump households and to give clusterwise on-the-spot training to maintain and repair the handpumps. This approach has been followed for many years already in the so-called female handpump-caretaker/mechanic training by UNICEF (Schenk-Sandbergen 2001).

9.3 FARM WOMEN TRAINING

The training of farmwomen was from the beginning accepted as a useful activity in the project, however the number of courses in comparison with the number allotted to men was only 10 per cent. 'More courses for women mean less courses for men, and as the land is in the name of the men, they are the eligible beneficiaries' was the line of thought of the male implementers. As it is perceived by the staff of the Agricultural Department that only 'beneficiaries' are entitled for training, it was difficult to bargain for an equal representation of women in comparison with men in the training programme. Finally, it was agreed to include courses on vegetables growing for farm women of a duration of five days. The course content was adjusted accordingly.

An impact study was conducted to investigate the use and effects of the training. A questionnaire was drawn up, and one very motivated male field investigator went to very remote villages to interview ex-trainees (103 men and 50 women) a few months after they had attended the course. It was out of the question that a woman investigator could be found to conduct the impact study among the 50 women respondents. We realize that would have been better, but the option was simply not available. The field-investigator often stayed overnight in the farm houses to continue the interviews next day as there was much to discuss.

9.3.1 Impact study on farmers/farm women training

Before we reveal the main findings of the impact of the training we shall briefly describe the demographic, social, economic and educational background of the 50 women respondents who have received the training. This would help us to know the type and qualification of the persons selected for the training and the improvements that can be suggested in the selection and training (see Report Research and Evaluation Unit no. 6, 1992, Parts 1 and 2).

Socio-economic and demographic profile of 50 trained farm women

Age and community: In the sample 60 per cent of the women respondents belong to Scheduled Caste communities, mainly Rajbansi and 40 per cent were Hindus. Most of the respondents (72 per cent) belong to the age group 20 to 50 years. Only one woman is above 50 years.

Educational level: 20 per cent of the respondents are illiterate which is far below the findings of the in-depth study and sample survey and tells us that the selection of beneficiaries has a bias for more educated women. Fourteen per cent have only primary education. The majority of the literates have read upto secondary or higher secondary level of education: 66 per cent of the sample. In our in-depth and sample survey study we could find hardly women with lower secondary education.

Household population: The population of 50 households of the 50 respondents is 348: males 174 and females 174. The average size of the family is 7 which is quite high and indicates that the selected women come probably from relatively well-to-do farmers' households. About 80 per cent of the respondents were married and the rest was unmarried or widows.

Occupation: 40 of the 50 respondents gave household work as their primary occupation though most of them (34) worked in their family farm. Three worked 'in service', two in business and five were girl-students. It is evident that at least 10 respondents who were selected for training did not have agriculture/household-work as their primary/secondary occupation. They were either students or private teachers, or engaged in business or service. It is possible that these women give a helping hand to family agriculture and certainly have helped in domestic work. But, as the training is intended for the beneficiary farm women it would be better to exclude such women from the purview of future training.

Economic condition and respondents: The distribution of the respondents' families into various agrarian classes is thus:

Marginal farmers (upto 2.5 acres)	22
small farmers (2.5-5 acres)	11
Middle farmers (5-10 acres)	12
Large farmers (above 10 acres)	1
Landless	2
Unknown	2
Total	50

The data show that the majority of the farm women trainees came from marginal/small farmer's families, around one/fifth are middle farmers, and only one woman from a big farmer family and two from landless families also. At least 34 of the 50 respondents take part in the agricultural activities of their family farm on a regular basis. This family farm is managed primarily by the male members of the households. Cultivation is done both in irrigated and unirrigated fields and types of crops grown in a season are similar to those described earlier. These families also use HYV/certified seeds, chemical fertilizer, irrigation and a few modern implements (sprayers, seed drills, pump sets).

Though the women respondents took part in different types of agricultural activities they asked the males of the households to help them answer questions about the size of the area cultivated, crops grown, output, quantities of fertilizer, etc., used, type of seeds, and such other points. It is difficult to say if this is a result of social expectations, or that they really do not know.

We focused on the information on the development of kitchen gardening, post-harvest technology, preservation of fruits/vegetables, etc. We are aware that with this focus, we reinforce the traditional women's role and limit the effort to bring women in the mainstream of agricultural development but the character of the training made this choice a viable one.

9.3.2 Extent of use of training

Kitchen garden: 44 out of 50 respondents (88 per cent) have a small kitchen garden attached to the dwelling huts. Others do not have a kitchen garden at all. The area of the kitchen garden is a very tiny plot, usually measuring a few decimals of an acre. The total area of 44 kitchen garden plots is 5.28 acres. The handpump provides irrigation in 28 cases (64 per cent) and dugwells in 16 cases (36 per cent). The kitchen garden were used entirely to produce vegetables (5.28 acres) in three seasons, but most of the produce was obtained in pre-*kharif* and *rabi* seasons.

The assumption was, that after the training in which the women were taught to plan and design the crop layout in three seasons, the entire area of the 44 kitchen gardens should be cultivated in a planned way as is done in regular farming. But in fact in most cases, a part of the kitchen garden was cultivated; particularly in the *kharif* season. Even then, assuring that half of the area was cultivated in pre-*kharif/rabi* seasons, the per acre production of vegetables is much less than that had been obtained in a regular farm of the report of male respondents. Poor output in the kitchen garden indicates unplanned cultivation, though 35 of the respondents said that they had cultivated the kitchen garden in a planned manner as Table 9.4 shows.

Most of the respondents were doing kitchen gardening even before the training. The training, it was hoped, would supplement their already existing knowledge and experience. But the survey does not reflect the effect of this training in terms of size of land used, design, or increased output from the kitchen garden.

Planting of fruits and other trees: The farm women were also trained on techniques of planting, grafting of fruit trees, growing other plantation crops (coconut, betel-nut and black pepper) and planting of trees for fuel. In the survey it was found that a small number of respondents have used the acquired knowledge in grafting fruit trees (14 per cent) and planting fuel wood trees (14 per cent), but proportionately a large number of respondents have planted fruit trees (72 per cent) (banana, mango, lemon, papaya both traditional and hybrid varieties) and other plantation trees (36 per cent) like coconut, betel-nut and black pepper. Planting of coconut, betel-nut and a few fruit trees is normal in a farming household. What is notable is that a few women

TABLE 9.4: APPLICATION OF TRAINING KNOWLEDGE IN KITCHEN GARDENING (N = 50)

Type of activity	No. of positive response
1. Planning	35
2. Cleaning, designing the crop layout	44
3. Preparing soil	44
4. Irrigating the filed	44
5. Using manure/chemical	40
6. Sowing seeds in recommended method	6
7. Weeding	42
8. Collecting seed in proper way	27
9. Harvesting crop	42
10. Storing of seed in recommended way	6
11. Preparing nursey bed for vegetable seedlings	41
12. Planting vegetable seedlings	44

respondents have used the technique of plant grafting, sown hybrid varieties of fruit trees, and planted fuel wood trees.

Other agriculture-related activities: Training was also given on a number of agricultural related activities-drying and preparation of storage bins, proper storage of crops seeds, cleaning and maintenance of sprayer, pumps and other agricultural implements, proper and safe keeping of insecticide/pesticide. The responses are noted below:

Activity	No. of positive response
1. Proper cleaning and preparation of storage bins	36
2. Drying and storage of agricultural products in the recommended way	36
3. Using seed bins	5
4. Storing of seeds in the recommended way	3
5. Safe storage of pesticide/insecticide and proper cleaning of the storage place	30
6. Maintenance of agricultural equipment (sprayer, wheel hoe, seed drill, paddy weeder)	25

Maintenance of the agricultural equipment means cleaning it after use, tightening a loose nut, if any, and application of oil in the shaft of the sprayer. About 72 per cent of the respondents said that they store the crops in the way recommended during the training, but seed storage in the recommended way is followed by very few. Unfortunately the reasons why they don't use seed bins are not clear to us.

Dairy and poultry development: Though keeping of fowl, ducks, goats and milch cows is quite common in a farm, very few households rear them in a scientific way. Only two respondents said that they have crossbreed cows for which they cultivate green fodder on the family farm. A few other households have few fowls, ducks (11 women) and goats (15 women) which are looked after by the women of the household. Only two women have a cow and are cultivating green fodder for them.

Poultry, ducks, pigs and goats are of local variety. No special care is taken for them. Besides almost every household has a cattle-shed, which is periodically cleaned by the women and small girls of the household.

Maintenance and repair of hand tubewell: A little over half of the respondents own a handpump (56 per cent). But only 24 of them said that they maintain the handpump properly. Maintenance here means keeping the area clean and seeing that the pump is properly used. Occasionally a loose nut may be tightened but when it breaks down or a washer is to be changed, the respondents said that they could not do the job. Perhaps a little more intensive practical training and supplying the handpump owners a small tool-kit may encourage the women to do simple repairs.

Aspects of home science: The farm women were also given training on food processing, preparation of jam, jelly, fruit preserves, cooking of nutritious and balanced food specially for children and expectant mothers. It seems shortly after the training some of the items were enthusiastically prepared at home but the interest after some time waned for several reasons. When the respondents were asked the question: How frequently you prepare the processed foods with seasonal vegetables and fruits? The response was, frequently-7, rarely-19, not at all-24 (N = 50). It seems 48 per cent of the respondents did not utilize the training knowledge of this activity even once. Only a small number of respondents have utilised the knowledge on a fairly regular basis.

Activity	(N = 50)	No. of responses
1. Preparing jam		2
2. Preparing jelly		17
3. Preparing pickles		18
4. Preparing papad		5
5. Preparing squash		3
6. Drying and preserving vegetables by using Janata refrigerator		8

Preparing pickles and fruits jelly seem to be more popular

than other types of food. One of the reasons for giving up the preparation of jam, jelly, squash is that the essential preservatives (sodium benzoate, potassium meta-bisulphate, pectin, etc.) are not locally available. The women are taught to add these preservative at the training.

On the question on the preparation of balanced and nutritious food the respondents were asked- how often you prepare balanced/nutritious food? The response was: frequently-2, seldom-16, not at all-32 (N = 50). So more than half of the respondents did not utilize this knowledge even once. Only two persons have prepared such foods frequently. Among those who had prepared such foods even once there is a difference in the number of responses according to the nature of activity.

Activity (N = 50)	No. of positive responses	%
1. Preparation of balanced dishes with locally available food ingredients	12	24
2. Preparation of nutrient food for expectant mothers, infants and pre-school children	16	32
3. Cooking vegetables maintaining their food value	11	22

One of the reasons of low response is that the informants often complained that food prepared by the recommended way is not liked by the members of the family. It is not tasty. Sometimes even children refuse to eat it.

Smokeless chulah: Only two respondents made a smokeless *chulah* in their home, but gave it up later as they found it inconvenient. In once case the house caught fire, which scared others.

9.3.3 Assessment of the training by the respondents

As discussed earlier the training seems to have made a mixed impact—the application of some items of training has been rather poor. The respondents were asked to explain the difficulties they had faced in implementing their training knowledge in their homes. A number of causes were given by them.

Possible constraints (N = 50)	No. of responses
1. Lack of capital for making foods in the recommended way	27
2. Materials not locally available	15
3. Cannot recall the training knowledge	3
4. Not very keen about proper application of knowledge	41
5. No time in hand due to heavy pressure of work	5
6. Members of the household do not like food prepared in the recommended way	43

While some of the reasons stated above (1, 2, 6) seem to be practical difficulties, overwhelmingly the respondents had a very casual attitude towards some aspects of training, particularly items of home science. Some way must be found that larger number of trainees take the training more seriously.

Despite the fact that the training knowledge was marginally used, most of the respondents liked to have this sort of training. To the question,—'Did you like the training though you are not utilizing/partly utilizing the knowledge?' 47 respondents out of 50 replied in affirmative. As to the reasons for taking this training they said:

Reasons for taking the training (N = 50)	No. of responses
1. Receiving training improves status among other women	44
2. Training is scope to go outside home and talk freely with educated persons	37
3. Training makes unknown things known	45
4. Through training a woman can become a good mother	31
5. A trained woman, if she wishes, can prepare processed foods	28
6. Trained women can help/direct farm agriculture in absence of menfolk	41

It is clear that most of the respondents are aware of the usefulness of the training and wish to have the training continued. We even came to know that in one case the status of a young unmarried woman who followed the training was so much raised that she became an attractive bride, and her father could reduce the dowry because of the value given to the 'training certificate' she brought to the in-laws house.

9.3.4 Teaching others

A number of respondents said that some women of the neighbourhood had come to them to know about planting of fruit trees, making of kitchen garden in a planned way, how to prepare jam, jelly or *papad*, planting and care of fuel wood trees, proper application of fertilizer, pesticide in vegetables and coconut trees. Of course, no woman wants to know all the above topics in one meeting. Usually, the trained woman goes to the most knowledgeable women in the neighbourhood to learn about one or two topics at a time. The important point is that some trained women are not only disseminating acquired knowledge among others, but also acting as promoters of new methods and skills.

To the question, What aspects of training do you recall most? Most respondents could recall the following topics arranged in order of their weightage.

1. Kitchen garden
2. Cattle rearing
3. Planting of fruit trees/fuel wood trees
4. Preparation of jam, jelly and making of nutritious food for children.

Similar order of answers were given for the question—what are the aspects of training you would like to utilize most?

About 84 per cent of the respondents wished to take further training. Those who said 'no' gave the reasons as: old age, no land to use the knowledge, inability to utilize the first training knowledge and wish to maintain the traditional practices.

Some respondents suggested an increase in the duration of the training period, diversification of the syllabus so as to give a more intensive training, and a small handbook written in Bengali for use at home.

Concluding, we can say that the reasons for taking training was more for an exposure to the outside world than anything else. But despite the poor application of training most respondents wished it to continue, and wanted a small handbook to carry home.

9.4 WOMEN EXTENSION WORKERS

It was strongly recommended on the basis of several obvious arguments that women be appointed as extension workers (two per block) in the 27 blocks of the districts, as the total extension work is carried out in the Terai area (and in the whole of Bengal) by male village extension workers, Krishi Prayukti Sahayak (KPS). In fact there was no objection in 1987 and we had good hopes that after some time a start would be made with the training of women in this line. To create labour opportunities for women in a male dominated field of employment might mean more chances for empowerment of women who will be appointed as extension workers, but also for the women who will be trained and informed by them.

It is a most laudable achievement of the project that nine women extension workers have been appointed since December 1992. They are in regular service of the Department of Agriculture and not funded by the Technical Assistance money of the project. As far as we know this is the only Indo-Dutch bilateral project where the appointment of female extension workers have been institutionalised within the department. The sustainable basis of the project has been strengthened very much, as the extension workers will continue their work in case the project will be phased out. An interview with a woman extension worker revealed that the selection for her appointment to the post was carried out through the usual official procedure. She was sent for an interview and written test by the District Employment Office. The training was six months in Calcutta. Her stipend was Rs 600 for six months which is extremely low. However, for six months training she had to spend Rs 5,500 from her own pocket: Rs 350 per month for food, to buy educational materials, the bus to Calcutta, and so on. She got Rs 1,000 from her father for the training and her parents-in-law also gave money. Her husband sold two cows (milkcow and calve) to meet the expenses.

Wednesday, 24 December 1993. Interview female KPS Nirmala Roy.

She is 31 years old, and has finished school [11th standard]. She was married in 1981 and went to a remote village, so she could not take the higher secondary examination. She has two daughters (9 and 7). Her husband looks after the agricultural work.

She lives in a nuclear family in the compound of a large joint family. There are 25 members in the compound [15 females and 10 males]. She does not know the total size of the family land. There are four brothers: brothers two and three have got their share of land, although the land is still in the name of her father-in-law. The eldest and youngest brother and father-in-law have communal property. So there are three shares of land. Her husband cultivates around 7 *bighas* of land with the help of a farm servant who is employed through the year on contract. Her husband pays Rs 1,200 a year plus food and cloth. Occasionally labourers are hired. She helps her husband during holidays. The produce of the paddy is not enough for the yearly consumption: there is a three- to four-month shortfall and they have to buy paddy from the local market. Since six months they got a hand pump under the Dutch Programme. She raises an additional income by selling vegetables and milk: 2 litres per day. There are several non-agricultural sources of income of the family. Younger brother is a school teacher. Two sisters-in-law are Integrated Child Development Scheme workers. She also became an Anganwadi worker and earned Rs 300 a month.

What is her agricultural experience? She did transplantation work in her father's house. After marriage she was sometimes engaged in agricultural work. She tried to harvest the rice this year.

She was registered in 1979 in the employment exchange in Siliguri. She is a Rajbansi and entitled to job reservation. She got a post card in 1988 from the employment exchange office after nine years to apply for a lady constable. She had to go to Darjeeling for a written and oral examination; she also had to run 400 m to test her physical fitness. Unfortunately, she was not selected because she had 2 kg underweight [she is 46 kg]. In 1991 she got her second call from the labour exchange office. She had a written examination in the office in Siliguri of Mr Chakraborty along with 20 other candidates. After one month she was called for an interview with 18 others. Out of 18 she was the only one selected. She went in March 1992 for training to Calcutta and stayed six months in the Ram Krishna Mission Ashram, Narendrapur, South 24-Paraganas. She had to go through six papers: fertilizers, animal husbandry, extension, crops, husbandry, plant protection. In the morning she had practicals, and in the afternoon theoretical lessons.

She was appointed in December 1992 in Kharibari-Phansidewa. The other eight women KPS were posted-four in Jalpaiguri, and four in Cooch Behar.

She has to cover eight units, three to four villages in each unit. In total she has to visit 24 to 25 villages. In each unit she has to contact farmers: total 80 contact farmers. They are hopefully the agents of change. Out of 80 contact farmers, 11 to 12 are women heads of households. She uses a cycle to reach the villages. She got a cycle from her father-in-law. Her area is 10 km from her house. She is from 11.00 till 16.00 in the Panchayat office. She has to collect the complaints of the farmers, to advise on the doses of chemicals to be given, what kind of seeds to be selected, etc. Now she is engaged in mini-kit distribution. She was prepared a work plan on wheat and potatoes. She is aware that she should support in particular work for the women in her villages. Her salary is Rs 1866. From her first salary she bought a nice sari, golden earrings for her daughter. With the next salary she plans to improve the house and to buy a cycle for her daughter.

9.5 GENDER AND WATER USERS' COMMITTEES

Raju (1997) writes that distribution of water to users within an irrigation system involves decisions including who is to get water, how much, at what time, etc. These decisions are usually made with the help of publicly recognized water distribution rules. There are two reasons for the existence of water distribution rules: to simplify decision making and to reduce potential conflicts. In West Bengal, there is an official memo of 1979 from the government in which it is stated that local committees for distribution of irrigation water should be reconstituted with the following members: local member of the Legalistic Assembly, Panchayat Samiti, Gram Panchayat, Agricultural Officer of the block and the Sub-Assistant Engineer of the block or the operator of the installation. In addition, the members will in their first meeting of the committee select and co-opt five representatives of the cultivators in the command area (not more than one representative from one spout): two representatives will come from the category of small and marginal farmers. A woman representative is not specifically mentioned.

The tasks of the Sub-Assistant Engineer (block level) include the formation of Beneficiary Committees at the deep tube well and river lift sites. The fact that the technical departments are in charge of farmers' participation, the formation of Water Users' Committees or Beneficiary Committees (BC) is remarkable. Often this merging of the two spheres is only achieved in other projects after many years, and with a lot of Technical Assistance or NGO input. Observation in the field indicates that the Assistant Engineers know the farmers, and show concern and interest in their problems as regards water use, operation and maintenance.

In the project area the Water Users' Groups (WUG) are known as BCs. The BC usually consists as stipulated in the official regulation four author-ities: the extension worker (from the Agricultural Development Office at the block level, ADO), Sub-Assistant Engineer (from the Block Development Office, BDO), a member of the Legislative Assembly, and the head of the Gram Panchayat (the pradhan).

Narayana (1986, p. 188) writes in his article on farmers' involvement in irrigation development in the so-called *warabandi* (rotational distribution of water) system in Andhra Pradesh, 'The village social structure, with all its inequalities and internal dynamics acts as a strong force against the distribution of water on equal basis.'

When we look at the class composition of the 'elected' members as representatives of the farmers of the BCs we have to conclude that, with some exceptions, the better-off farmers dominate the committees and that the role of the Secretary in water distribution decision making is crucial. The student research of Keulen/Dekker indicates that influential farmers who are nearly always the biggest farmers, are chosen by the other farmers in a plenary meeting: from each spout at least one BC member. In the river lift irrigation scheme investigated by them, they mention that after the formation of the BC three members were later added: two female beneficiaries and a prominent farmer. The women members of the BC were elected due to pressure from the Mahila Samiti of the CP(M). Keulen/Dekker remark, regarding the women members, 'that they hope that in the future, because of their membership, also female beneficiaries will attend the plenary meetings. The aim of these female members is to stimulate more women to work on the field and to learn them how to combine this with the household activities' (1992, p. 14).

Loeber (1991, p. 10) found in her study that in the deep tube well scheme she studied in detail the BC consisted of 15 members and she writes, 'Without exception the committee members are well-to-do villagers, either owning large landholdings or having a well paid job. There is no woman on the committee.'

The same trend was observed by Kranenburg (1994, p. 24). She states that the members of the BCs are 'mainly members of the relatively large farmers' households, who have power based on their properties (for example in their role as employers) and/ or have some status not necessarily linked to personal wealth (for example due to political functions or caste)'.

In Kranenburg's study the BC Secretary is a powerful person. More surprisingly, 60 per cent of the beneficiaries did not know anything about the BC, except the activities of the Secretary, who was described by one of them as the 'captain of the pumphouse'. The Secretary is usually the farmer who donated the plot of land for the pumphouse. In Loeber's study the Secretary was a panchayat member at the time of application. The BC is supposed to decide on the sequence of water supply and to maintain a serial order, following the dates of deposit of water fees as mentioned in the Requisition book. Kranenburg (1994, p. 12) writes, 'In practice the secretary of the BC is usually the person who composes the sequence of farmers to be observed in irrigation turns.'

It is observed that the richest farmers get priority in the distribution of water. Their fields are often near the pumphouse and they invite the operator and BC Secretary for tea and food.

Women farmers face special gender problems which are not recognized by the BCs. Loeber remarks that female farmers often refrain from irrigation since they can not go to the operator themselves or argue with male water users in order to get water. 'Women never set foot in the pumphouse, as it is considered a man's affair.'

It is obvious that cultural restrictions reinforce the already existing invisibility of women as water users. As mentioned, women are not the owners of land, and therefore are not perceived as water users and thus beneficiaries. This cuts them off from decision making institutions and irrigation water management in the larger government-owned irrigation schemes. But in principle it is the same in the small so-called 'collectively owned' shallow tube wells and pump dug well schemes. Male dominance as a result of patrilocal and patrilinear social organization is so pervasive that women are absolutely not considered as water users or water managers although they might do most of the farm work. Only the handpump scheme in which the pumps are privately owned by the households give women some control over the pump. Access to water for women is not the problem when it is released in the fields. The problem is that women have no control over when and where the water will be released.

On the other hand we also have to point to the fact that the formal composition of the BC does not offer much scope for a proper representation of interest groups (only a few members are accepted) and that also counts for male representatives of marginal- and landless households. In the command areas of the RLI and DTW in the Terai the research indicated that a considerable proportion of land and water is controlled by the middle and big farmers although in numbers the marginal and small farmers form the majority. The latter have in theory access to water but little control. Women have only indirectly access to water via their husbands and male family members and have also very little control over the management of the water. Therefore, it seems likely that poor farmers and women may fear in case irrigation devices are transferred, and 'privatization' will be pursued and successful, that their needs and interest will be subordinated to those of the more powerful in the BCs. The poor farmers and women have the least control over land and water. Even if it can be achieved that women's representation in BCs is fair, their control over resources is in practice not necessarily assured.

In principle it can be stated that the interests of the marginal farmers and women are more protected in the present Phase II with state owned and managed irrigation schemes as in principle the government procedures for acquizition of water are on paper very sound, and based on equity principles. Redressal of grievance is possible by complaining to the BDO, who is a neutral government official controlling the operator and staff in the RLI/ DTWs. As said, the uneven land ownership in the command area tends to favour the better-off farmers. It should be kept in mind that at present state mechanisms to redress this kind of social injustice are inherent in the procedures for access to water as the following example shows.

Kranenburg (1995) describes that disadvantages farmers, not getting water in the order of payment of water rates, protested and their action was successfully addressed. She describes that BC members went to the Block Development Office to complain. The cashier of the Block Development Office, who takes and administrates the water rates, told the operating staff to distribute water equally, and in the order of which the acquisition slip were received.

Under 'privatization' this kind of bureaucratic state protection will be absent and it is questionable whether the local panchayats can fulfil the corrective role when local social equality and class water conflicts are at stake. There will be no longer an incentive for accountability to the higher levels of policies and management. That might cause a stagnation in the strengthening of women by perpetuating the availing gender ideology. Will privatization lead to a hegemony of politics, and class and gender dominance? So far, we have found no sign that 'privatization' will make the productive role of women more visible, as they will become partners in paying the costs for the operation, maintenance and repair. The non-agricultural income generating opportunities are so minimal in the area, that first an 'employment revolution' has to be created to give women any chance to become visible.

In another case it happened that BC members favour

themselves by getting priority after a period in which no water could be released because of technical failures. It was observed that in any case, farmers with small amounts of irrigable land have to wait until the land of the larger farmers, who had deposited their water rates earlier, have been fully supplied.

However, it would not be fair to state that the water committees always favour those of their political party, or the rich and the powerful, in setting priorities for water release. Larger farmers are sometimes discouraged from requesting irrigation for all their land. A middle farmer stated to Kranendonk (1995) that he wanted irrigation for 8 *bighas* of mustard, but was told by the operator to request only half of this, as there were 'problems with the pumps', and there were several smaller farmers who wanted to receive some water as well.

Loeber (1991, p. 10) describes a case in which, as the pump had only a limited irrigation capacity (100 *bighas*), a ceiling (3 *bighas*) was fixed for the amount of *boro* that could be grown per farmer. It is also reported that operators and the Secretary of the BC sometimes agree to provide water to very poor farmers before payment of the water rates, assuming they will pay at a later stage. It was also observed during a field visit to Cooch Behar that in Bharya (deep tube well) the tribal Rabas are in-charge of the BC, and that they were very keen in on equity in water distribution.

Field notes of March 1993 (Report Euroconsult 16) shows the following illustrations of a very social aware BC in equitable water distribution,

> The water users' committee in Paschim Chapani [RLI] meets before each season to decide on an equitable distribution of water among the farmers having land in the Command Area. Last year farmers suffered big losses as many had invested in inputs to grow *boro*. However there was not sufficient irrigation water and the crop failed. As the demand for water to irrigate *boro* was this year [1993] again higher than the capacity of the RLI, a land ceiling was set for *boro* irrigation for each farmer, except for those who have income from service: they are excluded from *boro* irrigation but not of irrigation of other crops in other seasons. This decision of the water users' committee reflects an informal sense of social justice and may be an example for other water users' committees. To avoid illegal water use the five members of the

water users' committee control by rotation the illegal digging of *katcha* channels during the release of the water. With the list of names of farmers entitled to get water on a planned date, they walk around to supervise the water release.

9.6 CONSTRUCTION WORK AND FEMALE LANDLESS LABOURERS

The project generated some employment in construction as the pumphouses for the deep tube wells and the river lift irrigation have to be made. Four hectare units of at least 150 m brick and plastering work exist. The contractors should recruit unskilled labourers from the local population. In this way construction work should provide wage labour to local landless women (and men). Field visits reveal that this recommendations is also carried out by the responsible implementors.

Field visit 21 September 1989, Mainaguri, village Paschim Harmati.

The river lift irrigation pumphouse has been constructed and the underground tubes and pipes connected, recently, but the three engines have to be installed.

During construction local people were employed to do the unskilled labour. The ten women employed as construction labourers earned Rs 16 a day: the men Rs 20 a day.

Irrespective of the construction work that will create some employment for men and women of landless households, we have indicated that irrigation facilities generate more agricultural work. This is of utmost importance for the landless households and in particular the women. To survive they have to contribute to the family income, but the rigid division of labour has resulted in a segregated labour market, highly restricted both spatially and functionally. They do not face much patriarchal control over their labour by their own husbands but the men from rich households control the paid labour opportunities in the village and dictate the norms of *purdah* and status that discourage often women from seeking wage employment outside the village (Chen 1985, p. 25; Westergaard 1981, p. 14). Therefore, any traditional agricultural employment generated by the irrigation facilities can be an important contribution, but it can also give more means to landholding patriarchs to have more power in imposing control on the labour of landless women. The practical gender need and interests of this category of women are perceived and acknowledged by the officials and translated into the concrete demand to contractors to recruit local landless women in construction work. This in itself is again a small contribution to the creation of some labour out of the scope of traditional channels and shows the social and political sensitive climate of Bengal to be concerned with the weakest sections. However, wage discrimination for this group of women at all levels (in construction and agricultural wage labour) is obvious, as we have seen.

9.7 PRIVATIZATION AND SUSTAINABILITY

Finally, we want to indicate constraints and the views of some farmers in the Project area related to the new 'privatization' or 'handing over' approach and the withdrawal of the government that is pursued in the current phase of the project. What will be the consequences of this process for women, in particular of the marginal farmers?

To demonstrate the constraints regarding 'privatization' we have to reveal first the unequal agrarian structure in terms of classes of farmers, and their access to and control over land and water. In this context we also have to pay attention to the reported high degree of non-use of irrigation water of the deep tube wells and river lift irrigation and the reasons behind it. Some thoughts will also be given regarding the effects of withdrawal of the state subsidy and state management, in terms of erosion of the instruments for providing corrections where social injustice is at stake. This may be the more relevant as it can be stated that the socio political climate of West Bengal, and the Terai area, offers, in comparison with other states, the optimal setting to pursue equality in water distribution.

Let us look at the scenario of 'privatization' as envisaged in the 'pilot-project' in the next phase of the project. According to staff of the Department of Minor Irrigation the estimated operating costs of an river lift irrigation will be around Rs 2,00,000 annually. The subsidised water rate is now Rs 5 per acre/inch, the actual cost Rs 21 per acre/inch. This means that under 'privatization', the running costs for the farmers will increase by a factor of 4. The first target of the 'handing over strategy' will be to stop the salaries of the government appointed operators. So far, it is unknown what to do with the redundant government operators. It is the intention that in the future the farmers will pay the salary of the locally trained operator as well as that of the assistant-operator and the night-watch (at least Rs 5,500 monthly, personal communication with BDO (Coordination Report 18). The next steps are to withdraw the subsidy on diesel and ultimately to transfer all costs of operation and maintenance to the farmers. The BCs are assumed to be the carrying organizations of the whole enterprise as they will be the managers of the irrigation facilities. Ownership may be given to the Gram Panchayats.

And what do the farmers think themselves of this scenario? We spoke with the farmers in the river lift irrigation scheme, recently selected by the Bengal Government staff as a 'pilot-project'. They expressed their reservations on privatization. One of the sound arguments is that their products will be more expensive than those from subsidized (World Bank) river lift irrigation schemes in the nearby villages (only 30 of the 500 RLIs in the area are 'Dutch funded'). Inequality in prices and costs will increase: 'there will be no equal chances to sell our products'. That will be a big loss. This is a sound and valid argument which can not be solved in a pilot-project, but only at state level.

Besides, the farmers of the pilot RLI told us that they are confronted with an immense sand deposit in their command area due to the September 1993 floods. To remove the sand and to pursue measures to prevent such disasters (embankment of the river) is their first priority. Values such as 'independence in managing common irrigation facilities', 'striving' and 'risk-taking' are not very much encouraged under those conditions. In this context the folk story of the gift of the elephant (a metaphor for the deep tube well or river lift irrigation) from the maharaja to the successful entrepreneur is very illustrative. The point in the story is that finally the entrepreneur bagged the maharaja to take the elephant back, as it ruined him economically. People refuse the 'gift' of a deep tube well or river lift as they know it will be an elephant that will ruin them.

According to the farmers, a Farmers' Cooperative Association should first be established with a revolving fund to tackle collectively the serious financial problems of the weakest section of farmers with land in the Command Area. In the revolving fund, money, but also fertilizers, etc., can be deposited. They stated that the landholdings of the majority of the farmers are so small that they hardly can afford to use irrigation water, let alone accept a financial experiment of the scope as envisaged.

These statements can be underpinned by other findings of the research, indicating the poverty of the marginal farmers and related survival strategies and social aspects, the unequal landholding pattern in the command area and tendencies of unequal water distribution. Moreover, the findings of the river lift follow-up study are that over a period of three years there was an outflow of 20 per cent of marginal farmers, moving from agriculture to informal sector work in nearby towns. Even with the new irrigation facilities they could not sustain themselves.

Marginal farmers have not much scope to spend their money, as the study shows. In the river lift irrigation/deep tube well the food expenditures absorb 71 to 78 per cent of their income. With growth in income this proportion tends to fall. The proportion increases with the falling income of a household. Around 15 per cent of the marginal farmer households live below the poverty line (Rs 7,200 yearly in 1993).

Farmers with less land are more aware of risks, which they keep to a minimum. The following tactics are used:

- land fragmentation: some farmers have more than 20 tiny plots of land in the command area and outside the command area;
- small plots are prepared with maximum capacity to catch rain: bunds and embankment;
- if one plot is attacked by pest the other can be saved;
- transferring the risk of crop loss to somebody else by leasing land out;
- types of crops are cultivated with a minimum investment risk (leaving out *boro*) as wheat, jute, and *amon* which have remained the main crop. Farmers know that anyhow they will get back their investment costs;

TABLE 9.5: LANDHOLDING PATTERN IN THE COMMAND AREA OF RLI AND DTW ACCORDING TO CLASS IN PERCENTAGE IN THE SAMPLE SURVEY

Class	RLI		DTW	
	% farmers	% owned land	% farmers	% owned land
Marginal	63	35	70	45
Small	25	41	22	31
Middle	10	19	6	10
Large	2	5	2	14

- farmers will try innovations only on small plots, e.g. 1 *bigha* of High Yielding Variety tomatoes. In 1993 there were three cases of suicide of marginal farmers in the Terai area because of low market prices. They ruined themselves by taking too much land for High Yielding Variety tomatoes; when the prices came down they lost everything.
- they reduce the risk factor by growing early varieties of cauliflower, early variety Rs 150 for 40 kg and Rs 150 for 100 kg late variety.

Moreover, scarce savings can not be put back in agricultural production because of many social obligations such as the dowries for daughters. Households of marginal- and small farmers face problems when a daughter has to be married. As shown earlier dowries are also on the increase in the Project Area. The burden of dowry is one of the general reasons of loss of land, cows and other assets.

However, even more important than the just mentioned aspects to understand why marginal farmers express their reluctance to accept privatization are the prevailing patterns of landholding pattern and distribution of irrigation water.

The findings of the sample survey show the aggregate data on five river lift and three deep tube well schemes comprising 530 families. The landownership according to class of farmers in the command area of the farmers is tabulated in Table 9.5.

This shows that although the marginal farmers form the majority, they have control over only 35 per cent and 45 per cent respectively, of the land. This implies that 65 per cent and 55 per cent of the land is controlled by small, middle and large farmers, who, on a household basis, will benefit disproportionately.

Therefore, there is a risk that the real poor farmers' needs, interests and participation can become subordinate to those of the more powerful, often already dominant in the BCs. Translated in gender terms the danger is real that socio-economic polarization between various classes of women will increase in case of privatization under the prevailing conditions.

The conclusion that can be drawn from the data is that though as a class the marginal farmers are the biggest beneficiaries, the benefit distributed among the individual households is thinly spread among them. In the RLI/DTW schemes much less than 50 per cent of benefits of irrigation have gone to them. The net amount of irrigated land per household is very small for the marginal farmers compared to that of other classes. The marginal farmers of the DTW could irrigate 65 to 85 per cent of their Command Area land and the small farmers irrigated 57 to 91 per cent of their Command Area land in *rabi* season. This means that marginal/small farmers as a whole have received more benefit from the schemes than the other two classes in one season. But as the number of such beneficiaries is quite large the irrigated area actually averages only 1/3 acre for each marginal farmer and a little over 1/2 acre for each small farmer. Moreover, the use of water in pre-*kharif* remains far below expectation.

Besides, because of technical constraints the farmers are in no way assured of an optimal and timely irrigation water supply. To make investments under those conditions implies a lot of risk which they can ill afford. This is one of the reasons why the water use so far has remained below expectations.

NOTES

1. It is with sadness that we commemorate Mr Mitra, the real motivator and implementer behind the handpump programme. His untimely demise is a great loss for the project.
2. The complaint of too much iron in the water was tested immediately by the Director of Agriculture. The laboratory test showed that the iron content of the water was within permissible standards. The project area is outside the West Bengal belt in which arsenical poisoning of water has made many victims.

3. When the researchers reported this male-dominant control of handpumps immediate steps were taken by the Department of Agriculture to instruct the extension workers (KPS) to be alert on this point to convince men who removed the upper part of the pump that the it should be restored to relieve the women's work.

10. From Beneficiaries to Heroines?

10.1 BACK TO EMANCIPATION?

We started to put the gender analysis in a historical context in Chapter 2 by describing the prominent role of women in the revolutionary peasant movements which arose decades ago in the three districts of the small-scale irrigation projects. The first part of the title of this book, 'from Heroines to Beneficiaries' refers to the historical process in which the very emancipated women of the past became subordinated by processes of modernization and subsequent integration into the dominant Hindu culture and its related patriarchal dominance. The second part of the title and of this chapter, 'from Beneficiaries to Heroines?' hints at the future. How far can a development project like the North Bengal Terai contribute to the emergence of 'new' heroines, who will struggle again against old and new class and gender inequalities? It was stated that not many foreign and Indian consultants from other states, visiting the project field of the North Bengal Development Project, will be aware that the Rajbansi 'beneficiary woman' they talk with during their field visits, might be the daughter of a mother who was jailed, molested or shot in the Tebhaga or Naxalbari uprising. The mother fought for her right to get a fair share of the rice yield as *bargadar* (sharecropper) of the *jotedar* (landowner), or to get land to which she was entitled under the Land Reform Acts. Now, the daughter is the wife of a marginal farmer, and the allocation of a handpump is an important asset in her struggle for survival and emancipation.

The aim of this study was to assess the impact of Phase II of the small-scale irrigation North Bengal Terai Development Project (NBTDP) from a gender perspective. The main activities of the project were the implementation of handpumps, pump dug wells, shallow tube wells, deep tube wells and river lift irrigation schemes in three districts. In addition farmers' training, women's activities and a small pilot-project trial of the 'handing over' of an irrigation scheme to the local farmers were included. In short a whole range of technological, and some human-resource development interventions were introduced in a predominantly agrarian subsistence economy aiming to increase the production and income of in particular marginal and small farmers and to generate a better income distribution in the area.

The project content and the gender history of the project were sketched in Chapter 3. The considerations for, and the content of the planned gender impact study and activities were revealed therein.

For an insight into the impact, an intensive in-depth study was conducted in 1989, which started with a base-line of 273 households 'before' they used irrigation water. After the installation of the water device and its operational there was a follow-up of the households for three subsequent years till 1993. They were visited three times by the research field workers in the three seasons: *kharif*, *rabi* and pre-*kharif*. The sample survey of 1,524 households was undertaken to put the results of the in-depth study in wider perspective and thus covered the same fields. In addition, it tried to identify the various constraints—administrative, technical, social—which might have hindered the optimum use of the various schemes. The sample survey encompassed the entire project area and concerned the three agricultural seasons of 1992-3.

In this concluding chapter we will present a summary of the main findings of the basic gender data, and place the emerging trends of change in a theoretical perspective. We will reflect on the conditions which contributed to the success of the project in general, and specific for the gender component. Finally some general recommendations will be given which will hopefully contribute to a better operationalization of more 'emancipation-generating' empowerment strategies as a lesson learned.

10.2 SUMMARY FINDINGS ON GENDER IMPACT

We will first summarize our main findings of the gender impact of Phase II of the North Bengal Terai Development Project.

In Chapter 4 basic gender data were presented. We showed

the disadvantageous position of women in patrilocal and patrilineal social organization, the sex-ratio figures, higher mortality rates of women, bad health, lower literacy, early marriage, change from bride-price to dowry, and absence of inheritance rights.

The distribution of the households by community showed that the Rajbansis constitute a little less than half of the sample, followed by the Muslims, general Hindus, other Scheduled Castes, mainly Namasudras, and the Scheduled Tribes in order of numerical strength. There was no correlation between community and class. Most women in our study belong to the category of marginal farmers (60 per cent), followed by small (22 per cent), middle (14 per cent) and large farmer women (5 per cent). Women of 30 landless households in the in-depth study and 46 households in the sample survey were also included.

In our small sample of the follow-up study the numbers of males and females are basically too small to estimate a reliable sex-ratio. However, our finds show that there is reason for concern about the women's well-being in the Terai region. The sample survey in particular indicates an alarmingly low sex ratio, 876, far below the West Bengal rural average of 947 (Census 1981). The in-depth study sex-ratio is 944: about the rural average of the state.

Our data reveal that 95 per cent of the girls are married at the age of 15 years. Early motherhood in combination with a often dramatically weak physical condition and lack of ante- and postnatal care, and a high mortality risk during childbirth might be the major causes for the low sex ratios in the category of women above 15 years.

Patriarchy in the Terai is reflected in residence-, kinship-, and inheritance-patterns. Patrilocal residence patterns are almost an iron law. All the young brides migrate after marriage to the village of the bridegroom and parents-in-law. This makes the position of young women very vulnerable as they have to adjust to a new family, and are dependent on their acceptance and tolerance. Descent is fully patrilineal. Inheritance rights of land for women are almost unknown, unless the sibling composition does not allow any other option.

It seemed that only ten years ago the Rajbansis had a system of bride price in which the parents of the bridegroom had to give gifts to the parents of the bride as a compensation for their loss of a daughter and her labour. This system, reflecting high esteem for the girl, has turned some years ago the other way round, and we found that Rajbansis and also Namasudras, Muslims and even tribal groups gave dowries. The overall trend in increase of dowry has a detrimental effect on the existing already vulnerable position of women. The question how far the observed increase in dowries in the Terai area might have an impact on the worsening of the food priority and health care of girls cannot be answered. What we can indicate, however, is that dowries compel parents of daughters to sell, mortgage, or lease-out, the small plot of land they possess. With that they loose a basic survival resource.

The average household size in the project area is 6.2 persons in the in-depth study, and 5.7 in the sample survey. The in-depth study reveals a correlation between family size and economic status: the poorer the household, the smaller the family. The general trend is that of small nuclear families among landless (4.2 members) and marginal and small farmers (5.1), to larger joint and extended families in medium (9.7) and large farmers' households (6.5). The data show that there are not many differences in the general family size pattern per community, while during the timespan of the in-depth study not many differences could be traced.

Nuclear families constitute 64 per cent of the sample survey (average size 4.9), joint families 26 per cent (average size 7.3) and extended family 10 per cent (average size 6.7). However, reality is not so clear-cut as the formal classification suggests. In the selected villages it was often found that family units live together in one compound and can statistically be classified as nuclear. However, actually and functionally these families were in many respects joint: they pool the means of production and labour.

Out of 261 households, only ten are female headed in the in-depth study: nine women are widows and one is married. All women who are female heads of the family, except one, earn their own living as agricultural labourers, cultivators or maids. The percentage of female headed households in the sample survey is even less: only 4.5. Findings of the follow-up study show that female headed households can only be found in households of the landless and marginal farmers of the handpump scheme.

The literacy rates for the landless are very low: for men 56 per cent, and women only 22 per cent. The in-depth study shows that the literacy rates found are above the state average: 76 per cent for men and 54 per cent for women. The sample survey shows a more gloomy literacy rate: 66 per cent for men and women only 36 per cent. The gender gap in education between men and women is obvious.

10.2.1 Processes of change

In Chapter 5 the general achievements of the project in successfully reaching the poorest class and the socially weakest groups are revealed. The in-depth study indicates that there is no question of a growing land polarization in the area as a result of irrigation intervention. On the contrary, there is a slight trend indicating that some marginal farmers could climb up to the level of small farmers. Marginal farmers of the handpump scheme have increased their landholdings by 10 per cent over the three years of study. The increase in leasing-in of land by landless and marginal farmers in the command area (CA) indicates also a betterment in economic conditions. The farm production and farm income of the marginal and small farmers has increased though this is partly counterbalanced by inflation.

The findings in Chapter 5 also show that the participation of women in agriculture has increased, except in the handpump schemes. However, in the handpump scheme we also found a decrease in participation rate for the males. This implies that there is no question of gender specific withdrawal of women out of agricultural productive labour. General cultural notions on hire of wage labourers as circumstances allow, may have an impact on the participation of family labour of the handpump beneficiaries.

There is no indication that because of higher production and higher income women are withdrawn from productive agricultural labour and that consequently *purdah* ideology is reinforced. No process of domestication of landowning women in which they are kept more in the *bari* to enhance the prestige and esteem of the family, could be indicated.

Besides the actual participation rate of women in agricultural activities, we have asked about their perception of it in comparison with that of men. We have specified 20 different types of agricultural work and the data reflects the answers of 243 land owning women of the in-depth study. No woman participates in ploughing and marketing, which is in line with the division of labour in patrilineal societies. When men also have the monopoly on marketing, this guarantees that women have no access to or control over the local economy. That makes them dependent on men. This is the reality, but, as we have seen, poverty modifies male power, and in the marginal farmers households women sometimes also sell their vegetables in the market. The findings show that women feel that harvesting, threshing and storing are typical female activities; yet manure application, land and seed preparation, transplantation of paddy, weeding and in particular protection of crops are activities in which women assess that they contribute to a high degree.

In land preparation, protection of crops, and storing of crops, quite a number of women feel that they participate more than men. The overall picture indicates that the percentage of women perceiving that they do certain activities more than men has come down over the years of study. But the perception that they share the work equally with men has become more prevalent.

A closer look at the assessment of women in their role in irrigation reveals that only 38 per cent of women states that they are not engaged in irrigation activities. That implies that 62 per cent of the women participate in irrigation work. Around 40 per cent of them state that they do less work in irrigation compared with their men of the household, but 19 per cent state that irrigating the fields is carried out equally with men. Regarding the cleaning and maintaining of irrigation channels 54 per cent states not to be involved, 33 per cent less than men, 12 per cent equal with men and 1 per cent more than men. These warrant the conclusion that the majority of the women in our study can be considered water users although they have only indirect access to the water.

Chapter 6 shows that there is a greater workload for women of various classes. The women of marginal and small farmers are more engaged in agricultural production and post-harvest activities than at the time before the irrigation water came. The better-off women have to prepare more meals and drinks for the hired agricultural labourers. The custom to pay wages partly in kind and food is still prevalent although in some places it is quickly being replaced by cash. In particular women of marginal and small peasant classes have gained as their socio-economic condition has improved, and what is more important, there is no question of polarization between women, or marginalization of the poorest women by their becoming wage labourers. It is the opposite: the number of marginal- and small farm women doing additional wage labour is reduced as they have more work on their own farm. Observations during field visits reveal that the expansion of vegetable gardens and the growing of new vegetable crops has enlarged the freedom of movement of women of the better-off households: before the handpump came they were not working in the vegetable garden, but observations showed that now they do. The introduction of new crops not associated with traditional *purdah* restrictions has created a social space in which patriarchal control is, as yet, absent. This means that the reverse of domestication, a de-domestication trend, is taking place.

The process of change from a subsistence oriented economy towards integration in the market economy has so far not caused the well-known negative changes in the gender division of labour in which men are involved in the cultivation of 'modern' profit oriented cash crops, and women are left behind in 'traditional' food production. As many other studies show, this process implies that the status of women comes down as they do not produce visible surplus value in money terms. There is certainly so far no trace of this kind of marginalization. The first use of the irrigation water is to produce food for the family. The higher rice production is mainly used for home-consumption. Only the increase in vegetable growing allows families to sell the major harvest in the market. *Purdah* restrictions prevent women from selling themselves, and the men cash the money of their labour. But some men give the household purse to their wives.

The often mentioned process of 'feminization of agriculture' in which the men migrate to earn and the women stay behind to run the farm, is also not traceable in the Terai area. The land-holding sizes are too small, and the screaming lack of alternative employment for men in other parts of Bengal and other states, makes male 'out-migration' almost impossible. The conditions in the Terai constitute a pattern in which men, women and children work on their small family farm and have no option than to increase agricultural output to its maximum. The irrigation water is mostly used to grow vegetables which is a female associated crop, and *boro* rice which requires inputs of fertilizers, pesticides and HYV seeds. We cannot say that this process of modernization has caused a shift in control over production towards men, or that agriculture is 'taken away from women'. It is true that also in the Terai men go for bank loans, buy seeds, and purchase pesticides and fertilizers but they did that before the irrigation project started as well.

In the context of a changing division of productive labour, a detailed analysis was made on the role of women and men in domestic labour and the possible changes that have occurred as a result of the use of the irrigation water. The labour participation of women on their own farm has increased. As regards domestic responsibilities, in the handpump scheme there is a remarkable change in the share men take in child care. The figures in the base-line were, male/female ratio 20:80 but are now in 1992-3, male/female, the ratio is 45:55. This can be considered as a positive outcome and might indicate that men become more aware of their responsibilities in the domestic sphere, as their women do the same in the agricultural work that has to be done.

Forty-nine per cent of the women respondents felt in 1989-90 that they did mostly household work. In 1992-3 the percentage came down to 42. In line with this perception, 47 per cent of the women felt at the time of the base-line study that they participated equally with men in the agricultural work but in 1992-3 this has increased to 55 per cent. This might indicate that more women in all the schemes have become aware that they are not only housewife and mother, but that they equally participate with their husbands in their own farm. This is encouraging as perceptions of stereotype domestic roles are changing.

Chapter 7 shows that women of the landless class, even when they have a very small plot of homestead and/or farm land, have also gained from the distribution of handpumps and other irrigation devices. This has generated more wage labour although there is still a strong preference for men when it comes to hiring landless labourers. The employment ratio of women is half, or less than half in comparison with wage labour opportunities for men in all the schemes. The number of landless women doing wage labour has even reduced from half at the baseline to one-third at the last year of study. The reason might be that the project has generated more male agricultural wage labour, but it is also possible that because of more work, and more income of the men, the landless families could buy small pieces of land and are able to lease-in 1 *bigha* for one season. The landless women work therefore more on their own (leased-in) land than four years before, which is a positive effect.

Construction work related to the project has generated wage labour for local landless women (and men), as was stipulated in the document. Although the contractors were not informed that this was a rule, they hired local landless women, because they were the cheapest. Most landless women hold the view that irrigation has given them more days of employment, but not enough to keep them employed throughout the year. Increase in wages and work days have helped them to take small plots of land on lease/mortgage. The rate of wages has also increased according to the sample survey, both for men and women. However, the women workers remain unemployed for most of the year. They should get more days of employment.

Those who have some land wished to have regular supply of water from the scheme source (river lift irrigation/deep tube well) so that they could get a good yield.

In Chapter 8 we tried to answer the question if farm land-owning women (and men) of poor households can be strengthened (empowered) within the realm of small-scale irrigation development. The data reveal that in 1992-3, 69 per cent of the women have a negative attitude towards wage labour outside the home, and 31 per cent have a positive attitude. However there is a clear trend that the positive attitude is increasing over the years. In particular in the river lift irrigation and deep tube well schemes, more women are positive then three years ago. Only in the handpump scheme do women show a less positive attitude. Complementarily the negative attitude came down in river lift irrigation and deep tube well but increased among handpump beneficiary households.

On the other hand in the same target group of handpump households in the Terai project we met very emancipated Rajbansi women who are free and independent and do not conform to Hindu norms. On the contrary they earn money by smuggling goods as torches, shirts and pants from Nepal.

The figures indicate that the majority of women can spend money independently, and the percentage of those women has increased over the years. This indicates that wage earning women have a reasonably independent position. However, we have to consider for what purposes the women spend their wages. In line with outcome of many other empirical women's studies we found that 84 per cent spends on daily food; 69 per cent purchase clothes and 62 per cent spend on home improvement.

Another indicator of the independence of women was data on freedom of movement. Seven per cent go regularly to weekly markets, 48 per cent go sometimes and 33 per cent seldom; 12 per cent of the women never attend weekly markets.

The part of the decision making in agriculture and the household reveals that men remain dominant in decision making in agricultural matters, and somewhat less in family matters. The follow-up study indicated a trend over three years in which women seem to have more say in agricultural decision making, earlier an exclusively male sector. The same trend applies to important decisions in family matters. Concluding, we can state that the unequal gender relations in decision making have not worsened during the period of study, and that there is a slight trend that women are 'sometimes' more consulted. These outcomes more or less hide that it is likely that women, although not the formal decision makers in agricultural activities, exert their social influence in a more informal way.

10.3 CONCRETE GENDER ACHIEVEMENTS

In Chapter 9 the impact of the concrete gender activities in the project are assessed. Marginal women of households who got a handpump have gained a lot in terms of nutrition, health, saving of energy, increase in income, and more freedom of movement and more self-esteem. Female headed households have benefitted in a maximum way. Women of marginal and small farm households in the river lift and deep tube well command areas have gained less in these respects as no water facilities for domestic use were planned and designed in these schemes and they were not involved in any aspect related to decision making or management. The women of landless households and river lift irrigation and deep tube well expressed their wish to have better access to drinking water and water for domestic use.

Handpumps are extremely helpful for women in the area. Besides the objective of providing irrigation water they contribute to the relief of women's domestic labour, improve the nutritional status of the family and in particular of children; and contribute to the improvement of health. Many women respondents said that their children do not suffer from diarrhoea since they have started drinking water. Moreover the handpump water makes the environment more green and beautiful.

Instead of the 13,000 planned handpumps in the initial document for Phase II, almost 28,000 were installed by early 1995 as their multi-purpose use by women is fully acknowledged. In most cases the site of the handpump was selected in consultation with the women of the house. Research proves that poor female-headed households got priority in receiving pumps.

Costs of maintenance and repair have to be born by the owners as the pump is privately owned. The survey on the non-functioning of handpumps reveals that in general it is not major problem, although there are poor female headed households who cannot pay the costs. The philosophy of development experts, in particular with an economic orientation, that people only care when they have to pay for facilities, does not count.

The handpumps are 100 per cent subsidized, but very well looked after by the target group and particular by women who got the pump on their name. They expressed a sense of joy and well-being having such an important asset of their own: 'I look after it as my own child' a woman said.

Rare cases of documented non-functioning of handpumps are due to male dominance. Men dismantle pumps in the rainy season as they are not used for irrigation, not realizing that they disadvantage their wives who have to fetch water from the public wells. This has been corrected immediately by the Department of Agriculture.

The project regulation that women would get priority as handpump beneficiary when the land is in their name, has resulted in an unforeseen, but very positive side effect. Many men now transfer land into the name of their wives, since they then have a greater chance of being selected as a handpump beneficiary. The transfer of the land right document costs only Rs 10. Ten per cent of the handpumps were registered in the name of women in 1995, and it has gone up to fourteen per cent in Phase III.

We have also reported the considerable increase in gender awareness among the male staff of the departments of agriculture and irrigation. The attitudinal changes in awareness can be proved by the many tangible gender achievements of the project. Moreover, this has been accomplished as an integrated process. The emphasis on gender in the impact research has stimulated in general communication, debate and raised gender awareness among the implementing officials and managers at various levels. During the whole period of Phase II briefing meetings were organized for the staff in the office of the joint director of agriculture in Jalpaiguri. On those occasions the research supervisors and authors of this book presented the findings and asked the staff to comment on it.

A substantial achievement in the gender field is that nine women extension workers have been trained and appointed. The training curriculum is not gender specific but nevertheless interviews with them show that they particularly address particularly women, out of their own gender awareness. Groups of farm women have been trained in water management and repair of handpumps, for example. The only gender aim not achieved is the representation of a woman in the Advisory Committee of the project.

At the local level a few women are members of the water-users committees. They were elected due to pressure from the Mahila Samiti of the Communist Party (Marxist). However, it was explained in Chapter 8 that even a proper representation of women in BCs will in no way guarantee that women will get more decision making power and/or control over the management of irrigation water. The same counts for the fair representation of marginal male farmers. The skewed landownership in the CA and the power of the large farmers is a social reality and prevent equitable distribution of water in many places. However, it should be noted that in some places we found great social awareness. A field visit in 1993 revealed that farmers suffered big losses as many had invested in *boro* but there was not sufficient irrigation water and the crop failed. As the demand for water to irrigate *boro* was in 1993 again higher than the capacity of the river lift irrigation, a land ceiling was set for *boro* irrigation for each farmer, except for those who have income from service: they are excluded from *boro* irrigation but not of irrigation of other crops in other seasons. This decision reflects a sense of social justice and may be an example for other water users' committees. To avoid illegal water use the five members of the water users committee control by rotation the illegal digging of *katcha* channels during the release of the water. With the list of names of farmers entitled to get water on a planned date, they walk around to supervise the water release.

Cultural restrictions, we have seen, reinforce the already existing invisibility of women as water users. Men can freely approach the pump operator in his pumphouse and bargain or put pressure to release water in their fields, although this is considered an informal way of trying to get water. To follow this the informal way is difficult for women. Women are not the owners of land, and therefore are not perceived as water users and subsequently as beneficiaries that entitles them to water rights.

This cuts them off from the formal way to obtain water, and

the decision making institutions and irrigation water management in the larger government owned irrigation schemes as river lift and deep tube wells. But in principle it is the same in the small so-called 'collective owned' shallow tube wells and pump dug well schemes. Male dominance as a result of patrilocal and patrilineal social organization is so pervasive that women are not considered water users or water managers although they might do most of the farm work. Only the handpump scheme in which the pumps are privately owned by households gives women some control over the pump. In general we conclude that access to water for women is not the main problem. Men will give happily access to irrigation water to women, knowing they will work hard on their land to increase food production and generate more income. Control over water is the problem.

On the other hand, we also have to point to the fact that the formal recognized composition of the BCs does not offer much scope for a correct gender representation of interest groups (only a few members are accepted) and that also counts for male representatives of marginal- and landless households.

10.4 BEHIND THE COULISSE: COORDINATION AND COOPERATION

As said in Chapter 1, the nature of the project can be characterized as a simple, but solid 'old-fashioned' government project. We narrated that all kinds of modern innovative components which are part and parcel of current irrigation management projects as role of NGOs, community participation, training in all its varieties, environmental assessments, indigenous knowledge recording, alternative technologies, credit groups for women, were not included in Phase II of the Terai project.

We asked in the beginning if such an project without tooters and bells could be successful. Can such a project contribute to the empowerment of women without the support of a powerful and well-rooted women's NGO? We have shown that the answer will be 'yes': the project has succeeded in harvesting water, although not to the maximum possible, and the used irrigation water has contributed to the improvement of the life of poor-, and small marginal farmers' households. And the project has strengthened the women of these households to improve their economic position, to reduce patriarchal restrictions and to make them more independent and aware of their own important role in agricultural production.

In retrospect we can ask 'which factors have contributed to the success of the project and its gender component in Phase II.[1] Conditions contributing to this success are no doubt the dedication, commitment, integrity, professional skill, and personality of the people involved. But, the quality of people can only bloom when the carrying capacity of the institutional framework in which they function is a sound one and the basic ideology is mutually shared. Let us therefore look behind the coulisse of this old-fashioned project to understand the roots of its success behind the scene. There is more under the sky in projects than the usual hard- and soft ware as gender, environment and role of NGOs.

(1) The institutional setting in Phase II was that the implementation and management of the project was wholly carried out by the regular government departments,[2] and the local political institutions of the state of West Bengal (panchayats). This institutional set-up gave the project an autonomous character which is a strong point in its sustainability.

The individual farmers households (in case of handpumps and shallow tube wells) and the so-called BCs (in case of deep tube wells and river lift) played an important role in the water management at household and village level. The interplay between the three parties, state departments, political leaders, and users, has been successful although the extent of this success varies with the technology.

However the binding force in this interplay is the commonly adhered political and social ideology prevalent in the area. The area is mainly dominated by the Communist Party (Marxist) and the Forward Bloc, a coalition of various left parties. It is unmistakable that in their ideology 'social justice' and 'support for the poor' rank high. These values, notions and awareness were tacitly shared by the implementing staff and other involved people. The social commitment brought clarity of perspective and gave direction to the tasks to be implemented.

(2) There was clear coordination, resulting from the overall supervision by the Director of Agriculture, Jalpaiguri range. His authority as the final decision maker, carrying all responsibilities, provides a transparent and self-reliant focus in the project. Formal procedures, informal creativity, the 'workstyle', and authority of the director and his staff maintained the coordinating capacity.

(3) All parties cooperated with each other, mainly as a result of this articulate coordination and common shared ideological perspective in the project. The fact that the implementation of the physical targets was achieved in time, and some activities even before time, is the best evidence that can be given for a well planned scheme, a fine-tuned, and well functioning structure of clear communication and interaction. This crucial point has to be seen in the light of often defunct telephone connections, no computerization at all, bad roads, vagaries of the monsoon, and the overriding lack of means of transport, the main means being the bicycle and rickshaw.

The coordinating/cooperation lines and linkages were situated at three levels:

- *within* and *between* the various line departments.
- *between* the political and the bureaucratic institutions. Panchayat members participate together with the agricultural extension workers in the site selection of schemes, and the selection and mobilization of beneficiaries; they are members of the BCs of water users, and are involved in supporting activities for the project such as supplying governmental benefits like seeds or credit and informing villagers on government policies.
- *between* the political and bureaucratic institutions and the user households and beneficiary committees. Extension work, farm men and farm women training, demonstration plots, site and beneficiary selection, are some of the components which reflect the interplay between the three parties involved.

(4) The fourth crucial point (which is important in almost all projects) is the motivation, quality and dedication of the successive Joint-Directors of Agriculture and their staff. In Phase II even high-ranking officers refused to be transferred to better postings because of their dedication to the project.

As stated in Chapter 3 it was the conviction of the mission members who formulated the project that the best chances for success of social intervention in the Terai project could be expected by relying on the existing institutional set-up of the regular government departments, and the favourable socio-political climate in the project area. An effort from the Dutch side during the formulation mission of Phase II, to post a Dutch team-leader in the field was resisted by the Bengal authorities with self-confidence. The project was conceived in the spirit of self-reliance and autonomy in March 1987. This was an added incentive for the managers of the project to be motivated to demonstrate dignity, self-confidence, and professional quality.

Moreover, it cannot be denied that the long standing friendship between the Dutch coordinator and short-term gender/research experts, and their Indian counterparts had a positive impact on the motivation and work performance. During almost the whole second phase they were visiting the area regularly and that created continuity and mutual commitment and understanding in the relations. This experience shows the importance of the Indo-Dutch personal relations for success of projects. They can only emerge when the relations have had time to develop.

(5) For the implementation of the social aspects no 'outside institution' depending on foreign money (so-called Technical Assistants) existed. The project acquired its positive results on the basis of an 'intrinsic' institutional autonomy and social awareness. Gender and participatory aspects have been incorporated, and anchored in the work of the agricultural staff, the engineers and the panchayats.

Looking behind the coulisse we asked when we wrote the manuscript of this book in 1995, what are the weak points in the project set-up. Are there missing links? What recommendations do we make to strengthen women in irrigation development at the managing-, and line department level? Now this looks a little bit as 'mustard after the meal' as Phase III of the project is already going on for seven years. Therefore, we decided to delete our long list of practical recommendations related to technical, social and choice of technology aspects.

10.5 FROM HANDPUMP BENEFICIARIES TO HEROINES?

We have mentioned in our historical sketch the heroic role women played in the Tehbaga and Naxalite peasant revolts. In these peasant movements besides the general class struggle, women have, also struggled for gender equality and emancipation. Bottom-up women's organizations of the Communist Party (Marxist) have still the capacity to mobilize and organize women at the grass-roots.

A gender-specific empowerment strategy may highly enhance the sustainability of irrigation projects and contribute at the same time to the emancipation of women. However, in development circles this important pillar of sustainability is often ignored and neglected, and considered as an additional issue that should be integrated in the mainstream objectives. Sustainability is mainly conceived from the male view in terms of 'privatization', and the development of strategies for 'efficient and effective land-and-water packages' to hand over state owned irrigation devices to the farmers. Therefore, it is very encouraging that in the third phase (1995-2002) of the project an 'own' women and development programme is a strategic approach. The Project Support Unit facilitated the organization of economic groups among women who have been covered under various project components. More than 300 Self Help Groups have been formed to mobilize women around credit groups. This has enabled women to take up income generating programmes individually and collectively.

As a concluding remark, we want to express our hope that the wisdom that existed in the second phase of the North Bengal Terai Project in its autonomy and ideology, will not die as was the case with so many traditional water harvesting irrigation schemes in the past of India. The wisdom is documented in this book.

NOTES

1. See also the *Evaluation of the Netherlands Development Programme with India, 1980-1992.* IOV Evaluation Report 1994 (1994)
2. The selection, design, construction, operation and maintenance of a scheme is executed by the Department of Agriculture (DOA), and the Department of Minor Irrigation, subdivided in the Agri-Irrigation (DTW) and the Agri-Mechanical (RLI) wing. On Block level, the most important level of implementation, the Department of Home Affairs is represented by the Block Development Officer (BDO). Both the operator and assistant operator are employed (and paid) by Home Affairs but work under the command of Agri Mechanical (in case of RLI) or Agri-Irrigation (in case of a DTW).

ANNEXURE 1.1: CRITERIA FOR SELECTION OF SITES AND RESPONDENTS

In-depth Study

The general criteria for the selection of locations and respondents were:

- composition of the population according to community (Scheduled Castes and Tribes), and religion;
- landownership (marginal, small, medium and large farmer);
- location near, or far from, towns (market places);
- installation time of the irrigation facilities under Phase II;
- proportional representation of irrigation facilities over the two main districts Jalpaiguri, Cooch Behar and Siliguri sub-division and within the blocks of the district;
- the whole process of genesis and development of a scheme should be followed in the 'before-and-after' approach.

Sample Survey

The selection of the RLI and DTW sites was based on a list of RLI/DTWs that had been functioning for at least two years, given in the Project Coordination Report 14. Schemes that had been studied earlier during the in-depth study or in students' exhaustive work were excluded.

In the next step 5 RLIs from the short list were selected on the basis of their performance level as reported in the Coordination Reports. One RLI (Paschim Chapani) whose performance was very good, another whose performance was poor (Patramjote), two RLI whose performance was below average (Borokamath and Kodalkheti) and one whose performance was moderately good (Ghugarkuthi II) were chosen for the sample survey.

A similar exercise was undertaken for the DTWs and resulted in the selection of one DTW whose performance was reported to be very good (Madhya Boragari) another which was very poor (Satkhamar), the third which was just below the average (Bhareya). All households benefitting from the RLI or DTW were interviewed.

The sample HTWs were selected in a different manner.

In Phase II more than 24,000 HTW were sanctioned in 24 blocks of the Jalpaiguri and Cooch Behar districts and Siliguri subdivision of Darjeeling district. For the survey, one cluster consisting of about 25 HTW was taken from each block. Only in blocks where more than 1,000 HTW have been sanctioned were two clusters chosen. For each block a short list was prepared of villages with at least 20 HTW in operation for one to two years. This list was prepared in consultation with the Agricultural Department. From these short-lists either one of the villages were chosen systematically. None of the villages selected had been previously studied in the in-depth study nor by the Agriculture Department.

The STW were all located in the Dinhata II block of Cooch Behar district. Fifteen STW, located in the three villages of this area, were randomly selected from a list of STW provided by the Agriculture Department. The STW selected should have been in operation at least for two years prior to the survey. Eighteen STW used by 74 households were selected by this method from three villages in Dinhata II block.

Similarly, the PDW were concentrated in some blocks of the project area only. We selected Haldibari block of Cooch Behar district to draw the sample. From the list of PDW provided by the local office it was found that there were only 10 PDW which were in operation for a minimum period of one year. We included all the 49 households using 10 pump dug wells distributed in three villages of Haldibari block.

The landless labourer households that were interviewed were chosen in the RLI and DTW sites where the schemes had been operating successfully. Thus 26 landless labourer households in Madhya Boragari (DTW) and 20 households in Paschim Chapani (RLI) were included in the sample.

ANNEXURE 5.1: PERCENTAGE OF HOUSEHOLDS THAT PROVIDED HOUSEHOLD LABOUR IN AGRICULTURE IN 1992-3

Crops	RLI				DTW				HTW				STW				PDW			
	Marginal N=222	Small N=90	Middle N=34	Big N=8	Marginal N=124	Small N=38	Middle N=10	Big N=4	Marginal N=666	Small N=130	Middle N=27	Big N=2	Marginal N=15	Small N=38	Middle N=15	Big N=6	Marginal N=226	Small N=16	Middle N=7	Big N=0
Amon paddy	50	76	79	75	48	66	100	75	68	90	96	100	93	79	87	83	100	88	100	0
Aus paddy	29	47	50	75	16	26	20	50	39	58	44	50	13	26	47	17	4	0	14	0
HYV (*boro*) paddy	25	46	53	88	24	42	40	0	7	13	11	0	80	68	93	83	0	0	0	0
HYV (*K*) paddy	48	51	71	50	57	42	30	50	38	54	63	100	33	32	53	50	0	6	0	0
Jute	64	82	85	75	82	89	100	100	59	82	96	100	93	74	87	83	77	94	100	0
Oil seeds	36	41	74	75	21	61	70	25	10	18	26	0	67	58	93	83	0	0	0	0
Other cereal (*K*)	1	3	0	13	1	0	0	0	2	5	7	50	0	0	0	0	0	0	0	0
Other cereal (*PK*)	3	3	9	0	15	11	10	50	6	9	4	0	0	5	0	0	0	0	0	0
Other cereal (*R*)	13	13	26	50	4	5	0	0	4	5	11	0	0	0	7	17	0	6	0	0
Tobacco	2	4	6	0	2	5	0	25	15	25	30	0	13	5	13	0	0	6	14	0
Vegetables (*K*)	10	14	12	38	1	0	0	0	11	9	11	0	7	0	0	0	0	6	0	0
Vegetables (*PK*)	18	21	24	25	2	11	0	25	38	34	41	50	0	0	0	0	0	0	0	0
Vegetables (*R*)	56	82	76	50	69	66	60	50	82	88	89	100	0	29	47	17	92	94	100	0
Wheat	55	58	56	63	27	50	50	25	33	42	52	50	27	26	40	17	12	6	43	0
Sugar cane	0	0	0	0	0	0	0	0	0	0	0	0	0	0	0	0	0	0	0	0

ANNEXURE 5.2: RATE OF PARTICIPATION IN FARM AGRICULTURE BY HOUSEHOLD MALE WORKERS FORCE (15-59 YRS) IN 1992-3

(in percentage of the work force)

Crops	RLI				DTW				HTW				STW				PDW			
	Marginal	Small	Middle	Big	Marginal	Small	Middle	Big	Marginal	Small	Middle	Big	Marginal	Small	Middle	Big	Marginal	Small	Middle	Big
Amon paddy	83	82	89	94	87	78	70	100	93	95	93	80	100	96	96	100	94	87	83	0
Aus paddy	84	78	84	88	88	73	50	100	92	93	100	50	100	92	94	75	100	0	100	0
HYV (*boro*) paddy	84	83	86	91	83	73	44	0	89	92	89	0	100	95	96	100	0	0	0	0
HYV (*K*) paddy	87	87	80	82	96	100	86	67	90	94	84	80	100	100	94	100	0	100	0	0
Jute	84	81	85	89	92	86	70	82	94	94	93	80	100	92	96	100	96	83	83	0
Oil seeds	82	82	81	88	85	82	67	100	93	91	89	0	92	94	96	90	0	0	0	0
Other cereal (*K*)	100	78	0	50	100	0	0	0	92	83	71	100	0	0	0	0	0	0	0	0
Other cereal (*PK*)	80	100	100	0	94	83	50	67	93	86	100	0	0	100	0	0	0	0	0	0
Other cereal (*R*)	74	75	90	82	100	75	0	0	100	97	100	0	0	0	100	100	0	100	0	0
Tobacco	100	86	75	0	100	100	0	100	96	98	100	0	50	100	100	0	0	33	100	0
Vegetables (*K*)	79	74	67	89	100	0	0	0	91	93	100	0	100	0	0	0	0	100	0	0
Vegetables (*PK*)	91	84	88	71	60100	0	100		89	98	94	100	0	0	0	0	0	0	0	0
Vegetables (*R*)	84	84	89	100	96	88	85	71	92	94	93	80	0	100	92	100	94	88	83	0
Wheat	87	82	88	88	87	83	80	100	93	92	98	100	80	80	92	50	100	100	60	0
Sugar cane	50	0	0	0	0	0	0	0	0	0	0	0	0	0	0	0	0	0	0	0

ANNEXURE 5.3: RATE OF PARTICIPATION IN FARM AGRICULTURE BY HOUSEHOLD WOMEN WORKERS FORCE (15-59 YRS) IN 1992-3

(in percentage of the work force)

Crops	RLI				DTW				HTW				STW				PDW			
	Marginal	Small	Middle	Big	Marginal	Small	Middle	Big	Marginal	Small	Middle	Big	Marginal	Small	Middle	Big	Marginal	Small	Middle	Big
Amon paddy	80	77	72	54	91	85	88	71	94	92	100	80	100	96	100	86	94	100	100	0
Aus paddy	80	80	68	60	100	81	100	67	95	97	95	100	100	100	100	60	100	0	100	0
HYV (*boro*) paddy	90	81	73	61	98	88	100	0	96	97	100	0	100	93	100	71	0	0	0	0
HYV (*K*) paddy	83	82	64	80	86	96	75	80	95	90	100	80	100	100	100	90	100	0	0	
Jute	81	74	65	80	84	93	81	70	91	85	86	80	94	93	100	71	96	100	100	0
Oil seeds	80	85	70	60	83	89	75	50	94	78	83	0	100	92	100	79	0	0	0	0
Other cereal (*K*)	100	50	0	100	100	0	0	0	100	100	100	75	0	0	0	0	0	0	0	0
Other cereal (*PK*)	89	100	86	0	80	100	50	80	98	100	100	0	0	100	0	0	0	0	0	0
Other cereal (*R*)	83	93	93	60	100	100	0	0	100	100	88	0	0	0	100	100	0	100	0	0
Tobacco	100	100	83	0	100	86	0	100	93	95	82	0	100	100	100	0	0	100	100	0
Vegetables (*K*)	89	94	80	78	100	0	0	0	87	86	100	0	100	0	0	0	0	100	0	0
Vegetables (*PK*)	67	71	31	50	100	100	0	100	96	89	100	75	0	0	0	0	0	0	0	0
Vegetables (*R*)	82	77	69	60	90	89	82	57	94	93	100	80	0	89	91	80	94	100	100	0
Wheat	87	77	68	50	85	86	90	50	94	98	93	75	100	100	100	40	100	100	100	0
Sugar cane	0	0	0	0	0	0	0	0	0	0	0	0	0	0	0	0	0	0	0	0

ANNEXURE 6.1: PARTICIPATION OF WOMEN IN FAMILY FARM ACTIVITIES (PRE-*KHARIF*)

Participation rate (%)

Activity	Year	Summer paddy (Aus)					HYV paddy				Vegetables					Jute				
		RLI	DTW	HTW	STW	PDW	RLI	DTW	HTW	STW	RLI	DTW	HTW	STW	PDW	RLI	DTW	HTW	STW	PDW
1. Land, preparation (ploughing,	89-90	3	10	0	7	0	0	0	0	0	0	0	16	0	0	2	6	2	7	0
levelling etc.)	92-3	0	16	4	17	0	5	0	0	0	0	0	22	11	0	6	12	9	4	0
2. Seed selection/ preparation	89-90	0	1	0	0	0	0	0	0	0	0	0	0	0	0	0	0	0	0	0
of seed bed	92-3	0	0	5	0	0	5	0	13	0	0	0	14	0	0	0	0	0	0	0
3. Fertilizer/manure	89-90	7	2	17	11	0	0	0	0	0	0	0	40	0	0	5	7	3	4	0
application	92-3	0	14	10	33	0	10	23	0	0	0	0	23	22	0	0	18	15	4	0
4. Plucking of	89-90	0	0	0	0	0	0	30	0	0	0	0	0	0	0	0	0	0	0	0
seedlings	92-3	0	0	0	0	0	5	38	0	0	0	0	0	0	0	0	0	0	0	0
5. Sowing/	89-90	0	0	0	0	0	0	20	0	0	0	0	47	7	15	0	0	0	0	0
transplanting	92-3	0	0	0	0	0	10	0	0	0	0	0	45	22	0	0	0	0	0	0
6. Weeding	89-90	17	54	33	7	0	0	0	0	0	0	0	45	4	0	23	48	33	7	0
	92-3	7	38	33	33	0	0	0	0	0	0	0	37	11	0	22	49	38	4	0
7. Pesticide	89-90	3	0	0	0	0	0	0	0	0	0	0	2	0	0	0	0	0	0	0
application	92-3	0	0	0	0	0	0	0	0	0	0	0	0	0	0	0	0	0	0	0
8. Protecting crops	89-90	25	15	41	14	0	0	30	11	0	0	0	26	4	0	8	13	10	11	0
	92-3	36	15	49	33	0	50	38	13	0	0	0	32	22	0	42	22	31	42	0
9. Irrigating fields	89-90	0	0	0	0	0	0	0	0	0	0	0	21	0	0	0	0	0	0	0
	92-3	4	0	0	0	0	15	0	0	0	0	0	43	0	0	13	0	0	0	0
10. Preparation/	89-90	0	0	0	0	0	0	0	0	0	0	0	0	0	0	0	0	0	0	0
repair of bunds	92-3	0	0	0	0	0	10	0	0	0	0	0	0	0	0	0	0	0	0	0
11. Harvesting	89-90	2	16	3	0	0	0	50	11	0	0	0	79	29	23	23	0	27	4	0
	92-3	7	37	33	50	0	30	40	0	0	0	0	73	100	0	22	4	8	100	0

12. Drying of crops and straw	89-90	38	0	0	0	0	0	0	0	0	0	0	0	0	0	34	8	10	0	0
	92-3	71	0	0	0	0	65	0	0	0	0	0	0	0	0	52	27	65	0	0
13. Treshing	89-90	12	50	95	89	8	0	15	44	0	0	0	0	0	0	0	0	0	0	0
	92-3	9	49	51	67	36	20	15	38	0	0	0	0	0	0	47	0	0	0	0
14. Winnowing	89-90	33	50	0	80	8	0	50	0	0	0	0	0	0	0	0	0	0	0	0
	92-3	76	69	0	67	36	60	46	0	0	0	0	0	0	0	0	0	0	0	0
15. Storing	89-90	38	55	66	90	8	0	49	23	0	0	0	0	0	0	10	0	0	0	0
	92-3	89	98	79	83	36	60	46	63	0	0	0	37	0	0	63	17	62	100	0
16. Marketing	89-90	0	0	0	0	0	0	0	0	0	0	0	0	0	0	0	0	0	0	0
	92-3	0	0	0	0	0	0	0	0	0	0	0	2	0	0	0	0	0	0	0

Note: Participation rate is the percentage of women work force (adult) of the households growing the crop who had participated in the activity.

ANNEXURE 6.2: PARTICIPATION OF WOMEN IN FAMILY FARM ACTIVITIES (*KHARIF*) *Participation rate (%)*

Activity	Year	Winter paddy (Amon)					HYV paddy					Vegetables				
		RLI	DTW	HTW	STW	PDW	RLI	DTW	HTW	STW	PDW	RLI	DTW	HTW	STW	PDW
1. Land preparation	89-90	1	0	2	0	0	0	0	25	0	0	0	0	0	0	0
(ploughing, levelling, etc.)	92-3	7	5	2	4	0	10	6	29	4	0	0	0	64	29	0
2. Seed selection/preparation	89-90	6	17	41	4	0	0	14	32	4	0	0	0	0	0	0
of seed bed	92-3	11	23	32	33	0	14	17	0	33	0	0	0	0	0	0
3. Fertilizer/manure	89-90	1	14	16	18	0	2	13	3	18	0	0	0	0	0	0
application	92-3	7	17	19	8	0	10	12	20	8	0	0	0	12	29	0
4. Plucking of seedlings	89-90	42	51	0	0	0	2	2	0	0	0	0	0	0	0	0
	92-3	34	45	0	42	0	32	21	0	42	0	0	0	0	0	0
5. Sowing/transplanting	89-90	6	68	39	4	0	2	28	22	4	0	0	0	0	14	39
	92-3	12	49	36	4	0	16	23	31	4	0	0	0	12	76	0
6. Weeding	89-90	1	0	2	0	0	0	1	3	0	0	0	0	0	0	0
	92-3	1	0	16	0	0	1	0	16	0	0	0	0	41	0	0
7. Pesticide application	89-90	0	0	0	0	0	0	0	0	0	0	0	0	0	0	0
	92-3	0	0	0	0	0	0	0	0	0	0	0	0	0	0	0
8. Protecting crops	89-90	17	12	45	29	0	10	6	25	14	0	0	0	0	7	0
	92-3	49	25	37	13	0	55	19	29	13	0	0	0	6	41	0
9. Irrigating fields	89-90	0	0	0	0	0	0	2	0	0	0	0	0	0	0	0
	92-3	0	0	1	0	0	0	0	23	0	0	0	0	47	18	0
10. Preparation/repair of	89-90	0	1	0	0	0	0	0	3	0	0	0	0	0	0	0
bunds	92-3	20	0	0	0	0	21	0	0	0	0	0	0	0	0	0
11. Harvesting	89-90	13	44	19	0	0	10	33	13	0	0	0	0	0	43	40
	92-3	14	43	37	0	0	15	33	42	0	0	0	0	76	94	28

12. Drying of crops and straw	89-90	60	0	0	0	0	2	0		0	0	0	0	0	0	0
	92-3	80	0	0	0	0	82	0	0	0	0	0	0	0	0	0
13. Threshing	89-90	44	97	81	100	31	32	77	70	82	0	0	0	0	8	0
	92-3	12	95	50	71	44	16	63	63	71	27	0	0	0	82	0
14. Winnowing	89-90	65	91	0	80	30	41	54	0	0	0	0	0	0	0	0
	92-3	88	79	0	50	44	88	73	0	50	36	0	0	0	0	0
15. Storing	89-90	69	99	83	100	8	20	76	67	50	0	0	0	0	0	0
	92-3	85	98	67	100	44	86	77	76	100	36	0	0	6	0	28
16. Marketing	89-90	0	0	0	0	0	2	0	0	0	0	0	0	0	0	0
	92-3	0	0	0	0	0	0	0	0	0	0	0	0	6	0	0

Note: Participation rate is the percentage of women work force (adult) of the households growing the crop who had participated in the activity.

ANNEXURE 6.3: PARTICIPATION OF WOMEN IN FAMILY FARM ACTIVITIES (*RABI*)

Participation rate (%)

Activity	Year	Wheat					Tobacco					Vegetables					Oil seeds				Pulses	
		RLI	DTW	HTW	STW	PDW	RLI	DTW	HTW	STW	PDW	RLI	DTW	HTW	STW	PDW	RLI	DTW	HTW	STW	RLI	DTW
1. Land preparation (ploughing,	89-90	6	3	3	0	0	2	18	25	0	0	11	3	25	0	0	0	0	0	0	0	0
levelling, etc.)	92-93	6	22	28	46	0	12	33	52	44	0	19	24	40	29	0	0	7	2	29	0	0
2. Seed selection/ preparation	89-90	0	0	0	0	0	36	14	7	0	0	10	3	12	0	0	0	0	0	0	0	0
of seed bed	92-93	0	0	5	0	0	21	20	48	44	0	8	7	18	0	0	0	0	7	0	0	0
3. Fertilizer/manure	89-90	0	5	0	0	0	13	58	48	0	0	25	11	18	0	0	11	0	0	0	0	0
application	92-93	15	33	25	63	0	43	61	69	88	0	38	43	35	29	0	0	42	0	33	0	0
4. Plucking of seedlings	89-90	0	0	0	0	0	2	0	0	0	0	0	0	0	0	0	0	0	0	0	0	0
	92-93	0	0	0	0	0	55	0	0	0	0	14	0	0	0	0	0	0	0	0	0	0
5. Sowing/ transplanting	89-90	0	0	0	0	0	26	6	5	0	15	35	39	6	14	0	11	0	0	0	0	0
	92-93	1	0	0	0	0	43	9	10	0	0	52	43	35	76	0	0	0	0	0	0	0
6. Weeding	89-90	6	13	3	0	0	6	0	0	0	0	24	45	37	0	0	0	0	0	0	0	0
	92-93	1	32	32	13	0	52	2	12	0	0	47	52	40	0	0	2	25	0	0	0	0
7. Pesticide	89-90	0	3	0	0	0	0	0	0	0	0	3	0	1	0	0	0	0	0	0	0	0
application	92-93	0	0	0	0	0	0	0	0	0	0	0	0	0	0	0	0	0	0	0	0	0
8. Protecting crops	89-90	6	5	27	0	0	30	20	7	0	0	27	74	22	7	0	22	0	0	0	17	0
	92-93	62	21	42	29	0	67	40	10	33	0	71	70	46	41	0	34	0	33	10	0	9
9. Irrigating fields	89-90	9	13	7	0	0	13	63	48	0	0	16	47	13	0	0	0	0	0	0	0	0
	92-93	37	26	24	42	0	33	59	33	28	0	35	48	50	18	0	3	0	0	52	0	0
10. Preparation/repair	89-90	0	0	0	0	0	2	0	0	0	0	0	0	0	0	0	0	0	0	0	0	0
of bunds	92-93	0	0	3	0	0	0	0	0	0	0	0	0	10	0	0	0	0	0	0	0	0

11.	Harvesting	89-90	14	53	33	0	0	43	54	23	4	0	40	82	65	43	9	0	0	0	11	0	30
		92-93	26	40	41	50	0	33	51	36	33	4	61	87	66	94	28	12	42	45	57	0	90
12.	Drying of crops and straw	89-90	0	0	0	0	0	43	74	59	14	0	0	0	0	0	0	0	0	0	0	0	0
		92-93	72	0	0	0	0	50	72	52	100	0	0	0	0	0	0	46	0	0	0	0	0
13.	Treshing	89-90	25	68	90	43	8	0	0	0	0	0	0	0	0	0	0	11	0	0	0	0	0
		92-93	18	72	59	54	0	0	0	0	0	0	0	0	0	0	0	7	33	60	86	0	0
14.	Winnowing	89-90	34	53	0	50	4	0	0	0	0	0	0	0	0	0	0	3	0	0	0	0	50
		92-93	85	58	0	92	0	0	0	0	0	0	0	0	0	0	0	68	58	0	14	0	95
15.	Storing	89-90	40	68	90	54	8	51	74	41	14	0	17	0	0	8	0	4	0	0	0	0	46
		92-93	72	77	75	96	0	81	87	74	100	14	66	17	57	82	28	68	75	67	100	0	90
16.	Marketing	89-90	0	0	0	0	0	0	0	0	0	0	3	0	5	0	0	0	0	0	0	0	0
		92-93	0	0	0	0	0	0	0	0	0	0	3	0	3	0	0	0	0	0	0	0	0

Note: Participation rate is the percentage of women work force (adult) of the households growing the crop who had participated in the activity.

Bibliography

Afshar, Haleh ed. (1987). *Women, State and Ideology. Studies from Africa and Asia*, Macmillan Press, London.

Agarwal, Anil and Sunita Narain, eds (1997). *Dying Wisdom: Rise, Fall and Potential of India's Traditional Water Harvesting sSstems, State of India's Environment*, A Citizens' Report. Centre for Science and Environment, Delhi.

Agarwal, B. (1986). Women, poverty and agricultural growth in India, *The Journal of Peasant Studies*, Vol. 13, No. 4, pp. 165-220.

Agarwal, B. (1994). *A Field of One's Own. Gender and Land rights in South Asia*. South Asian Studies 58. University Press, Cambridge.

Bandyopadhyay, Sekhar (1994). Development, differentiation and caste: the Namasudra movement in Bengal, 1872-1947, in Bandyopadhyay, Dasgupta and Schendel eds (1994), *Bengal: Communities, Development*, Manohar, Delhi, pp. 43-65.

Bandyopadhyay, Sekhar, Abhijit Dasgupta and Willem van Schendel eds (1994). *Bengal: Communities, Development and States*, Manohar, Delhi.

Banerjee, Nirmala and Devaki Jain eds (1985). *Tyranny of the Household, Investigative Essays on Women's Work*, Shakti Books, Delhi.

Basu, Amrita (1993). *Two Faces of Protest, Contrasting Modes of Women's Activism*, Oxford University Press, Delhi.

Basu, Swaraj (1994). The colonial state and the indigenous society: the creation of the Rajbansi identity in Bengal, in S. Bandyopadhyay, A. Dasgupta and W. van Schendel eds (1994), *Bengal: Communities, Development and States*, Manohar, Delhi, pp. 43-65.

Beneria, Lourdes ed. (1982). *The Sexual Division of Labour in Rural Societies*, Preager, New York.

Bharadwaj, K. (1990). *Irrigation in India, Alternative Perspectives*, ICSSR, Research in Economics, Second Survey. Monograph 3, Delhi.

Bhave, Sumitra (1988). *Pan on Fire: Eight Dalit Women tell their Story* (translated by Gauri Deshpande), Indian Social Institute, Delhi.

Bowles, Gloria and R. Duelli Klein eds (1983). *Theories of Women's Studies*, Routledge & Kegan Paul, London.

Carney, Judith A. (1988). Struggles over crop rights and labor within contract farming households in a Gambian irrigated rice project, *The Journal of Peasant Studies*, Vol. 15, No. 3, pp. 334-49.

Centre for Women's Development Studies (1990). *National Colloquium on Role of Women in Water Resource Management*, Report, CWDS, Delhi.

Chakrabarti, S.B., B.R. Ghose and A.K. Danda eds (1985). *Agrarian Situation in India*, Vol. II, Anthropological Survey of India, Calcutta.

Chakrabarti, S.B. ed. (1988). *Social Science and Social Concern: Felicitation Volume in Honour of Professor B.K. Roy Burman*, Mittal Publications, Delhi.

Chambers, R. (1987). *Managing Canal Irrigation: Practical Analysis from South Asia*, Oxford University Press, Delhi.

Chen, Martha Alter (1986). *A Quiet Revolution, Women in Transition in rural Bangladesh* (rpt. 1993), BRAC Prokashana, Dhaka.

Choudhury, N.C. and Rajatsubhra Mukhopadhyay (1988). Irrigation opportunities, agrarian Class and Rural Development, in S.B. Chakrabarti ed. *Social Science and Social Concern: Felicitation Volume in honour of Professor B.K. Roy Burman*, Mittal Publication, Delhi.

Chowdhury, A.K.M. Alauddin (1985). Maternal nutrition in rural Bangladesh, in N. Banerjee and D. Jain, eds *Tyranny of the Household*, Shakti, New Delhi.

Dasgupta, Satadal, Seana Hennessey and Rajat Subhra Mukhopadhyay (2002). Caste and Agrarian Structure in West Bengal: Implications for Rural Development, in *Man and Development*, Vol. XXII (2), pp. 45-62.

Dove, Michael R. and Carol Carpenter eds (1992). *Sociology of Natural Resources in Pakistan and Adjoining Countries*, Vanguard, Lahore.

Epstein, Scarlett T. (1962). *Economic Development and Social Change in South India*, Manchester University Press, Manchester.

Etienne, M. and E. Leacock eds (1980). *Women and Colonization*, Praeger, New York, pp. 25-42.

French, Marilyn (1995), *From Eve to Dawn: A Women's History of the World*, Meulenhoff, Amsterdam.

Ghose, A.K. (1986). Agrarian reform in West Bengal: Objectives, achievements and limitations in Ghose ed. (1986), pp. 91-137.

Ghose, Ajit Kumar ed. (1986). *Agrarian Reform in Contemporary Developing Countries*, Croom Helm, London and Canberra.

Ghosh, Chitra (1991). *Women Movement Politics in Bengal,* Chatterjee, Calcutta.

Golde, Peggy ed. (1970). *Women in the Field, Anthropological Experiences*, Aldine, Chicago.

Gooneratne, W. and S. Hirashima eds (1990). *Irrigation and Water Management in Asia*, Sterling, Delhi.

Gopalan, C. (1995). The mother and child in India, *Economic and Political Weekly*, Vol. XX, No. 4, 26 January, pp. 159-66.

Groverman, Verona and Edith van Walsum (1994), India, Women may lose or gain: expected impact of irrigation projects, in Vera Gianotten, Verona Groverman, Edith van Walsum, Lida Zuiderberg, *Assessing the Gender*

Impact of Development Projects, Case Studies from Bolivia, Burkina Fasso and India, Royal Tropical Institute, Amsterdam, pp. 71-94.

Gulati, Leela (1975). Female work participation—A study of inter-state difference, *Economic and Political Weekly*, Vol. 10, Nos. 1-2, pp. 35-42.

Gupta, Tilak D. (1995). And promises to skip, *The Telegraph*, Wednesday, 8 February, p. 9.

Harding, Sandra and Merill B. Hintikka eds (1983). *Discovering Reality, Feminist Perspectives on Epistomology, Metaphysics, Methodology, and Philosophy of Science*, D. Reidel Publishing Company, Dordrecht, Holland.

Hommes, E.W. (1970). *Over de evaluatie van plattelandsplanning in India,* Publikatie Nr. 14. Afdeling Zuid- en Zuidoost Azië, Antropologisch-Sociologisch Centrum, Universiteit van Amsterdam.

Illo, Jean Frances (1988). *Irrigation in the Philippines: Impact on Women and their Households*, The Aslong Project Case, The Population Council, Bangkok, Thailand.

IOV Evaluation Report 1994 (1994). *India, Evaluation of the Netherlands Development Programme with India, 1980-1992,* Netherlands Development Cooperation, Operations Review Unit, The Hague.

Jeffery, Patricia, Roger Jeffery and Andrew Lyon (1989). *Labour Pains and Labour Power, Women and Childbearing in India*, Zed Books, London/ Manohar, Delhi.

Jeffery, Patricia, Roger Jeffery and Andrew Lyon (1987). Contaminating states: midwifery, childbearing and the state in rural north India, in H. Afshar ed. (1987) *Women, State and Ideology. Studies from Africa and Asia*, Macmillan, London, pp. 152-69.

Kahnert, Friedrich and Gilbert Levine (1993). *Groundwater Irrigation and the Rural Poor, Options for Development in the Gangetic Basin,* A World Bank Symposium, World Bank, Washington, D.C.

Kelkar, G. (1981). *Impact of Green Revolution on Women's Work, Participation and Sex Roles*, ILO Tripartite Asian Regional Seminar, Rural Development and Women, Mahabeshwar.

Kelkar, Govind (1992). *Women, Peasant Organisations and Land Rights: A Study from Bihar, India.* Gender and Development Studies, Asian Institute of Technology, Bangkok.

Kelkar, Govind and Dev Nathan (1991). *Gender and Tribe: Women, Land and Forests in Jharkhand*, Kali for Women, Delhi and Zed Press, London.

Keulen, A. and R. Dekker (1992). *A Study at Field Level of Two Irrigation Schemes of the North Bengal Tera Development Project.*

Kohli, A. (1987). *The State and Poverty in India, The Politics of Reform,* Cambridge University Press, Cambridge.

Kothari, R. (1993). *Growing Amnesia*, Viking, Penguin Books, Delhi.

Kranenburg, M. (1995). 'Still Waters Run Deep, Bengali Women and Small-scale Irrigation in North Bengal Terai Development Project'. Master's

Thesis, University of Amsterdam, Department of Anthropology.

Krishnamurthy, S. (1981). *The Dowry Problem, A legal and social perspective*, IBH Prakashana, Bangalore.

Kumari, Ranjana (1989). *Women-Headed Households in Rural India*, Radiant Delhi.

Leacock, Eleanor Burke (1981). Women, development and anthropological facts and fiction, in *Myths of Male Dominance: Collected Articles on Women Cross-Culturally*, Monthly Review Press, New York, pp. 310-17.

Lieten, G.K. (1992). *Continuity and Change in Rural West Bengal*, Sage, Delhi.

Lieten, G.K. (1994). Rural development in West Bengal: views from below, *Journal of Contemporary Asia*, Vol. 24, No. 4, pp. 515-29.

Lieten, G.K. and Prabhat Datta (1995), Panchayats in Dealing with Natural Disasters, 1993 Floods in Jalpaiguri, in *Economic and Political Weekly*, 15 April, pp. 828-32.

Loeber, A.M. (1991). *The North Bengal Terai Development Project, A Detailed Study of two Irrigation Schemes,* University of Amsterdam, Euroconsult.

Maloney, Clarence and K.V. Raju (1994). *Managing Irrigation Together, Practice and Policy in India*, Sage, Delhi.

Mies, Maria (1983). Towards a methodology of women's studies, in Gloria Bowles and R. Duelli Klein eds. *Theories of Women's Studies*, Routledge and Kegan Paul, London.

Miller, Barbara D. (1981). Differentials in Child Care, in *The Endangered Sex, Neglect of Female Children in Rural North India*. Cornell University Press, Yale.

Moser, Caroline (1989). Gender planning in the third world: meeting practical and strategic gender needs, *World Development*.

Mukherjee, Raktima and S.B. Roy (1994). *Influence of Social Institutions on Women's Participation in PMF: A Case Study from Sarugarh, North Bengal,* Indian Institute of Bio-Social Research and Development (IBRAD), Working Paper No. 17, Calcutta.

Mukhopadhyay, R.S. (1990) *The Rajbansis of North Bengal: A Comparative Demographic Profile.* (Mimeo), Department of Sociology and Social Anthropology, University of North Bengal.

Narayana, G. (1986). Farmers' involvement in irrigation development: a study of Warabandi system in a village setting, in M.V.K. Sivamohan ed., *Issues in Irrigated Agriculture and Command Area Development*, Ashish, New Delhi.

North Bengal Terai India; Small scale irrigation and soil conservation and soil improvement projects, March 1987.

Report of the Evaluation Mission Phase I, in 3 Vols:

* Volume 1: Main report
* Volume 2: Draft Project Document Phase II
* Volume 3: Annexes of Vol. 1.

Pal, Surajit Kumar (1985). Agrarian relations in a village in Cooch Behar District, West Bengal, in Chakrabarti, Ghose and Danda eds (1985).

Paul, Madan Chandra (1955). *Dowry and the Position of Women in India, A Study of Delhi Metropolis*, Inter-India Publications, Delhi.

Rahman, Mahbubar and Willem van Schendel (1997), Gender and the Inheritance of Land, Living Law in Bangladesh in: Jan Breman, Peter Kloos and Ashwami Saith eds, *The Village in Asia Revisited*, Oxford University Press, Delhi, pp. 237-76.

Rights of Women to the natural resources land and water (1997), Working Paper 2, Women and Development, Netherlands Development Assistance (NEDA). Development Cooperation Information Department, Ministry of Foreign Affairs, The Hague.

Roy, Debal K. Singha (1992). *Women in Peasant Movements, Tebhaga, Naxalite and After*, Manohar, Delhi.

Samanta, A.K. (1984). *Left Extremist Movement in West Bengal, An Experiment in Armed Agrarian Struggle*, Firma KLM Private Limited, Calcutta.

Sanyal, Charu Chandra (1965). *The Rajbansis of North Bengal (A study of a Hindu Social Group)*, The Asiatic Society, Monograph Series, Vol. XI, Calcutta.

SAWA (1993). *Gender and Irrigation, a manual for the planning and assessment of small scale irrigation projects* (Lisette van der Wel), Ede.

Schenk-Sandbergen, L. Ch. (1986). Waarom worden er bruiden verbrand in India? De bruidsschat en het geweld tegen jonge bruiden [Bride burning in India, dowry and violence against young brides], *Tijdschrift voor Vrouwenstudies*, 25, pp. 30-46.

Schenk-Sandbergen, Loes (1991). Empowerment of women: its scope in a bilateral development project — a small-scale irrigation project in North Bengal, *Economic and Political Weekly*, Vol. XXVI, No. 17, 27 April, pp. WS 27-35

Schenk-Sandbergen, L. Ch. (1992). *Gender in Field Research: Experiences in India*, IDPAD 2, Occasional Papers and Reprints, New Delhi/The Hague.

Schenk-Sandbergen, L. Ch. (1994a). Sustainability for whom ? Lessons from the North Bengal Terai small scale irrigation project, in Skutsch, Opdam and Schulte Nordholt eds (1994).

Schenk-Sandbergen, L. Ch. (1994b). *Main Findings of the Socio-economic Impact Study, North Terai Development Project, Phase II*, Euroconsult, Report No. 15 of the Research and Evaluation Unit, Arnhem, The Netherlands.

Schenk-Sandbergen, L. Ch. ed. (1995). *Women and Seasonal Survival Migration in India*, Series, Indo-Dutch Alternatives in Development, Sage, Delhi.

Schenk-Sandbergen, L. Ch. and N.C. Choudhury (1994a). Women and Irrigation, Report No.12. Final Report of the Follow-up Study (1989-90 to 1992-3). Research & Evaluation Unit, Bagdogra.

Schenk-Sandbergen, L. Ch. and N.C. Choudhury (1994b), *Overview Main Findings: Socio-Economic Impact Study,* North Bengal Terai Development Project, Report No. 13. Research & Evaluation Unit, Bagdogra.

Schenk-Sandbergen, L. Ch. and Outhaki Choulamany-Khamphoui (1995). *Women in Rice-Fields and Offices in Laos, Gender Specific case-studies in four villages*, Empowerment, Heiloo.

Schenk-Sandbergen, L. Ch.(1998). *Gender, Culture and Land Rights in Rural Laos*, Asian Institute of Technology, Bangkok.

Schenk-Sandbergen, L. Ch. (1997) *Some Gender Dimensions in Managing Water Scarcity*, paper IDPAD-Seminar, Managing Water Scarcity: Experiences and Prospects, Amersfoort.

Schenk-Sandbergen, L. Ch. (2001), Women, Water and Sanitation in the Slums of Bangalore: A Case Study of Action Research, in H. Schenk ed. *Living in India's Slums, A Case Study of Bangalore*, Manohar, Delhi, pp. 185-216.

Sivamohan, M.V.K. ed. (1986). *Issues in irrigated Agriculture and Command Area Development.* Ashish, Delhi.

Skutsch, Margaret M., J. Hans M. Opdam and Nico G. Schulte Nordholt eds (1994). *Towards Sustainable Development*, A liber Amicorum for Enno W. Hommes, University of Twente, Enschede.

Sen, Amartya and Sunil Sengupta (1985). Malnutrition of rural children and the sex bias, in Banerjee and Jain eds (1985).

Sen, Gita (1982). Women workers and the Green Revolution, in Lourdes Beneria ed. (1982).

Sen, Gita (1985). Women's work and women agricultural labourers—A study of the Indian Census, *Economic and Political Weekly*, Vol. 20, No. 17, pp. WS 49-56.

Sen, Sunil (1985). *The working Women and Popular Movements in Bengal, From the Gandhi era to the Present Day*, K.P. Bagchi & Company, Calcutta.

Sengupta, Nirmal (1991). *Managing Common Property, Irrigation in India and the Phillippines*, Indo-Dutch Studies on Development Alternatives 6, Sage, Delhi.

Sharma, Ursala (1980). *Women, Work and Property in Northwest India*, Tavistock Publishers, London.

Shiva, Vandana (1989). *Staying Alive: Women Ecology and Development*, Zed Books, London.

Singh, Andrea M. and Neera Burra eds (1994). *Women and Wasteland Development in India*, A study prepared for the International Labour Office within the framework of the World Employment Programme, Sage Publications, Delhi.

Singh, Prakash (1995). *The Naxalite Movement in India,* Rupa & Co., Delhi.

Stanbury, Pamela (1992). *Women and Water: Effects of Irrigation Development in a North Indian Village*, in Dove and Carpenter eds (1992), pp. 372-99.

Stanbury, Pamela (1984). Women's Role in Agriculture: 1984 Diagnostic Analysis Workshop, Dahod Tank Irrigation Project, Madhya Pradesh, India. Water Management Synthesis project, University Services Center, Colorado State University, Fort Collins, Colorado.

Stroes, Jiska (1997), Tussern 2 Werelden, MA thesis, University of Amsterdam, Cultural Anthropology/Non-Western Sociology.

Trivedi, Harshad R. (1976). *Scheduled Caste Women, Studies in Exploitation, with reference to Superstition, Ignorence and Poverty*, Concept Publishing Company, Delhi.

Uphoff, Norman, Priti Ramamurthy and Steiner Roy (1991), Managing Irrigation, Analysing and Improving the Performance of Bureaucracies, Sage, Delhi.

Van Koppen, Barbara and Simeen Mahmud (1996). *Women and Water-pumps: the impact of participation in irrigation groups on women's status*, Intermediate Technology Publications, London.

Van Koppen, Barbara (1997). *Gendered Poverty Alleviation under Water Scarcity,* Paper IDPAD Seminar, Managing Water Scarcity: Experiences and Prospects, Amersfoort.

Van Wijk, Christine, Esther de Lange, David Saunders (1996). Gender aspects in the management of water, in *Natural Resources Forum*, Vol. 20, No. 2, pp. 91-103.

Viegas, Philip and Geeta Menon (1994). Bringing government and people together: Forest Protection Committees of West Bengal-role and participation of women, in Singh, M. Andrea and Neera Burra eds, *Women and Wasteland Development in India*, A study prepared for the International Labour Office within the framework of the World Employment Programme, Sage, Delhi, pp. 171-210.

Visaria, Pravin and Leela Visaria (1985). Indian households with Female Heads: their Incidence, Characteristics and Level of Living, in Devaki Jain and Nirmala Banerjee eds., *Tyranny of the Household, Investigative Essays on Women's Work*, Shakti Books, Delhi.

Warren, Carol A.B. (1988). *Gender Issues in Field Research*, Qualitative Research Method Series 9, Sage, Delhi.

Westergaard, Kirsten (1981). Marxist government and people's participation: the case of West Bengal, *Journal of Social Studies*, Vol. 38, pp. 95-113.

White, Sarah W. (1992). *Arguing with the Crocodile, Gender and Class in Bangladesh,* University Press Limited, Dhaka.

Whitehead, T.N. and M.E. Conaway eds (1986). *Self, Sex and Gender in Cross-Cultural Fieldwork*, University of Illinois Press, Urbana and Chicago.

Wolf, Eric R. (1982). *Europe and the People without History*, University of California Press, Berkeley.

Zwarteveen, Margreet (1993). *Gender and Irrigation Management: Issues and Challenges*, Paper presented for SIDA Workshop on Gender and Water

Resources Management: Lessons Learned and Strategies for the Future, Stockholm.

Zwarteveen, Margreet Z.(1997), Water: From Basic Need to Commodity: A Discussion on Gender and Water Rights in the Context of Irrigation, in *World Development*, Vol. 25, No. 8, pp. 1335-49.

PROJECT REPORTS AND DOCUMENTS

Base-line Studies Reports, Nos. 1 to 5.

Report No. 1. River Lift Irrigation Scheme, Paschim Harmati, Jalpaiguri district.

Report No. 2. Deep Tubewell Irrigation Scheme, Jamadarerbos, Cooch Behar district.

Report No. 3. Hand Tubewells- Bhangni-II (Dinhata I); Bagjan (Maynaguri); Velkujote (Kharibari); Khuniapukri (Kharibari).

Report No. 4. Part I STW (Kalamati); PDW (Panisala): Part II Landless labourers.

Report No. 5. Women of Beneficiaries and Landless labourers' households.

Report No. 6. Study of impact of beneficiary farmers' training programme organized by Krishi Vigyan Kendra, Ramshai, Jalpaiguri district.
Part 1: Socio-economic background of the beneficiary farmers trained in 1990-1. Research and Evaluation Unit, January 1992.
Part 2: Main Report; results of field-survey, October 1992.

Reports In-depth Study, Nos. 7 to 12.

Report No. 7. Report of the First Round Follow-up Study, 1990-1. Research and Evaluation Unit, March 1992.

Report No. 8. Report of the Second Round Follow-up Study (1991-2). Research and Evaluation Unit, October 1992.

Report No. 9. Final Report of the Follow-up Study (1989-90 to 1992-3). RLI (Paschim Harmati) and DTW (Jamadarerbos). Research and Evaluation Unit, January 1994.

Report No. 10. Final Report of the Follow-up Study (1989-90 to 1992-3). HTW in three villages (Bhangni-II, Bagjan, Velkujote). Research and Evaluation Unit, January 1994.

Report No. 11. Final Report of the Follow-up Study, (1989-90 to 1992-3).
Part I : STW (Kalamati) and PDW (Panisala).
Part II: Landless Labourers, Research and Evaluation Unit, January 1994.

Report No. 12. Final Report of the Follow-up Study (1989-90 to 1992-3).

Women and Irrigation, Research and Evaluation Unit, January 1994.

Report No. 13. Summary In-depth Study (1989-90 to 1992-3), Research and Evaluation Unit. May 1994.

Report No. 14. Report of the Sample Survey (1992-3), Research and Evaluation Unit, May 1994.

Report No. 15. Overview Main Findings Socio-Economic Impact Study, Euroconsult, Arnhem, September 1994.

Report No. 16. Abstract of different surveys (1989-93), North Bengal Terai Development Project, Phase-II (in Bengali). Research and Evaluation Unit, April 1994.

Research contributions in Euroconsult, Arnhem, Project Coordination Reports.

1989, Report No. 3, pp. 21-30.

1989, Report No. 5, October 1989, pp. 15-18. A4-A10.

1990, Report No. 6, April 1990, pp. 18-23, A1-A11.

1990, Report No. 8, October 1990, pp. 18-22, Baseline Survey; some findings, F1-F19.

1991, Report No. 10, April 1991, pp. 23-33, A9-A16

1992, Report No. 11, January 1992, pp. 24-36, A2-A9.

1992, Report No. 13, July 1992, pp. 23-31, A6-A8.

1993, Report No. 15, January 1993, pp. 27-37.

1993, Report No. 16, April 1993, pp. 23-33, A7-A12.

1993, Report No. 17, October 1993, pp. 24-39, A5-A6.

1994, Report No. 18, February 1994, pp. 28-31, A1-A5.

1994, Report No. 19, May 1994, pp. 28-29.

Index